LIBERALISM'S RELIGION

Liberalism's Religion

Cécile Laborde

Harvard University Press

Cambridge, Massachusetts
London, England

2017

First printing

Library of Congress Cataloging-in-Publication Data

Names: Laborde, Cécile, author.

Title: Liberalism's religion / Cécile Laborde.

Description: Cambridge, Massachusetts : Harvard University Press, 2017. | Includes bibliographical references and index.

Identifiers: LCCN 2017012577 | ISBN 9780674976269 (alk. paper)

Subjects: LCSH: Religion and state. | Liberalism—Religious aspects.

Classification: LCC BL65.S8 L325 2017 | DDC 322/.1—dc23 LC record available at https://lccn.loc.gov/2017012577

Contents

Introduction

Can a liberal state establish a particular religion in its laws and institutions? Can state officials appeal to religious convictions in justifying laws? Can majority religious symbols be displayed in the public sphere? Can churches have male-only clergy? Can faith-based businesses deny services to LGBTQ citizens? Should conscientious objectors be exempted from the application of general laws? Should religious minorities be protected against discrimination on the same grounds as racial minorities?

In this book I aim to provide reasoned solutions to these, and similar, controversies. But I also take a step back, to reflect on more foundational issues about the place of religion in liberal political theory. The notion of religion is central to the historical elaboration of Western liberalism, from the European wars of religion onward. Yet, strangely, it has remained under-theorized by liberal political philosophers. *Liberalism's*

Religion aims to fill this gap. I argue that controversies such as those referred to above are not best explicated and resolved in relation to a vague concept of "religion." Rather, each relates to particular, discrete dimensions of (what we call) religion. When we think about the moral dilemmas that such controversies present us with, our focus should not be on the rights of "religion" as such. Instead, it should be on how liberal laws and institutions relate to the variegated manifestations of religious life that different controversies make salient—religion as cognitive statements of truth, identificatory symbols, comprehensive ways of life, modes of voluntary association, moral and ethical obligations, vulnerable collective identities, and so forth. Each facet of religion raises its own set of normative questions. The chief argument of this book is that we should *disaggregate* religion into a plurality of different interpretive dimensions.

Let me be clear about the scope of my argument. By suggesting that the category of religion can be dispensed with in political theory, I do not mean to deny that religion is a central, indeed indispensable, category of our ethical, spiritual, and social experience. Nor do I deny that the semantic category of religion is a useful heuristic device in a range of scholarly endeavors. What I do suggest, however, is that the category of religion is less than adequate *as a politico-legal category.* We can explicate the values implicit in freedom of religion, equality between religions, and neutrality of the state toward religion—to mention just a few of the relevant liberal ideals—without direct recourse to the semantic category of religion at all. What we need, as political and legal theorists, is not a semantic or a descriptive notion of religion but, rather, an interpretive one: We need to articulate the multiple values that particular dimensions of religion realize. My theory of liberalism's religion, therefore, is interpretive—it eschews the term "religion" to focus on the values it realizes. And it is also disaggregative—it suggests that the values (and disvalues) of religion are plural and multidimensional.

The advantages of such a theory should be evident. It breaks with the long-standing tradition, in Western political theory at least, to think of religion as a discrete sphere of life deserving uniquely special politico-legal treatment—in the form of special protection (religious exemptions) and special containment (religious nonestablishment). My reworking of liberal theory implies that religion is not uniquely special: whatever treatment it receives from the law, it receives in virtue of features that it shares with nonreligious beliefs, conceptions, and identities. Disaggregating religion, then, allows us to treat religious and nonreligious individuals and groups on the same terms, as expressions of ethical and social pluralism. Nor is this all. Disaggregating religion also allows us to dispense with the Western-, Christian-inflected construal of religion that liberal political theory relies on. Instead of assuming that separation between state and religion is a requirement of liberal legitimacy, for example, I shall identify the different dimensions of religion that directly engage the legitimacy of the political order. The upshot is that, when particular instances of religion do not exhibit those dimensions, then liberalism does not mandate Western-style strict separation. *Liberalism's Religion,* then, aims to reformulate liberalism to defend it against critics who denounce its ethnocentric, Christian understanding of what religion is. As a result, it offers a novel answer to the question of how universal theories of both secularism and religion can be; and of how to rethink equality in complex pluralistic societies.

A note on method. I think of political theory as an immanent and dialogical exercise. Much of my argument emerges as a product of fairly extensive and detailed engagement with existing literature, both in analytical philosophy and in (what I shall call) critical religion. Although I write in the analytical, normative tradition of political theory, I share with Continental-influenced, poststructuralist critics a deep-seated interest in the opacity and ambiguity of language. One of the paradoxes I explore is that, for all its commitments to clarity and precision, Anglo-American analytical political philosophy has relied on a strikingly vague understanding of religion—an imprecision carried over to the loose analogue of "conception of the good" popularized by John Rawls. By clarifying some of the presuppositions of liberal philosophers' use of such terms, I aim to provide a finer-grained conceptual account of one of the key, indeed foundational, notions of liberal political philosophy. The account I provide, importantly, is not idiosyncratic. It is one of the aims of my work to demonstrate that something like the interpretive, disaggregative approach is discernible, in embryonic form, in existing liberal theories. Likewise, I try to show that critics of liberalism implicitly rely, for the plausibility of their critique, on those normative liberal criteria that they otherwise eschew. In sum, my reworking of liberal theory illuminates the deeper common ground there can be, between different philosophical traditions, over liberalism's religion.

Throughout this book, my argument takes its distinctive shape by engaging with two distinct bodies of thought: critical theorists of secularism and religion, on the one hand, and liberal egalitarian theorists of justice, on the other. In brief, I try to convince theorists of justice that critical theorists have identified genuine blind spots in liberal theory. And, in turn, I try to convince critical theorists that liberalism can be reworked so that it is less vulnerable to their pertinent criticisms. Let me draw the argumentative arc of my argument. Critical religion theorists (such as Saba Mahmood, Stanley Fish, Steven Smith, and Winnifred Sullivan) offer a root-and-branch critique of liberalism. Liberalism, for them, is bound up with inadequate, ethnocentric, and Christian understandings of what religion is. The liberal secular state, far from guaranteeing freedom of religion for all, arbitrarily produces and shapes legitimate religion, and in the process inevitably marginalizes religious minorities. I agree that this criticism is valid against the uses and abuses of the rhetoric of secularism and liberalism in actual public debates. But in this book I demonstrate that the *philosophical* school of liberal egalitarianism is less vulnerable to it. Drawing on the work of John Rawls, liberal egalitarians argue that religion need not be singled out in the liberal state. The liberal state provides a framework of justice within which all citizens can pursue their conception of what makes life good. Freedom of religion and the nonestablishment of religion by the state are interpreted through general ideals of equal liberty and state neutrality. The state respects and protects religion, but only as one of the ways in which citizens live a life they think good. And the state does not officially establish or endorse any religion, but only because it does not establish or endorse any conception of the good in general. Liberal egalitarians, then, construe religion as a subset of a broader category, which they refer to as "conceptions of the good" or "the good."

I endorse the broad liberal egalitarian project yet I also show that, in its current formulations, it does not adequately answer the challenge of critical religion. My chief ambition in this book is to develop a more robust theory of liberal egalitarianism. First, instead of *analogizing* religion with an equally vague category of "conceptions of the good," I argue that we should *disaggregate* religion into a plurality of relevant normative dimensions. In line with my sympathetic reading of other theorists, however, I show that something like the disaggregative approach is already present in the writings of authors such as Ronald Dworkin, Charles Taylor, Jonathan Quong, Christopher Eisgruber, and Lawrence Sager. When they seek to conceptualize freedom of religion or the nonestablishment of religion, they—consciously or otherwise—pick out several different dimensions of religion, and rarely work with an undifferentiated view of religion as a conception of the good. Second, I reformulate liberal egalitarianism so that it can adequately respond to the two most serious challenges posed by critics.

The first of those challenges is *ethical salience*. This posits that liberalism, for all its claims to neutrality, cannot dispense with an ethical evaluation of the salience of different conceptions, beliefs, and commitments. I agree with the critique, and show that liberals must be clearer about what it means to treat religious and nonreligious commitments equally. Once we have identified the different metrics of equality, we can specify the multiple yet restricted domains in which neutrality applies. The second challenge is that of *jurisdictional boundary*. Liberalism, critics point out, grants the sovereign state the final authority to delimit the boundary between the religious and the nonreligious, the public and the private, the right and the good. Again, I agree with the critique, and I

6 INTRODUCTION

show that liberals must think harder about the ultimate sovereignty of the state and its legitimacy in enforcing specific terms of liberal justice, in a context of reasonable democratic disagreement about justice itself. Here is how the argument unfolds in detail. The book is divided into two parts. Part I, "Analogizing Religion," analyzes existing literature and introduces the liberal egalitarian response to the critical religion challenge.

In Chapter 1, on liberal egalitarianism and the critique of religion, I explore the ideas of an eclectic group of writers, such as Talal Asad, William Cavanaugh, Peter Danchin, Stanley Fish, Saba Mahmood, Hussein Agrama, Elizabeth Shakman-Hurd, Steven Smith, and Winnifred Fallers Sullivan. Their common claim is that the liberal attempt to define the "just bounds" between the state and religion is "mission impossible," to use Fish's memorable phrase, because there is no nonarbitrary way to single out, and fairly regulate, a stable, self-contained sphere of religion. I distinguish three versions of the critique, the *semantic* critique, the *Protestant* critique, and the *realist* critique. I show that liberal egalitarianism is able to deflect the most radical versions of the critique, because it does not single out religion as uniquely special. The liberal egalitarian strategy of extension by analogy is a promising attempt to rethink equality in an age characterized by a deep pluralism of values, beliefs, and identities. However, in the rest of this book I suggest that it is vulnerable to subtler and more challenging versions of the critique, which I call ethical salience and jurisdictional boundary.

In Chapter 2, on liberal egalitarianism and the exemptions puzzle, I introduce the ethical salience problem by examining liberal egalitarian theories of religious exemptions. The puzzle is this: If religious and nonreligious beliefs and identities are treated equally, how do we justify providing special exemptions from general laws to some individuals (religious and nonreligious) but not others? When, and why, is religion—and its analogues—ethically salient? I examine three strategies to resolve this puzzle. The first, the *dissolving* strategy, has been developed by Ronald Dworkin, who rejects exemptions on the grounds that no defensible distinction can be drawn between religious and nonreligious ethical views. The second, the *mainstreaming* strategy, is associated with Christopher Eisgruber and Lawrence Sager, who analogize religion with existing protection-worthy categories, such as disabilities, vulnerable identities, or close associations. The third, the *narrowing* strategy, analogizes religion with a specific subset of conscientious duties, and has recently been articulated by Charles Taylor, Jocelyn Maclure, and other liberal egalitarians. In this chapter I explain the limits of each strategy in turn. Such limits are instructive, however, because each strategy identifies an ethically salient dimension of religion and, therefore, points to the need for a more complex, disaggregated account of religion, as well as of the justice of exemptions, both individual and collective.

In Chapter 3, on liberal egalitarianism and the state neutrality puzzle, I further explore the ethical salience problem, and introduce the jurisdictional boundary problem, by looking at questions of nonestablishment of religion and state neutrality. Why should the state be neutral about the good? Which dimensions of the good are unsuitable for state endorsement? Why should the state not establish religion, or the good? I identify three theories of neutrality as "generalizing nonestablishment." The first, *ethical usurpation,* is associated with Dworkin, who argues that the state should not usurp the judgment of individuals and should respect their ethical independence. The second, *civic disparagement,* has been developed by Eisgruber and Sager, who argue that the state should not endorse some identities over others because this would infringe on equal citizenship. The third, *foundational disagreement,* has been articulated by Jonathan Quong, who suggests that the state should be neutral about the good because of the particularly intractable nature of disagreement about the good. I show that each strategy identifies an important dimension of religion and the good, but that they do not provide a fully satisfactory account of the grounds of state neutrality in relation to the ethical salience problem. I also show that they have a blind spot about how the boundary is drawn between the good and the right, the religious and nonreligious, and the public and the private. Liberal egalitarians have focused on issues of justification (What is a public reason?) and justice (Who gets what?) but have neglected issues of jurisdiction (Who decides who gets what?).

In Part II, "Disaggregating Religion," I put forward a more satisfactory solution to the ethical salience and the jurisdictional boundary problems, by disaggregating religion more systematically and developing a more differentiated theory of exemptions and state neutrality.

In Chapter 4, on the disaggregation of religion and the question of nonestablishment, I ask in what sense, if any, there should be a separation between state and religion. Instead of drawing on vague notions of neutrality or secularism, I identify three central liberal values and map them onto three specific dimensions of religion or the good. The *justifiable* state appeals to the idea that laws should be justified only by reasons that are accessible to citizens. The *inclusive* state is a state that honors the equal status and citizenship of all. The *limited* state respects individual self-determination in private matters. Each picks out a different feature of disaggregated religion: religion as *nonaccessible;* religion as *divisive;* and religion as *comprehensive.* Disaggregating religion allows me to specify that religion is not uniquely special: nonreligious ideologies and practices can be inaccessible, divisive, and comprehensive too. This also means that the state need not be separate from religion when religion is not divisive, inaccessible, or comprehensive. One question, however, remains. Who is to decide what belongs to the private and the public, to the personal and political, to the religious and nonreligious? Theories of liberal justice do not address problems of jurisdiction.

In Chapter 5, on state sovereignty and freedom of association, I address the jurisdictional boundary problem head-on. I do so by engaging with recent theories of church autonomy and jurisdictional institutionalism, such as those of Richard Garnett, Steven Smith, and Victor Muniz-Fraticelli. I argue that liberal egalitarianism relies on a presumption of sovereignty of the secular democratic state in deciding contested questions of the boundary and scope of freedom of religion. I then go on to show that even though the state does not share sovereignty with other institutions, it must respect associational autonomy. I then apply my theory of disaggregation to the general puzzle of collective religious exemptions from antidiscrimination laws. I agree with liberal egalitarians that whatever rights religious associations have should be derived from the liberal value of freedom of association. However, I argue that freedom of association itself is an internally complex idea. I disaggregate the values it protects, so as to justify some of the collective rights claimed by religious groups. I set out two salient associational interests: what I call *coherence* and *competence* interests. I argue that although many associations can appeal to coherence interests to defeat the application of some general laws, only some can, in addition, appeal to competence interests. Disaggregating associational interests in this way allows me to explain why religious associations (but not only they) can have some latitude in choosing their personnel.

In Chapter 6, on the disaggregation of religion and the question of free exercise, I return to the issues of individual religious exemptions and the ethical salience problem. I defend three liberal principles, and map them onto three dimensions of religion. The first principle is that of negative freedom and state noninterference. Citizens have a general right to pursue their preferences, commitments, and conceptions of the good; and it is wrong, as Dworkin argues, for the state to target, or discriminate against, some conceptions just because it considers them inferior. Yet justificatory neutrality is not sufficient: Liberal states often appeal to good, neutral reasons to enforce general laws that incidentally burden some groups of citizens. Which class of preferences and commitments should *pro tanto* be candidates for exemptions from such laws? I argue that the ethically salient category is that of *integrity-protecting commitments* (IPCs). These further subdivide into obligation-IPCs and identity-IPCs. I articulate two cases of fair exemptions, which broadly map onto each IPC. Fair exemptions for *disproportionate burden* are required when the pursuit of some state regulatory interest makes it impossible for some citizens to fulfill an obligatory requirement of their faith or culture, yet they can be relieved of the burden without excessive cost. Fair exemptions for *majority bias* are required when majority citizens are able to combine the pursuit of a socially valuable opportunity with an identity-IPC, yet minority citizens are unjustifiably denied an equivalent opportunity set. My theory provides an integrated account of the ethical salience both of *religion* and *culture,* and therefore bridges the gap between the literature about multiculturalism and cultural recognition, on the one hand, and freedom of religion and conscience, on the other. I conclude with a conceptual map of liberalism's religion, which shows that my theory of liberalism need not be wedded to a culturally specific conception of what religion is. If liberal values are contestable, they need to be challenged on their own ground—not on the dubious ground that they rely on an inaccurate or ethnocentric view of religion.

I

ANALOGIZING RELIGION

1

৪০৫৪

Liberal Egalitarianism
and the Critique of Religion

In this chapter, I introduce what I call the liberal egalitarian theory of religion and the state. Its main idea can be stated simply. Religion need not be singled out in the liberal state. The liberal state provides a framework of justice within which all citizens can pursue their conception of what makes life good. Freedom of religion and the nonestablishment of religion by the state are interpreted through general ideals of equal liberty and state neutrality. The implications of liberal egalitarianism for the place of religion in the state are twofold. First, the state respects and protects religion, but only as one of the ways in which citizens live a life they think good. Second, the state does not officially establish or endorse any religion, but only because it does not establish or endorse any conception of the good. Liberal egalitarianism, then, construes religion as a subset of a larger category: "conceptions of the good" or "the good." It is egalitarian in the specific sense that it treats religious and nonreligious individuals and groups on the same terms—as expressions of ethical pluralism—instead of singling out the religious for special protection or containment. Liberal egalitarian theorists of religious freedom draw on John Rawls, and include Ronald Dworkin, Charles Taylor, Christopher Eisgruber, Lawrence Sager, Micah Schwartzman, and Jonathan Quong.[1]

In this book I endorse the liberal egalitarian approach. I agree that religion need not be uniquely singled out in the liberal state, and that it can adequately be regulated through a framework of equal liberty. I argue, however, that the analogy between religion and "conceptions of the good" (or similarly loose terms) is unsatisfactory, and that the slogan "equal liberty" sometimes obfuscates what is being equalized. I aim to revise the liberal egalitarian theory of religion and the state, providing a more complex picture of what religion is *like,* by identifying an array of politically or legally relevant dimensions of religion—beyond the simple and vague analogy of "conception of the good." The main purpose of this book, then, is to engage with, and improve on, existing liberal egalitarian theories. Instead of a simple analogy between religion and the good, I will—in due course—propose a more complex egalitarian strategy of disaggregation of religion.

In this chapter I set the stage for the argument, in order to show the initial plausibility and appeal of liberal egalitarianism. I do this by suggesting that it offers a promising line of response to an influential critique of the liberal treatment of religion. According to the critical religion school, the liberal ambition to define the just place of religion in the state is fatally compromised by the inadequacy of the concept of religion it relies upon. In the first section of this chapter, I explicate this critique and explain why it must be taken seriously by liberal political theorists. In the second section, I show that liberal egalitarianism is a promising—though not yet fully developed—answer to it. In the rest of this book, I will refine liberal egalitarianism in order to provide a robust answer to the critical religion challenge. Critical religion theorists ask probing questions about liberalism's religion—the concept of religion at the heart of liberalism—and it is vitally important that liberal political philosophers adequately respond to it.

The Critical Religion Challenge

A sensible place to locate the building blocks of the liberal political theory of religion is in its classic statement by John Locke in his 1689 "Letter Concerning Toleration." Religion, Locke thought, is about the aspirations to salvation of the individual soul. The state has no authority to shape or control such aspirations: it cannot effectively compel inward belief, nor does it have the competence and wisdom to distinguish true from false belief. The state should, therefore, adopt a policy of toleration of religious beliefs. Its role is limited to the care and protection of "outward things, such as money, land, houses, furniture, and the like." In such domains, churches are in turn incompetent, and should not meddle with the business of government. What is "above all things necessary," Locke famously wrote, is "to distinguish exactly the business of civil government from that of religion, and to settle the just bounds that lie between the one and the other."[2] In contemporary liberalism, this basic intuition has evolved into what Amy Gutmann has called "two-way protection": protection of religion from the state, and protection of the state from religion.[3] Both find paradigmatic expression in the First Amendment of the U.S. Constitution, which begins: "Congress shall make no law respecting an establishment of religion, or prohibiting the free exercise thereof."

The liberal distinctions between the religious and the secular, the private and the public, the individual and the community, and the personal and the political have had their fair share of critiques. Here I shall focus on a recent, distinctive strand of critique, which I call critical religion, that points to the indeterminacy and inadequacy of the liberal construal of religion itself. This critique has been developed by an eclectic group of writers, among whom Talal Asad, William Cavanaugh, Peter Danchin, Stanley Fish, Timothy Fitzgerald, Saba Mahmood, Elizabeth

Shakman-Hurd, Steven Smith, and Winnifred Fallers Sullivan.[4] These are anthropologists, sociologists, philosophers, historians, lawyers, and comparative politics and religious studies experts, all versed in methodologies that openly reject the claims of normative liberal political philosophy—Foucauldian, Schmittian, postcolonialist, pragmatist, or realist. Their main claim is that the liberal attempt to define the "just bounds" between the state and religion is a "mission impossible," in Fish's memorable phrase, because there is no nonarbitrary way to single out, and fairly regulate, a stable, recognizable sphere of religion.[5] Given that these writers are skeptical about liberalism generally, does it make sense to isolate their critique of liberalism's religion? Does their critique of liberalism not stand or fall alongside their critique of religion? It does not. I shall argue that critics are right to press liberals on their concept of religion, but that the liberal project can be rescued from their critique.

Liberalism is not fatally discredited by the critics' blanket condemnation of liberalism because those critics often miss their target. Critical theorists and normative philosophers tend to talk at cross-purposes, and even though they discuss the same topics, they do not often discuss them with one another. So let me first briefly clarify two common misunderstandings, which are relevant to the critical religion writings. First, critics of liberalism tend to confuse genesis with justification: they think a *historical* critique can serve as a *philosophical* critique of liberalism. Recent historical scholarship has powerfully debunked the myth of the origins of liberalism: namely, the idea—found in Rawls and others—that the liberal state, by eschewing appeal to religious truth, provided a peaceful solution to religious violence.[6] Historians have shown that early modern toleration was not a philosophical achievement but, rather, a pragmatic and often grudgingly negotiated social practice; that it did not prefigure modern notions of individualism, freedom of conscience, and state neutrality but instead deployed a "circumstantial casuistry" of historically embedded, conflicting concepts; that it was connected, not to the emergence of liberal states, but to the formation of confessional, absolutist modern states; that it was deeply rooted in Christian theology;

and that it did not tame religious violence as much as it legitimized a new form of violence—nationalist, secular, and political.[7] Historians have offered a penetrating critique of mainstream liberal discourse and of the popular, "enchanted" story of the liberal state. Insofar as the liberal myth is "a story told about the past to explain or justify a present state of affairs,"[8] it has too often been used to equate religion with persecuting fanaticism (notably of the Oriental, specifically Muslim, "Other")[9] and to take for granted Western individualism, secularism, and pluralism as universal models.

But how damming is this critique for *philosophical* liberalism? Liberal philosophers do not justify their commitments to toleration, individual rights, and state neutrality by appeal to history (although they too at times invoke history in a casual and rhetorical fashion). It is highly probable that what Mark Lilla calls the "Great Separation" (between religion and the state) did not actually happen in quite the way it is imagined; but this does not mean that a principle of separation cannot be defended.[10] It is a fact that religious freedom emerged in its modern form within a pervasively Christian society, but it does not mean that liberalism is irremediably Christian (this would be as absurd as discrediting mathematics because it was a great achievement of Arab civilization). To be sure, the historically specific genesis of liberalism has generated problematic philosophical blind spots, as the rest of this book will investigate. But simply to conjure up the tainted history of liberalism does not suffice to discredit it: a more extensive engagement with its philosophical argumentative structure is required.

Second, critics of liberalism tend to judge liberal theory through the lens of liberal practice. They rightly point out how actual states pay homage to religious freedom and equality yet maintain and aggravate the vulnerability of minorities in the state. In a richly documented and insightful article, for example, Peter Danchin and Saba Mahmood have explored the unexpected similarities between Islamic Egyptian and secular European courts' appeals to notions of public order to police the boundaries of acceptable religiosity. In both public spheres, and in very similar ways, majoritarian sensibilities have shaped legal responses to minority demands.[11] The implication is that the contrast between liberal secular Europe and nonliberal, religious non-Western contexts is not as stark as is commonly thought. Middle Eastern and Western states share a structurally similar *secular* project—whereby the state pervasively shapes and gives form to claims of religious difference and equality.[12] The point is well made, and well taken.

But it is not clear what normative implications follow. Liberals are well aware that the structurally secular nature of a state is no guarantee of its liberal credentials—whether in the Middle East or in Western societies. They have been highly critical of European appeals to cultural majoritarianism, the heritage of Christianity, and utilitarian notions of public order, especially as these are mobilized to target Muslim minorities. Normative appeals to freedom and equality do not function only as legitimizing ideological discourses for the arbitrary exercise of state power: they also serve as shared, if contested, discursive resources for the critique of such power. Critical theorists denounce normativity as a system of ideological domination; but they miss out on the critical potential of normative philosophy. Nor are they themselves averse covertly to deploying evaluative, normative categories, as when certain configurations of power are castigated as "unfair" or "oppressive."[13] Generally, critics of liberalism are not explicit enough about the normative basis of their own critique—if pushed, it usually turns out to be some version of liberal equality, freedom, or pluralism.[14]

That said, with these misunderstandings out of the way, it remains the case that critical religion theorists have developed three compelling lines of criticism of the liberal treatment of religion. I call them the *semantic* critique, the *Protestant* critique, and the *realist* critique. Let me distill them in turn, drawing on major writings of the critical religion school.

     1. The *semantic* critique, baldly stated, is that there is no stable, universally valid empirical referent for the category of religion.

This claim might be surprising, as the word "religion" is widely used both in ordinary language and in specialized academic discourse. Religion is commonly seen as a culturally mediated yet universal feature of the human condition; a set of convictions, held by individuals, that constitute multiple paths to spiritual salvation or flourishing. As comparative historians of religion have evocatively illustrated, however, this is a distinctively modern and Western notion. It was born, from the sixteenth century onward, out of a mix of Christian disputes about truth, European colonial expansion, and the formation of nation-states. Although we tend to think of the term as being transhistorical and transcultural, scholars have shown that there is no such thing as ancient religions—at best, the term is an anachronistic redescription. The Roman term *religio* referred to the performance of social rites. It was later applied to the *monastic* dimension of Christian life. The Arabic work *din* is awkwardly captured by modern translations such as "religion" and "faith"; it is best rendered as *lex* or "law," what we would today call social order, law, ethics, or morality—closer here to the Latin *religio* or the Greek *threskeia*. The word *islam* is not the name of a new community, but instead a verbal noun: a *muslim* is someone who submits to the Law (some of the members of the early community of believers or *umma* were Jews and Christians; and for eighth-century Christians, Muslims were not members of a separate religion but Christian heretics).[15]

The idea that the world is divided into different religions offering competing ways of individual salvation was born during the European Renaissance and Reformation. With the Wars of Religion, and the tumultuous beginnings of the modern system of nation-states, a political consensus (slowly) emerged that political stability could be achieved, not by settling arguments about which kind of Christianity was true, but by isolating beliefs about God in the private sphere and elevating loyalty to the legal codes of developing nation-states.[16] Embryonic in Bodin and the writings of the *politiques,* the new concept of religion was clearly articulated by Locke. Locke argued that churches are voluntary associations of individuals who adhere to a particular doctrine of salvation—a sphere of life that can be isolated from other spheres, notably that of the public interest of the state. By the end of the seventeenth century, it was common to confine *religio* and the religious to the realm of the inner self, as when Locke postulated that "true and saving *religio* consists in the inward persuasion of the mind [*in interna animi fide*]."[17]

At the same time as the genus of religion was coming to be thought of as an internal, private, depoliticized entity, interactions with previously unknown peoples through foreign exploration and colonization were beginning to create new species of individual religion. In each society, Europeans noticed, people venerated invisible beings; had stories not unlike Christian scriptures; had people who resembled clergy and buildings that resembled temples; and though the natives did not group these items together, Europeans did do so for comparative purposes. Thus it was, famously, that Hinduism was invented as an ancient, venerable faith—in fact, a parceling out of the social life and customs of the people living near the Indus river (the origin of the term *hindu*) into "religious" and "nonreligious" practices. The nineteenth century saw the foundation of an academic discipline of "religion" and its corollary, "world religions," based on an interiorized—and supposedly universal—concept of mental representation, which allowed a notion of European universalism to be "preserved in the language of pluralism." In parallel, Enlightenment rationality invited a growing distinction between science, reason, and natural religion, on the one hand, and ritualism, superstition, and prejudice, on the other. Throughout the period, the true and natural religion of Christianity was compared and contrasted to inferior, material, and ritualistic religions.[18]

Partly because of the checkered history of the category of religion, it lacks conceptual coherence as a classificatory scheme. It is impossible to discern any common core or essence to all the world religions, as W. C. Smith pointed out in 1962.[19] There is no feature, or set of features, that all religions share. Christianity, Islam, Judaism, Buddhism, and Shintoism have nothing in common—and no feature that would allow us to distinguish them from nonreligious ideologies, such as nationalism.

Some religions do not have any deity; others are community- rather than belief-based; the boundary between them and other social practices is porous; and there is no epistemically reliable way of distinguishing a religious from a nonreligious proposition or belief. Twentieth-century sociologists have elaborated sophisticated theories of religion—functional and substantive—but the consensus among scholars is that such definitions are either under-inclusive or over-inclusive, and do not adequately track ordinary language.[20] The category of religion, in sum, fails to capture a universally recognizable or semantically coherent reality. As Elizabeth Shakman Hurd puts it, "Religion is too unstable a category to be treated as an isolable entity, whether the objective is to attempt to separate religion from law and politics or design a political response to 'it.'"[21]

2. The *Protestant* critique focuses on the political and legal treatment of religion and argues that liberal law is based toward individualistic, belief-based religions.

This critique, developed most influentially by writers such as Talal Asad and Saba Mahmood, interrogates the way religion is deployed in legal and political practice. Asad, in *Genealogies of Religion,* has challenged the "insistence that religion has an autonomous essence—not to be confused with the essence of science, or of politics, or of common sense . . . [and that it is] a trans-historical and trans-cultural phenomenon."[22] But he adds the more specifically legal critique that, as a result of the implication of the concept of religion in the formation of Western, secular modernity, it is biased against non-Protestant religion.[23] Modernity is Protestant in two complementary senses. First, it coincides with the emergence, in the aftermath of the Protestant Reformation in Europe, of a newly secular mode of political governance, which relies on a set of foundational and mutually reinforcing binary oppositions: between divine obligations and civil obligations, between belief and reason, between thought and action, and between mind and body.

Second, drawing on the Protestant rejection of Catholic ritualism, it sees true religion as firmly located on the first side of each opposition: religion is about mind, belief, and thought, and about the individual's freedom to interpret the nature of her religious obligations—echoing Martin Luther's argument that salvation is "by faith alone" *(sola fide)* and not by ritual works. For Locke, it referred to "that inner worship of the heart which God demands." Although necessarily expressed by the outward actions of the body, these were by definition "subject to the discretion of the magistrate," for they are "indeterminate and indifferent to [superior] law." Here Locke draws on a staple of Reformation political controversy, the grounds of the magistrate's authority to determine *adiaphora,* or "indifferent things." These are things that were not strictly necessary for salvation. They included a host of social practices embedded in ordinary life, as well as the specific rituals of worship and imposed ceremonies. Through a literal separation of mind and body, spiritual capacity and worldly action, ritual was seen by Locke to require merely bodily acts, and therefore was not essential to religion.[24] This conception of religion "emphasizes the priority of belief as a state of mind rather than constituting an activity in the world."[25] And it understands religious freedom as being centrally about the freedom to assent to truth propositions.[26] Two traditions, the Christian creedal tradition and modern analytic discourse, combine to teach us that religious belief means the affirmation of certain propositions.[27] In sum, "religion—'true' religion, some would say—on this modern Protestant reading, came to be understood as being private, voluntary, individual, textual, and believed."[28]

This construal of religion has found its way in both national and international law, and in public discourse. Consider, for example, three popular arguments advanced about the regulation of Islamic veiling in Europe. The first is that Muslim dress can be regulated because it belongs "merely" to the realm of practices *(forum externum),* not to the realm of belief *(forum internum).* The second is that veiling is not a religious obligation strictly speaking: it is not one of the five pillars of Islam, and there are disagreements, within the Islamic community, as to whether it is required by the faith or whether it is an adiaphorous act. The third common argument is that veiling is not endorsed freely by women, and therefore does not respect their status as autonomous beings.[29] On this view, authenticity rests on the modern subject's ability to choose her beliefs and act on them. This conception of belief as singular and inaccessible to other locations reinforces the idea of an autonomous "buffered" subject able to separate itself from objects by contemplation, reasoning, and interpretation.[30]

The Protestant critique echoes the communitarian critique of the liberal self as radically detached from its ends and from the communities and habits that form and sustain it. As Michael Sandel pointed out, "not all religious beliefs can be described without loss as the product of free and voluntary choice by the faithful."[31] Saba Mahmood's ethnographic descriptions of the pious self show that it is not empty or unencumbered but is, rather, constituted and shaped by specific virtues and dispositions. In her pathbreaking *Politics of Piety,* she contrasts the liberal model of religion—a set of propositions that one accepts or rejects—with a richer, Foucauldian, and neo-Aristotelian account of the religious life as a life shaped by the cultivation of bodily disciplines, inherited or naturalized through habitus and manifested in social practices and public institutions.[32] A great deal of religious practice—ritual observance, dietary habits, dress, and bodily behavior—has little to do with creedal proposition or with personal sincerity.[33] For example, a Hindu "may be a theist, pantheist, atheist, communist and believe whatever he likes but what makes him into a Hindu are the ritual practices he performs and the rules to which he adheres, in short, what he does."[34] In Hinduism, Judaism, Islam, aboriginal religions, as well as several forms of Christianity, practices and community are more important than belief and individuality.[35] The liberal state arbitrarily privatizes and individualizes areas of social life that are intrinsically social, communal, and public.

One implication of the Protestant critique is that, once the religious experience is seen as an embodied, practice- and community-based way of life, it is difficult to single it out in relation to other social practices. It is no longer clear what is special about religion. In an influential book suggestively entitled *The Impossibility of Religious Freedom,* Winnifred Sullivan has shown that the U.S. First Amendment Free Exercise clause is quite incapable of protecting the popular, unruly, ritualized religiosity she saw at work in baroque funerary displays in a Florida cemetery. Sullivan suggests that lived religion is too complex, too comprehensive, and too multifaceted to be adequately captured by the law of the liberal state.[36] The law, in her view, has established an excessively narrow understanding of religion and a strained ghettoization of religion from the rest of life. In an age where "religions seems to be bursting all over, . . . in complicated ways: fundamentalisms, new age, neo-pagans, Muslims, voodoo, millennialists,"[37] there is no justification for privileging a high-minded, textualist understanding of "true" religion. She concludes that "legal protection for religion is certainly theoretically incoherent and possibly unconstitutional"[38] (because it is incompatible with the nonestablishment of religion) and she argues instead for a regime, not of special treatment, but of equality.

> 3. The *realist* critique points out that liberal regulation of religion
> amounts either to the naked exercise of arbitrary power, or to the
> establishment of an alternative religion, that of liberalism.

Talal Asad has aptly summarized the realist critique of liberalism: for him, liberalism is not a principle of state neutrality toward religion, but instead it entails the sovereign prerogative of the state to regulate and police religious life.[39] There are three versions of this critique.

First, liberalism is incoherent because it constantly produces what it denies: the state is unavoidably entangled with religion, and there is no meaningful separation between religion and state. The moment when the law is faced with deciding which practices are religious and which are secular, it engages in a theological exercise and gives up on its own secularity.[40] All states "establish" religion, formally or informally: instead of honoring the autonomy of a (nonexistent) predefined spiritual sphere, they shape, structure, and manage religion, bringing to bear background cultural assumptions, cosmologies, anthropologies, and institutions.[41] Recent scholarship has eloquently illustrated how North American and European nations are currently modeling and managing religion worldwide, via state-sponsored intervention in the name of the global politics of religious freedom.[42] Second, liberalism is arbitrary because the regulation of religion is ultimately harnessed to the promotion of state purposes—not to some lofty ideal of toleration or freedom. In the theoretically perceptive works of critics such as Hussein Agrama, Arvind Mandair, and Marcus Dressler, religion appears purely as an effect of secular state power. Seemingly religious states such as Egypt, and secular states such as Turkey and India, as well as Western states, all operate within the same problem-space of modern secular power, which works by continually politicizing those traditions and practices it designates as religious—notably via the deployment of statist categories such as public order.[43]

A third version of the realist critique posits that liberalism itself is a religion. Liberalism cannot impartially govern the religious because it is a rival metaphysics or substantive way of life, one that—unlike traditional religion—cannot own up to the contested character of its own commitments. This critique has achieved wide currency in conservative, often Christian-inspired, legal circles as well as among agonistic, antifoundationalist critics of liberalism. On that view, liberalism is a "secular fundamentalist" and normalizing project, one that designates heretics and dissidents as "unreasonable"—a loose, rhetorical category that designates those who do not agree with its articles of faith.[44] A variant of this thesis is found in Carl Schmitt, who argued that the modern liberal state is grounded in a distinctive *political theology* that mobilizes the structural categories of metaphysics and theology to bolster and consolidate the higher identity of secular citizenship. The secular separation between a privatized, individualized sphere of religion and a public, social, rational sphere of politics has obscured the way in which the state, the nation, and the law operate as the modern sacred.[45]

The Liberal Egalitarian Answer

In this section, I show that liberal egalitarianism can adequately answer the most radical challenges of critical religion. (In the rest of this book, I shall show that it remains vulnerable to subtler versions of this critique, and I shall endeavor to reformulate it to provide a more robust version of liberal egalitarianism.) Before I do so, I need to clarify exactly what I mean by a liberal egalitarian theory of religion and the state—*liberal egalitarianism*, for short.[46] Earlier I defined liberalism by appeal to what Amy Gutmann has called "two-way protection." The thought is that, in a liberal state, the state protects freedom of religion and abstains from establishing, endorsing, or promoting any religion. Religion is protected from the state, and the state is protected from religion—a dispensation nicely captured in the two religion clauses in the First Amendment to the U.S. Constitution, the Free Exercise Clause and the Establishment Clause. This is the sense in which religion is (originally) special in the liberal state.

Contemporary liberal egalitarians deny such special status, but this is not because they seek to downgrade the status of religion. Rather, they seek to extend and generalize the protections and burdens traditionally associated with religion (when these are justified) to broader categories of secular doctrines, practices, and ways of life.[47] In the 1970s and 1980s, a number of theorists attempted to sum up the essence of liberalism in terms of a principle requiring the state to refrain from taking sides on disputed religious and ethical questions. This constituted a break from the traditional liberalism of Locke, Kant, and Mill, all of whom grounded their commitment to liberalism in foundational, comprehensive philosophies about the existence of God, the nature of reason, and the destiny of the human individual. By the mid-twentieth century, many philosophers had come to doubt whether such comprehensive philosophies could legitimately be part of political morality, given the depth and intractability of ethical pluralism. Ronald Dworkin, for example, influentially suggested that the state does not treat people as *equals* if it draws "on a particular conception of the good life or what gives value to life."[48]

What is called neutrality in contemporary liberal philosophy should be seen as a generalization of the original ideal of religious toleration.[49] As John Rawls saw it, toleration is not only the historically notable solution to the religious wars of early modern Europe but the paradigmatic political principle for a social condition characterized by a "diversity of doctrines" and a "plurality of conflicting and . . . incommensurable conceptions of the good affirmed by the members of existing democratic societies." His "intuitive idea" was to "generalize the principle of religious toleration to a social form, thereby arriving at equal liberty in public institutions."[50] The liberal state is no longer required merely to be neutral between religions; it has to be neutral also between almost all aspects of its citizens' conceptions of the good, whether these are spiritual or secular.[51]

This liberalism is *egalitarian* in two senses. First, because it is not rooted in a comprehensive secularist worldview, it does not exclude religious believers from its constituency of justification. Political liberalism, in particular, is explicitly designed to be acceptable not only to secular citizens but also to citizens with religious beliefs. Rawls hoped that citizens otherwise deeply divided in their comprehensive, ethical and religious, commitments, could converge on a political conception of liberal justice. Religious worldviews could offer different paths toward an overlapping consensus on basic principles of political morality, which would themselves be justified by appeal to public reason. The upshot is that the liberal state does not single out religious views and conceptions as uniquely problematic for purposes of legitimacy. It does not separate itself uniquely from religion but, rather, refrains from endorsing or promoting any controversial or comprehensive conception of the good.

Second, the liberal state does not uniquely protect *religious* beliefs and practices from intolerance, repression, and discrimination. Philosophers such as Rawls and Dworkin articulated their distinctive vision against the backdrop of the struggles of the 1960s around African American civil rights, conscientious objection to war, women's rights to contraception and abortion, and the recognition of sexual minorities and indigenous groups. Liberal democracies, on their view, are committed to a fundamental principle of equality. A commitment to egalitarianism permeated their theories of distributive social justice. But it also affected their interpretation of basic liberal freedoms. They dislodged what they saw as the unjustifiable primacy of freedom of religion in traditional liberal thought. Religious freedom is only one instantiation of a more basic right—a right to personal freedom or ethical independence, which is also at stake in other controversies around war, conscience, sexuality, and abortion.[52]

There is nothing special about religion, such that religious citizens should receive uniquely privileged treatment in the law—say, in the form of exclusive exemptions on the ground of religious belief. Religious beliefs and activities might be *specially* protected, but not *uniquely* so: if and when they are, it is as a subset of a broader category of respect-worthy beliefs and activities. Liberal egalitarians concede that religion may be paradigmatic of beliefs, identifications, and practices that people have a particular interest in pursuing in their own way, individually or collectively. But they insist that, while religion is a paradigm of those valuable concerns, it does not uniquely capture them. As leading political philosophers have argued, it is the human capacity for moral or spiritual agency, not for leading good lives with a determinate, perhaps religious, content, that should ground the respect that the state owes to persons *qua* persons. Rawls, for example, treats free religious exercise as part of a broader notion of "equal liberty of conscience" that extends both to "moral and religious claims."[53] More recently, Dworkin has suggested that religious freedom is not *sui generis* and is only one implication of a right to "ethical independence in foundational matters."[54] What matters to egalitarians is that all citizens—traditionally religious or not—are treated with equal concern and respect, as free and equal citizens of a democratic society.

This egalitarian turn of liberalism mirrors a parallel shift, within U.S. constitutional doctrine, from a *separationist* to a broadly *neutralist* perspective.[55] At stake in this debate is the question of whether religion deserves constitutionally special treatment, or whether it can be analogized with nonreligious conceptions, practices, and institutions.[56] A separationist approach points out that religion is special, in terms of both protection and exemptions (the Free Exercise Clause) and containment and separation (the Establishment Clause). In the 1960s and 1970s, the U.S. Supreme Court developed such an interpretation of the two clauses. On the Free Exercise side, the "compelling interest" test enshrined in *Sherbert v. Verner* (1963) required religious practices to be exempted from certain laws—a treatment that was not enjoyed by other forms of belief and action. On the Establishment side, the "Lemon test" adopted in *Lemon v. Kurtzmann* (1971) prohibited laws that did not have a secular purpose, that had the effect of advancing or inhibiting religion, or that fostered excessive entanglement of the state with religion.[57]

Separationism came under intense pressure from the 1980s. In *Employment Division v. Smith* (1990) the Court abandoned the compelling interest test, denying a right of religious exemption from laws that are valid, neutral, and generally applicable. The Lemon test was also displaced in favor of a looser test centered on equality. In terms of state funding, the government should be "evenhanded" in its funding of religious groups pursuing public-interest activities and should treat religious speakers exactly as all other speakers. In terms of *state* speech, it should avoid endorsing messages that conveyed disparagement of any citizen, in particular minority believers or nonbelievers. One of the most influential justifications for this stance of state neutrality was rooted in egalitarian principles. In their important book *Religious Freedom and the Constitution* (2007), Christopher Eisgruber and Lawrence Sager rejected the view that religion is a "constitutional anomaly," and instead developed an egalitarian account in which religion is treated no worse, but also no better, than other forms of human experience.[58]

Having sketched the main outlines of liberal egalitarianism, I now show that it offers a promising answer to the critical religion challenge. Let me respond to the three lines of criticism in turn.

The Semantic Critique

Recall that the semantic critique points out that, because there is no stable semantic reference for the term "religion," it cannot be apprehended or regulated by law and the state. In what follows, I suggest that liberal egalitarianism is not vulnerable to the semantic critique because it deploys an interpretive, *not a semantic,* conception of religion. Before I develop this point, let me first mention another sense in which the semantic critique is not as damaging as its proponents suppose. It might be true that there is no essence to religion: no set of features that all religious beliefs, practices, and activities share. But we can apply to religion what Ludwig Wittgenstein said about games: that they have no common feature, but rather exhibit "family resemblances."[59] This has been creatively applied by prominent constitutional scholars such as Kent Greenawalt, who has defended an analogical approach to the definition of the legal concept of religion—a methodology for deciding whether a belief system is or is not a religion, rather than a definition in the dictionary sense.[60] Courts have usually employed a version of this analogical approach, and in practice have had little difficulty identifying what ordinary language would recognize as religion (including non-Western, nontheistic, and unfamiliar religions).[61] There might be borderline cases: humanism, transcendental meditation, and Scientology, to name the most extensively discussed—but these limit cases only reproduce the fuzziness of the ordinary, semantic use of "religion." The law, then, can adequately track the semantic meaning of religion, if we adopt a non-essentialist, broadly Wittgensteinian theory of linguistic use.

However cogent the semantic critique is, it nonetheless misses the mark as a challenge to liberal egalitarianism, which points to a different, nonsemantic approach. The question liberal egalitarians ask is not whether the law adequately captures what is ordinarily meant by religion. From a normative perspective, this begs the prior question: namely, what is it about religion that is protection-worthy? What deeper normative values underpin protection of freedom of religion? In line with Dworkin's interpretive theory of law, the basic thought is that legal concepts cannot be reduced to their semantic meaning.[62] Consider: The law of free speech does not protect *all* that ordinary language calls speech (such as libel) and it does not *only* protect what ordinary language calls speech (such as flag burning). As George Letsas has put it: "We cannot infer simply on the basis of the text that all religious practices are *pro tanto* worthy of protection, any more than we can infer from the basis of the text that all speech is *pro tanto* worthy of protection."[63] Legal and semantic meanings do not overlap, because the law has a specific normative purpose. This is important because not all values can, or indeed should, be expressed by the law. Just as we would not want the law to express the whole of the value of marriage or the family, for example, so we would not want the law to capture of the whole of the value of religion. At best, the law will put forward an interpretive notion of marriage or the family, or of religion. The fact that a particular law or theory does not capture the semantic meaning of religion (or marriage, or the family, or speech) is not, in itself, a sufficient objection to it. What matters is that the law, or the theory, expresses and protects the correct underlying values.[64] It is at this more fundamental level that interpretive approaches must be assessed and evaluated. The right question, for interpretive theories, is not what religion is but, in Dworkin's words, "what makes a belief religious for purposes of the First Amendment" (or, more generally, for purposes of equal liberty).[65]

Because liberal egalitarianism does not single out religion as an area of uniquely special concern, it does not need to get embroiled in controversial definitions of what religion is. All citizens deserve equal

respect as citizens, whatever their particular conception of the good—
be it a life of intellectual reflection, of pious devotion, or of consumerist
hedonism. Ronald Dworkin suggested that everyone possesses some
such conception, from the "scholar who values a life of contemplation"
to the "television-watching beer-drinking citizen" who has never given
the matter much thought.[66] Liberal egalitarian philosophers have been
able to bypass the debates about the category of religion, and therefore
are not vulnerable to the semantic critique. They have generalized the
notion of "religion" to a broader, vaguer, and therefore less ethnocentric
and biased category. The liberal state protects individuals' moral powers
(notably their ability to form and live by a conception of the good); and
it itself does not endorse any such conception of the good. Religion is
morally and politically salient only as one of the conceptions of the good,
ethical worldviews, ways of life, and so on, that make up the pluralism of
contemporary societies.

The Protestant Critique

Recall the two main strands of the Protestant critique: first, liberalism
singles out religion as such; second, liberalism privileges belief-based religious life. It should be clear by now that liberal egalitarianism is not
vulnerable to the first critique. It is egalitarian precisely in the sense that
it does not single out religious believers and groups for special regulation. It rejects the special status of religion in two ways. First, because
freedom of religion protects a generic capacity, it can be adequately guaranteed through basic liberal freedoms such as freedom of thought, speech,
and association: it need not be thought of as a distinctive interpretive
category.[67] Whatever rights religious citizens have, they have in virtue
of a feature that is not exclusive to religion. For example, if there is a
right of conscientious objection from compulsory military service law,
such a right should apply to citizens with both religious and secular
conscientious convictions. Second, the state abstains from endorsing or
supporting any particular religion, but only because it does not endorse

any particular conception of the good. There is no uniquely special separation of state and religion: what matters to state action is how it justifies its policies and institutions, and whether it treats all citizens with equal respect. As a result, religious believers and groups neither enjoy nor suffer exclusively special legal treatment; they are treated under a broader regime of equality, in line with Sullivan's own injunction at the end of *Impossibility of Religious Freedom*.

Let us now turn to the second charge: that liberal egalitarianism is biased against both practice-based and unchosen conceptions of the good. We saw that this charge was pertinent in relation to some recent legal political controversies in Europe, notably veiling controversies. But it is unclear that it applies to philosophical liberalism, let alone to its egalitarian version. The great bulk of philosophical hard cases in academic discussions has concerned exemptions from laws that burden religious *practices:* Shabbat and Friday prayers; religious dress and symbols; the ingestion of peyote; ritual animal slaughter; and so forth. Legal and political philosophers have disagreed over the legitimacy of exemptions for such (mostly non-Protestant) practices. But this is not because they doubt they are properly religious. Rather, disagreement has focused on the justifiability of exemptions generally. To use the terminology of Article 9 of the European Convention of Human Rights, disagreement is not about Article 9(1)—whether the practice counts as an exercise of religion in the first place—but rather about Article 9(2): whether the practice can be legitimately restricted by appeal to other values.[68] No doubt the legitimacy of minority practices is too often screened through majoritarian sensibilities. The European Court of Human Rights freedom of religion jurisprudence has notoriously been lenient toward practices of Christian establishment and overtly intolerant toward the presence of Islam in the public sphere.[69] But I am not convinced that such majoritarian prejudices can be traced back to a liberal *philosophical* bias in favor of belief-based, voluntarily chosen religious practices.

Two considerations must be adduced here, one about choice, and the other about belief. First, it is correct that liberals value *choice,* but the reason they do so is not because they think that what is good about religion is choice. Instead, choice is what is good about legally protected *freedom* of religion. This is very different, and an interpretive theory of religion in the law explains why. Consider again my earlier example of marriage. Marriage realizes goods such as intimacy, love, and commitment. Yet it is true, as Michael Sandel noted in his influential critique of the liberal conception of the self, that when the law deals with the social practice of marriage, it makes it a matter of contractually enforceable rights and duties, notably in relation to divorce, child care, and so forth.[70] More recently, Sandel has developed a similar critique of the notion of freedom of religion: he has argued that the law reduces the richly ethical notion of freedom of religion to mere freedom of conscience, understood as individual choice.[71]

Sandel might be right about the ethical value of marriage and religion, but he is wrong about the role of the law. On the interpretive theory of the law defended here, it is not the business of the law to express and protect the full ethical value of any given social institution. The law should not affirm what is good about marriage, or religion: because people disagree on how best to realize these goods, the law is there to make sure that they are pursued within a fair framework that protects the rights of all. The reason we need a law of divorce is because sometimes marriages do break down and spouses fight, not because marriage is (ethically) a contractual arrangement. By analogy, the reason we need a law of freedom of religion is because religious coercion and persecution is bad, not because religion is a voluntary choice. What the law protects is the right not to be coerced into changing or abandoning the beliefs or way of life that one in fact has. On this view, it does not matter how religious commitments were acquired, provided people identify with them.[72] People might experience being "called" by a divine presence or "claimed" by a community, instead of "choosing their religion." There is nothing in the liberal law of freedom of religion that contradicts or hampers the depth and variety of religious experience. As Will Kymlicka has rightly pointed out, choice is not important *per se:* what matters is that lives are "led from the inside"—that individuals identify with their ends and commitments, however these were acquired. We could go further. There is a paradox in the critical religion attack on the presumed liberal bias toward chosen beliefs. The paradigmatic case of religious exemptions, for generations of liberals, has been exemptions on grounds on *conscience* and *duty.* As Martin Luther put it, "Here I stand, and I cannot act otherwise."[73] We will get back in due course to this duty-based conception of religion. Suffice here to say that it has enough pull on liberals to throw doubt on the blanket criticism of the liberal's presumed bias toward choice.

The second misconception entertained by otherwise astute critics is about the importance of *belief* in the liberal construal of freedom of religion. Mahmood and Danchin, for example, argue that the liberal law of religious freedom only protects *forum internum* and arbitrarily regulates *forum externum,* because practices (by contrast to beliefs) automatically fall under the civil interests of the state. I shall say more about the role of the state in Chapter 5 (where I agree with Mahmood, Danchin, Asad, and Agrama about the central place of state sovereignty in secular liberalism). But at this point it is worth noting that the liberal state does not regulate *forum externum* just because it is *externum.* This is a necessary but not a sufficient condition. In both Locke and Mill, we find the notion that religious practices can only be interfered with *if* they injure or harm others, or otherwise infringe on their rights.[74] To take up again the critics' favorite example of Muslim veiling: Few liberals would argue that there can be a justification for direct bans on practices that do not infringe on the rights of others. Such bans have usually been justified in relation to specifically French-influenced conceptions of *laïcité* and secularism—but these differ from the liberal egalitarianism I discuss in this book.[75] Liberal philosophers have been as vocal as critical theorists in denouncing infringements on freedom of religion in the name of public order, majoritarian sensibilities, or mere offense to others.[76] And—as this section has briefly illustrated—philosophical liberalism is not committed to the implausible view that religion is essentially about belief not practice, or that it has to be chosen to deserve respect.

The Realist Critique

There are two variants of the realist critique, which we may call *liberalism-as-power* and *liberalism-as-religion*. There is no space here to do justice to both, which would require going deep into methodological and substantive disputes between critical theorists and normative philosophers. But let me, as a way of laying the foundations for my own argument, briefly dispel some common misunderstandings.

According to the first charge, liberalism is a mode of state governance based on the constant and arbitrary reconfiguration and regulation of religion in the interests of secular state power. All states—whether formally secular or religious—produce regimes of religious normativity, to use Foucault's phrase. It is no coincidence that states as otherwise different as France, Turkey, and Egypt are heavily involved in defining and regulating "proper" religion. Such regulation—the objection continues—contradicts liberal states' commitment to separation of state and religion.[77]

What are we to make of this criticism? Critics sometimes write as though state definition and regulation of religion is *per se* troubling or embarrassing for liberals. But it is not. First, there is nothing self-contradictory about the state, or the law, defining the area or activity to which it applies (this "competence," as we shall see in Chapter 5, is in fact constitutive of sovereignty). To protect freedom of speech, the state must define the scope of speech (that is, interpret the value of speech); to subsidize the arts, it must define the arts; to combat racial hatred, it must define both hatred and race. Those definitions are problematic and contested, of course, but it does not mean that they are self-defeating.[78] It is unconvincing to suggest, as some have, that the mere fact that states define what religion is amounts to "establishment" of religion. On the interpretive view that I defend, we will need finer-grained distinctions—of establishment, of what is impermissible about it, and why.

Second, the fact that regulation of religion is normative in a Foucauldian sense—it shapes the way that people experience the world—does not mean that it is impermissible in a liberal normative sense. It may be true that both Saudi Arabia and France define and regulate religion; just as it is true that both the UK and Uganda define and regulate homosexuality. But it is not good enough to point out that power is everywhere, and that everywhere it is normative: just ask members of sexual and religious minorities in Uganda or Saudi Arabia. As Nancy Fraser sharply argued in her incisive critique of Foucault, there are good and bad, better or worse exercises of power, and a radical sweeping critique of state norms does not empower, but rather blunts, the edge of critique.[79]

Third, critics take the idea of separation too literally. They write as though liberals, insofar as they are committed to "neutrality," are committed to something like a "separate sovereignty" view of church-state relations. Thus Peter Danchin writes that "the neutrality thesis is no longer tenable. Rather than withdraw from the religious domain, the modern secular state . . . intervenes and . . . reconfigures substantive features of religious life."[80] But this confuses neutrality—a normative abstract principle—with separation—a particular institutional and political framework. As Eisgruber and Sager have argued, the metaphor of a "wall of separation" between state and religion is descriptively and normatively unhelpful.[81] The liberal state intervenes in religious life—as in social life—in myriad ways, and often does so permissibly. For example, states extend their fire services protection to churches, mosques, and synagogues; they do not exempt religious officials from the purview of criminal law; they provide financial support to a range of religious associations and charities; they recognize the cultural and social role of religion. Such activities may breach strict separation, but they are not *ipso facto* incompatible with neutrality.[82] Critics fail to see that liberal neutrality refers either to the *justification* of specific arrangements or politics, or to the principle of *equal treatment* of different conceptions of the good and ways of life. Both raise intriguing puzzles for the liberal treatment of religion—which I will come back to in due course. But these cannot be reduced to a simple contradiction between separation and neutrality.

Finally, and connectedly, critics mistake liberal neutrality for liberal skepticism. Liberals are not committed to value-free neutrality (or separation or abstention). Rather, these are best seen as derivative, downstream principles: principles that follow from higher-order commitments to substantive (if thin) liberal ideals. Roughly, liberalism is based on the idea that all individuals should enjoy as much freedom as is compatible with the freedoms of others, and—in its egalitarian version—it distributes a set of primary goods (such as rights and opportunities) according to principles of justice. This is not an ethically neutral ideal. As liberal egalitarians do not embrace skepticism, they should not be worried by Fish's charge that the state is not neutral when it forces a basic liberal education on religious fundamentalists.[83] This is not an arbitrary violation of non-neutrality, but instead a logical implication of liberal political morality.

This nicely takes us to the second main realist charge—that liberalism is merely another religion. This suggests that liberalism is "anything but impartial . . . it is [a] notion of the good, as contestable as any other."[84] It cannot claim to regulate and arbitrate between diverse religions and conceptions of the good because it is itself a religion. This is a familiar critique of liberalism, and in the rest of this book I shall directly respond to some of its most sophisticated versions. Here I'll just briefly dispel the crudest variants of it. The first variant is purely semantic. There are ways in which liberalism is "like" a religion, which, however, do not affect its normative claim to provide a fair framework for living together under conditions of pluralism. The point is semantic because it depends on which referent is used for the word "religion." To say that liberalism is the religion of this or that state may simply imply (in one sense of religion) that it provides the fundamental set of principles that the state claims to live up to. Individuals may also see liberalism as their religion—rights activists, trade unionists, political dissidents, and such organize their lives around liberal ideals, profess their truth, form liberal lobbying associations, and so forth. We can also say that liberalism rests on sacred values such as rights: they are sacred in the sense that they are not to be weighed, bargained, and balanced in a utilitarian trade-off, but instead are pursued with total commitment regardless of loss and sacrifice.[85] Liberalism can also be called a faith—an array of aspirations and hopes that one is moved by, but that is not anchored in a foundational, rational argument. Liberalism can be as intransigent and fundamentalist as any religion, as when it enforces the rights of suspected terrorists against majoritarian populism. And, of course, liberalism has deep religious roots—ethically, spiritually—and it is constantly revitalized, sustained, and fed by diverse religious traditions of thought.[86] All of these are perfectly legitimate uses of the term "religion." But they depart from the interpretive sense of "liberalism's religion" that I seek to pin down in this book, which relates to the specific politico-legal values of free exercise and nonestablishment.

Second, then, there is a serious philosophical point. This is that the political philosophy of liberalism has no valid claim to provide a framework for the fair coexistence between different religions (and conceptions of the good), because it is itself a religion. It is, in a sense, judge and party. What is the dimension of religion that Fish picks out in the sentence above? On the one hand, Fish might mean that liberalism is a controversial doctrine: it is not universally shared. This is correct, but need not trouble liberals. Political liberals, following Rawls's later work, seek to justify liberalism to a wide consistency of individuals holding diverse conceptions of the good, but, as we saw, no liberals (not even political liberals) claim that liberalism is uncontroversial, or that it can be justified to those who reject its central norms. If this is what is meant by the idea that liberalism is a religion, liberals are guilty as charged, but the charge is trivial.

On the other hand, Fish might mean that liberalism is a religion in the thicker sense that it is a rival metaphysics and a comprehensive way of life—it is a direct competitor to traditionally religious doctrines and therefore cannot claim to accommodate them fairly. This is a more damaging charge, and is indeed a valid criticism of one variant of liberalism—one inspired by Enlightenment ideals of rationality, individual autonomy from religion, and substantive secularism (such as, for example, a version of French *laïcité*).[87] This, however, is not the liberal tradition I associate with. Liberal egalitarianism, much in the spirit of Rawls's political liberalism, seeks to provide a fair framework of coexistence between citizens holding a variety of doctrines, religious and nonreligious. It is not itself grounded in any comprehensive metaphysical, ontological, or ethical doctrine. It does not seek to enforce a substantively liberal and secular way of life on citizens, but instead affirms political principles of justice, notably the fair distribution of "primary goods" (goods that everyone values, whatever else they value), such as freedoms, rights, and opportunities. As a political doctrine, it can be endorsed—so political liberals hope—from a variety of otherwise conflicting conceptions of the good. The liberal framework promises the fairest way of living together under terms that preserve the equal freedom of all. The onus is on critics of liberalism to explain how any political alternative might be defensible at all. There has been no shortage of radical critiques of philosophical liberalism, but few have positively defended attractive alternatives—from agonistic, relativist, or truth-based perspectives.

This does not mean, however, that philosophical liberalism is not riddled by significant tensions. In the rest of this book, I shall explore—and attempt to address—some of them. In doing so, I shall follow the lead of the critical religion school. It is correct, as they suspect, that some of the blind spots of liberalism emerge from its insufficient reflection on the concept of religion. In particular, I shall argue that the liberal analogy between religion and "conception of the good" is unsatisfactory. To defend liberal egalitarianism, we will need to work with a more complex, disaggregated conception of religion and the good. The liberal state is not—should not be—neutral toward "religion" or "the good" in general. Rather, reflecting on the interpretive values of liberalism allows us to pick out different values associated with religion and the good.

In Chapters 2 and 3, I show that liberal egalitarians such as Dworkin, Taylor, Eisgruber and Sager, and Quong have in fact a much more layered and structured view of what "religion" stands for within liberalism. Through a close reading of their texts, I shall show that liberal egalitarians work not with one simple analogy (of religion and "conceptions of the good") but with a plurality of interpretive analogies. They in fact rely on different interpretations of what religion is, for purposes of freedom of religion and nonestablishment. This points the way toward a more complex strategy of defense of liberalism, which I will pursue in Part II. Once we have a clear grasp of the implication of my alternative *disaggregation* strategy, we will be able to come back to, and address, two salient critical religion challenges. The first, which I shall call the ethical salience problem, is that liberal egalitarians cannot avoid evaluating the normative salience of different kinds of beliefs, practices, and identities. The second, which I shall call the jurisdictional boundary problem, is that liberal egalitarians cannot avoid granting the state the authority to delimitate the proper boundaries of religion. Both objections throw doubts on the liberal egalitarian promise of neutrality toward religion. The shift to neutrality does not dissolve the substantive question of where to draw the line between the religious and the nonreligious, and of what is valuable (or problematic) about religion, even on an interpretive theory. If we are to defend liberalism, we will have to give up, or at least modify, some claims made on behalf of liberal neutrality. This much we will have learned from the critical religion challenge—and it is, I shall suggest, a salutary lesson.

2

୫୦୦ଛ

Liberal Egalitarianism
and the Exemptions Puzzle

In Chapter 1, I introduced the liberal egalitarian theory of state and religion. Its main starting point is that there is nothing special about religion, such that religious citizens should receive uniquely privileged treatment in the law—say, in the form of exclusive exemptions on the ground of religious belief. Religious beliefs and activities might be *specially* protected, but not *uniquely* so: if and when they are, it is as a subset of a broader category of respect-worthy beliefs and activities. But what exactly is this broader category? What is it made of? What is religion *like,* and why is it ethically salient? Liberal egalitarians have not been forthcoming in their response to what I call the ethical salience challenge. It is easy to understand why. Liberal egalitarians' main criticism of religionist accommodationists is that singling out religion is incompatible with commitment to neutrality about the good and equality between all citizens.[1] So it is understandable that liberal egalitarians should be uneasy about identifying a class of ethically salient commitments to which religious (though not only religious) practices belong. Isn't *any* judgment of ethical salience straightforwardly incompatible with neutrality and equality?

In this chapter, I explore these tensions by analyzing the liberal egalitarian solution to the puzzle of exemptions. Legal exemptions abound in Western law, and most (if not all) are granted on the grounds of religious belief. Think of exemptions from food regulations, dress codes, health and safety regulations, military service, educational and medical requirements, antidiscrimination laws, and so forth. Are there grounds, as a matter of justice (not merely expediency), for exempting some citizens, on grounds of their beliefs or conceptions of the good, from the burdens of general laws? If exemptions are not exclusive to religion—if they are granted on the basis that religion is a subset of a broader category of beliefs or practices that themselves qualify for exemption—then religious exemptions might be permissible. But how can exemptions be compatible with neutrality and equality? How do we justify providing special exemptions from general laws to some individuals but not others? When, and why, is religion—or its analogues—ethically salient?

I will examine three strategies that have been proposed to resolve this puzzle: *dissolving* religion, *mainstreaming* religion, and *narrowing* religion. The *dissolving* strategy has been developed by Ronald Dworkin, who bites the ethical salience bullet and rejects exemptions on the grounds that no defensible distinction can be drawn between and among religious and nonreligious ethical views. The *mainstreaming* strategy is associated with Christopher Eisgruber and Lawrence Sager, who analogize religion with existing protection-worthy categories, such as disabilities, vulnerable identities, or close association. The *narrowing* strategy analogizes religion with a specific subset of conscientious duties, and has recently been articulated by Charles Taylor, Jocelyn Maclure, and other liberal egalitarians. I explain the potential and limits of each strategy in turn. These limits, however, are instructive: each strategy zooms in on one ethically salient dimension of religion, which is necessary but—I shall argue—not sufficient. Liberal egalitarians have underestimated the internal complexity of the referent of "religion." I will conclude that we need a more complex, disaggregated account of religion, as well as of the justice of exemptions, both individual and collective.

Dissolving Religion

The first strategy is the most consistent in following through on the starting assumptions of liberal egalitarianism. It proposes to broaden religion into a maximally inclusive category that comprises preferences, commitments, identities, beliefs, worldviews, and so forth. Religion is not so much analogized with them as dissolved into them. This means that neither religion nor the more inclusive category it falls under needs to be defined precisely, because their boundaries and scope are irrelevant for the purpose of egalitarian treatment. Logically, therefore, because there is no specific category that displays identifiable features that would justify differential treatment, there is no justification for exemptions from the law.

A particularly articulate and sophisticated exponent of this strategy is Ronald Dworkin. In a posthumous book entitled *Religion without God* (2013), Dworkin explains what, for legal and political purposes, we should interpret religion to be. Religion, Dworkin notes, is not easy to define. Either it is defined too narrowly (as theistic religion) and the protections of religious freedom are unjustifiably denied to atheists. Or it is defined too broadly (as "religion without God," or any sincere conviction about what gives meaning to life) and it would "cover too much." Instead, Dworkin suggests a different, nonsemantic approach—applying his interpretive theory of law and policies to the treatment of religion.[2] Instead of "fixing attention on the subject matter in question" (the semantic question of what religion is), we should, for legal and political purposes, "fix on the relation between government and its citizens: . . . [and] limit the reasons government may offer for any constraint on a citizen's freedom at all."[3]

This shift of focus—from subject matter to reasons—allows Dworkin to draw on a crucial distinction between "general" and "special" rights.[4] The government protects general rights when it does not directly and deliberatively violate the freedom in question, but it can regulate that freedom if it appeals to appropriately neutral reasons—reasons that respect citizens' ethical independence. So government must not appeal to the superiority of one way of life over another; but it can appeal to neutral reasons such as just distribution or environmental protection to justify policies that interfere with citizens' way of life—including religious ways of life. Special rights, in turn, require a higher level of protection. They protect special interests and can only be regulated if government offers a "compelling justification" for doing so. Freedom of speech, for Dworkin, is one example of such a special right: government cannot routinely constrain it in the pursuit of its otherwise legitimate goals. So even speech that would seriously undermine a government's economic and distributive strategy must not be abridged.[5]

Freedom of religion, in turn, should be seen as a general right.[6] It is a general right to ethical independence, which is formulated as a principle of reason-giving or justification. Government must not appeal to the truth or untruth of one religion or ethical view in the pursuit of its goals. But freedom of religion does not require a "high hurdle of protection and therefore its compelling need for strict limits and careful definition."[7] To declare that freedom of religion is a special right would be, for Dworkin, "troublesome." This is so for two main reasons. First, if the notion of religion is understood to include nontheistic beliefs and commitments, then freedom of religion would be "out of control."[8] As there is "no compelling distinction" between a religion and some other general kind of attitude toward life (Dworkin cites secular pacifism, views about the permissibility of abortion, and even "devout materialism" as possible religious attitudes), special rights of protection would be—absurdly—extended "to all passionately held convictions."[9]

Second, granting special rights of exemptions would exacerbate the risk that the government would discriminate between citizens on arbitrary grounds. To illustrate his claim, Dworkin approvingly cites the landmark decision of the U.S. Supreme Court in *Oregon v. Smith* (1990). Should members of a Native American community be entitled to an exemption from drug use regulations because they use a hallucinogenic drug called peyote in their ritual ceremonies? Dworkin thinks not: first, because the purpose of the law is general and nondiscriminatory and is intended to protect all citizens against a substantial health risk, and second, because there is no principled way of distinguishing between religious and other uses of a drug (for example, that of the hippy adepts of Aldous Huxley).[10] In sum, Dworkin concludes, "if religion cannot be restricted to theism, the priority of non-discriminatory government legislation over private religious exercise seems inevitable and right."[11]

The logic of the dissolving strategy could not be explicated more clearly. If there is no ethically salient boundary between religious and other kinds of attitudes to life, it becomes impossible to carve out a specific area of protection from the law. Freedom of religion is not a special but a general right—an instantiation of a more general right of ethical independence, which requires government not to appeal to particular conceptions of the good to justify its action.

In what follows, however, I argue that Dworkin did not successfully circumvent the ethical salience challenge, because of hidden tensions and internal contradictions within his theory. The first tension is between Dworkin's non-exemption stance and his concern for special burdens. The second is between his commitment to broad neutrality of justification and his more specific ban on appeal to "religious" matters. I examine them in turn.

First, recall that what distinguishes a special from a general right is that, whereas the former protects a specially valuable interest from the burden of a general law, the latter requires only that neutral justifications be appealed to justify the law. This means that the fact that a particular practice, say a religious practice, is incidentally burdened by a general law (as in the peyote case) does not mean that the right to freedom of religion has been violated. What matters is that the justification for the law is suitably neutral and nondiscriminatory and pursues a valid general interest. Here Dworkin draws very close to a position famously endorsed by Brian Barry, according to whom, if a law is otherwise legitimate and justified, we should not worry about the unequal incidental burdens it creates for certain groups of citizens (this position is also that of the French republican conception of equality and *laïcité*).[12] This position relies on a firm distinction between the justification of a regulation, on the one hand, and its effects and impact, on the other.

Yet, on closer inspection, Dworkin has a far more complex position of what counts as a neutral justification: it turns out to be one that must also take effect and impact into account. Dworkin writes that a justification is not neutral if it "directly, indirectly or covertly" presupposes the superiority of one ethical view over another.[13] Let us focus on "covert" non-neutrality. A justification is "covertly" non-neutral if, albeit facially neutral, it "ignores the special importance of some issue to some citizens" and thereby constitutes a failure of equal concern. Dworkin goes further, in passing, in his discussion of the peyote case: "Equal concern requires the legislature to notice *whether the activity it proposes to prohibit or burden is regarded by any group as a sacred duty.* If any group does, then the legislature must consider whether equal concern for that group requires an exemption or other amelioration."[14]

But this, of course, was precisely the reasoning of critics of *Smith* in the peyote case. Dworkin finds that, *on balance,* the exemption is not defensible, because the interest pursued by the state (drugs control) is a weighty one. But this is different from saying that there is no special right to freedom of religion *on principle.* Dworkin himself seems to concede that *if* something is considered by a group as a sacred duty, a legislature can only ignore it if it can demonstrate a compelling state interest. Perhaps drug policy is such an interest. Dworkin unfortunately avoids any further discussion of whether (and which) religious exemptions from general law might be defensible if the interests pursued by the law are less than compelling, and yet the duty burdened is held by some group as sacred. But it is precisely *this* discussion that is needed if we are to assess whether freedom of religion is a special right. As soon as it is conceded that a justification cannot be fully neutral if it fails to take into account some duty held sacred by some group, the distinction between neutrality as reason and neutrality as impact (and the refusal to consider the nature and weight of burdens) breaks down.

Dworkin evades the ethical salience problem in another passage of *Religion without God*. Commenting on some recent French and Belgian legislation, he writes that the wearing of religious signs, being an essentially "private" matter, should not be forbidden by law.[15] But he avoids the more difficult question, whether this private matter may be *incidentally* burdened by the application of general laws. What if an organization—say, the police force—has a policy that requires all its members to wear a suitable uniform, and be bareheaded and clean-shaven? The policy clearly has a neutral, nondiscriminatory justification. Yet some would say that it is unfairly burdensome, insofar as it ignores the claim by some of members of the police force—Sikhs, Jews, and Muslims—that the wearing of beards or special headwear is a sacred duty for them. Is this a case of covert discrimination, in Dworkin's view? How can we know this without assessing the particular weight of the interest in question? It looks as if, on Dworkin's own theory, freedom of religion will sometimes generate special rights of protection. But if that is the case, we will need a workable theory of what counts as a *burden* on freedom of religion. And we will not be able to evade the difficult question—which Dworkin sought to sidestep—as to whether a religious use of drugs is more respectable, from the perspective of the liberal state, than a recreational use of drugs. This is the heart of the ethical salience problem.

In sum, the extension of the category of religion to cover godless beliefs and commitments, and the appeal to a general right of ethical independence, do not by themselves resolve the question of where to draw the line between those activities that it is wrong to burden, even incidentally and unintentionally, through ordinary legislation, and those activities, which are less ethically salient, that can permissibly be so burdened. Dworkin hoped that broadening the notion of religion to godless beliefs would allow him to solve the question of the legitimacy of exemptions, essentially by dissolving it. Yet by conceding that liberal justification is not neutral if it "indirectly or covertly" discriminates against some practices considered as "sacred"—by conceding, in effect, that liberal justification should concern itself with impact, not only with reasons[16]—Dworkin has not so much solved the question as reformulated it at a higher level of generality.

This is, so, secondly, because a version of the ethical salience challenge also reappears at the level of justification. It is important to see this, because it could be argued that I have exaggerated the significance of Dworkin's ambivalent stance about *Smith* and the justice of exempting Native American practices. Dworkin's unexpected concession to advocates of exemptions could be interpreted as a strategic intervention in political debates about the First Amendment religion clauses in the U.S. Constitution. He could be understood as denying that there is a constitutional right to exemptions but accepting (in line with *Smith*) that exemptions may be granted by legislatures; as well as affirming that, *if* exemptions are legitimate, they are legitimate for non-Christian and nontheistic religions too. But these should be seen as minor pragmatic exceptions to a firmly stated general philosophical principle: namely, that once religion is dissolved into a broader category, the principled case for exemptions collapses, and the ethical salience challenge is answered.

In response, I shall suggest that, even if Dworkin's stance on exemptions is more pragmatic than principled, the ethical salience challenge reappears at the level of principled justification. This is because the shift to second-order justification does not eliminate the need to interpret the properly "religious." Why not? As we shall see in Chapter 3, Dworkin thought that the state must be neutral about the good because it should not usurp people's own decisions about matters that touch on the meaning of life and death, intimate decisions about birth, sexuality, and family, and so forth. In *Life's Dominion*, he famously argued that the state should not regulate people's decisions about abortion or euthanasia, because these are *religious* matters.[17] In the first section of *Religion without God*, Dworkin further expanded his interpretive notion of religion by showing that atheistic liberals, too, hold religious views—views about what is sacred about human life and human existence. If that is the case, then there *is* an ethically relevant distinction between what is religious and what is not (even if religion is defined broadly). What this means is that the respect we owe "religion" is respect we owe to any sincere search for the meaning of human life in a profoundly mysterious, baffling, but also beautiful universe. Yet in the second section of *Religion without God*, Dworkin insisted that such distinctions of ethical salience should have no political implication. As a political principle, liberal neutrality demands that the state does *not* discriminate between what is religious and what is not.

But this cannot be correct. A Dworkinian state discriminates between religious and nonreligious worldviews: it cannot permissibly appeal to the former in the justification of its laws, but it can appeal to the latter. So we need to know what is, and what is not, relevantly religious, for the purposes of public justification. I conclude that even if Dworkin can successfully dispense with a definition of what is religious for purposes of exemptions, the ethical salience challenge reemerges at the level of justification.[18] I shall explore this issue in Chapter 3, when I turn to the issue of state neutrality and nonestablishment.

Mainstreaming Religion

An alternative strategy, which I call the "mainstreaming strategy," analogizes religion with comparable categories that also deserve egalitarian concern. This strategy is more promising than the dissolving strategy, insofar as it accepts that, although religion is not uniquely special, it can be protected by analogy with other protection-worthy categories.

The most sophisticated exposition of the mainstreaming strategy to date is Christopher Eisgruber and Lawrence Sager's *Religious Freedom and the Constitution*.[19] In this book-length commentary on recent religion clause jurisprudence of the U.S. Supreme Court, Eisgruber and Sager vigorously defend the view that religious believers should enjoy "equal not special liberty." Religion should not be seen as "a constitutional anomaly, a category of human experience that demands special benefits and / or necessitates special restrictions."[20] Instead, religious commitments should be treated as part of a broader class of commitments and projects that people care about, whether religious or not. Eisgruber and Sager deny that such commitments and projects, however morally weighty and significant, generate *pro tanto* rights against the state. The relevant political question is whether the government, in coordinating different life projects, shares benefits and burdens fairly among people.[21] This allows the formulation of a discrimination-centered account of religious freedom: "Persons [should] not be treated unequally on account of the spiritual foundations of their deep commitments."

Contra critics of exemptions,[22] they argue that exemptions might be demanded by the ideal of equality, insofar as a government enacting generally applicable laws "may be hostile or insensitive to the needs and interests of minority faiths."[23] It is as members of groups that are discriminated against or disparaged, not as holders of intrinsically valuable religious beliefs and practices, that minority religious believers deserve special consideration under the theory of equal liberty. Their interests should not be *privileged* as religious, but instead *protected* on similar terms as comparably serious nonreligious interests.[24] The aim, as Eisgruber and Sager put it, is equality, not privilege. This is an attractive proposition for egalitarians, who worry that formal legal equality leaves minority interests at the mercy of majoritarian preferences yet see little justification for a McConnell-style privileging of religious interests *qua* religious.[25]

We can distinguish three different kinds of cases of application of this principle in Eisgruber and Sager's discussion. In the first set of cases, the contested law already provides for exemptions for nonreligious interests, to which minority religious interests can easily be analogized. Eisgruber and Sager use the example of two Muslim policemen, Faruq

Abdul-Aziz and Shakour Mustafa, who challenged the Newark police
department's requirement that officers be clean-shaven, on the ground
that their faith demanded that they wear a beard.[26] Given that the
Newark department already exempted officers with skin disorders, such
as folliculitis, that made shaving painful or promoted infection, its refusal to accommodate the Muslims' request constitutes a failure of equal
regard.[27] In the second set of cases, the contested law does not directly
provide exemptions, but is applied against a broader regulatory background that advantages mainstream or majoritarian interests. The *Sherbert
v. Verner* decision (1963)—a landmark case in the U.S. constitutionalization of religious freedom—falls into this category. Adell Sherbert, a
member of the Seventh-Day Adventist Church, was denied unemployment compensation on the grounds that no "good cause" justified her
unwillingness to comply with her employer's demand that she, like other
employees, accept Saturday work. Eisgruber and Sager argue that denying compensation would have entailed unjustly discriminating against
Sherbert. This is because, *unlike similarly situated workers,* she faces an
unfair dilemma: either complying with the job's requirements or obeying
the demands of her faith (and losing her claim to compensation). The
state of South Carolina had strict Sunday closing laws, which meant
that mainstream Christians were not forced to choose between exercising
their religious rights and performing the demands of their job. So Adell
Sherbert was discriminated against when her claim for compensation
was denied.[28]

    In the third, most complicated, set of cases, the contested law is fa-
cially neutral and generally applicable. Here, Eisgruber and Sager suggest that government may be held to a standard that measures a claim
for a religious exemption against *hypothetical* exemptions. For example,
in the case of *Lyng v. Northwestern Cemetery Protective Association* (1988),
the Supreme Court considered Native American claims that construction of a logging road on federal land would disrupt vision quests, sacred
rituals that depend on isolation and immersion in wilderness. There
were no ready-made comparisons, but Eisgruber and Sager speculate that

the Forest Service would not have constructed the road had mainstream religious ("a site sacred to a small but well-acknowledged group of Catholics or Orthodox Jews") or secular ("killing off some of the last great redwood trees") interests been at stake. In light of that hypothetical comparison, they say, the case is revealed as a problem of unjust inequality that should have been decided in favor of the plaintiffs.[29] In sum, through a creative use of analogical and hypothetical reasoning, Eisgruber and Sager suggest that, even though religious interests are not presumptively entitled to unique constitutional immunity from otherwise valid laws, they should enjoy robust protection on the basis of equality. It is because minority religious interests are "vulnerable to hostility and neglect" that they should receive special solicitude.[30] The underlying value of such an antidiscrimination approach is "parity, not advantage."[31]

But what exactly is being equalized here? Which category of beliefs and identities is protection-worthy in the first place? Many things are alike and unlike in different respects, so the relevant comparison requires an underlying substantive theory of equality. If equality is not to be an empty, purely formal notion,[32] theories of equality and nondiscrimination must specify in respect of what people must be treated equally. The claim that religion and nonreligion should be treated equally is too vague: What is nonreligion? As Woljciech Sadurski has put it, "You cannot, without running into absurdity, be neutral between X and everything that is non-X, including those things which are totally irrelevant from the point of view of X."[33] The category of nonreligion is too loose and imprecise to serve as a comparator to that of religion.[34]

Theories of equality are not self-standing: they rely on a prior account of which relevant features of existing states of affairs are to be the proper object of comparative evaluations of unfair treatment. For example, it would be implausible to assert that marriage laws unfairly discriminate against business associates or frequent tennis partners, just by virtue of those "couples" being excluded from its benefits. By contrast, they can be said to discriminate against same-sex couples insofar as the latter exhibit the valued features (intimacy, stability, commitment) that marriage is supposed to protect. Or, alternatively, marriage laws can be said to be indefensible in the first place because they arbitrarily single out, protect, and privilege values associated with the traditional family and a conservative social order, and therefore discriminate against non-conventional families and single-parent households.[35] In sum, to be able to claim that tennis partners, same-sex couples, or single parents are discriminated against by marriage laws, we need to provide both (1) an account of the features singled out and promoted by those laws and (2) an account of what it means to be "similarly situated" in relation to these features. Religion, in this respect, is no different from marriage.

In what follows, I argue that Eisgruber and Sager have not settled for a single criterion of comparability between religion and nonreligion, and instead oscillate between normatively distinct criteria.[36] The first criterion is that of *vulnerability to discrimination*. Religious minority identities, like other minority identities, are vulnerable to hostility and disregard from the majority. On this first criterion, religion is a marker for any kind of belief or practice that is particularly vulnerable to invidious discrimination (or neglect) by majorities. But what kind of hostility and disregard counts as unfair discrimination, and which identities are ethically salient?[37] The easiest case is that of actual *inequality* in the treatment of different religions, and official disregard of minority religions. An example here is the way the state of Oregon treated the religious uses of alcohol and the drug peyote in the run-up to the *Smith* case. The state laws limiting alcohol use included an exemption for communion wine, but the laws limiting peyote use contained no such exemption. Christians benefit from an exemption from laws restricting alcohol use to facilitate their religious practice, but members of the Native American religion, which makes sacramental use of peyote, do not. Eisgruber and Sager plausibly argue that failing to exempt sacramental peyote use—a minority practice—therefore violates equal regard.[38] On this reading, *Smith* would constitute a straightforward breach of neutrality and equality.

However, crucially, equal liberty requires equality not only between majority and minority religions, but also between religious and secular commitments and projects. But which nonreligious commitments are ethically salient, such that they can be analogized with religion? What is the criterion of comparability? One answer provided by Eisgruber and Sager is the *depth of commitments*. As they note in an earlier article, "religion does not exhaust the commitments and passions that move human beings in deep and valuable ways."[39] For exemption purposes, they claim, religious interests should be protected in virtue of being "deep," "serious," "spiritual," "moral" commitments held by individuals. Although those terms are not elaborated upon, they are pivotal to their theory. They allow Eisgruber and Sager to draw a wedge between religious freedom and the protection of "frivolous" interests, such as fashion or aesthetic preferences.[40] As Andrew Koppelman has suggested, Eisgruber and Sager therefore rely on something like Taylorian "strong evaluation."[41] Even though they deny it, they need an account of the ethical salience—in their view, the "depth"—of religious and nonreligious commitments.

One secular claim sufficiently resembles traditional religion to be accommodated on this ground: nonreligious conscientious commitment. Those who have a sincere, deep, nonreligious conscientious commitment to pacifism are entitled to the same exemptions as those whose pacifism is religiously grounded. In two important Vietnam War decisions, *Seeger* and *Welsh,* the U.S. Supreme Court exempted secular pacifists from military service on the ground that they had "a sincere and meaningful belief which occupies in the life of its possessor a place parallel to that filled by the God of those admittedly qualifying for the exemption."[42] Unsurprisingly, the *Seeger-Welsh* jurisprudence has become a point of reference for liberal egalitarian theorists, as the paradigm of accommodation extended from religious to nonreligious moral commitments.

There are two difficulties with the depth criterion, however. The first question is whether it provides a sound basis for extending accommodation *from* nonreligious *to* religious interests. Eisgruber and Sager answer that it does, in cases when the government accommodates "serious . . . secular interests but refuses to provide an equivalent accommodation for the comparably serious interests of minority religious groups or individuals."[43] They argue that certain arrangements provide benchmarks by which we can judge whether the religious and the secular are treated equally. One such benchmark is the provision made for medical conditions, as in the Newark police case. Here, religious interests are explicitly analogized with disabilities and other "comparably serious" or "sufficiently compelling" interests.[44]

One advantage of this view is that it sidesteps the sterile debate about whether the ethical salience of religious commitments must be connected to whether they are products of "chance" or "choice."[45] What matters is that they are weighty and serious: regardless of how they were acquired, they are generally not contingent, negotiable personal preferences. If they are not treated with the same consideration as equally serious interests, their bearers may reasonably experience a loss of civic standing.[46] Yet Eisgruber and Sager trade on an ambiguity between two senses of "serious." Medical conditions are "serious," but they are not "spiritual," "moral" commitments held by individuals. It makes a moral difference that people (by and large) positively endorse and embrace their religious convictions, whereas they (by and large) prefer not to suffer from a disability.[47] Medical conditions and disabilities are not "important projects and commitments" with "spiritual foundations." It is not clear, therefore, what it is, in virtue of which they are "secular interests" that are "comparable" to religion. Religious commitments may in some case be treated like disabilities, but it is not in virtue of being conceptions of the good or deep moral commitments.

The second difficulty is that the depth criterion, in itself, does not invite any search for a comparator group. It may be wrong to burden religious interests, regardless of whether medical conditions, or other interests, are protected. What if a general law burdens only minority religious interests with no obvious comparator group? Consider, again, the *Sherbert* case. Sherbert might in fact have been victim of a double wrong. It is true that mainstream Christians in South Carolina who refused to work on their day of rest were protected from adverse consequences that they might otherwise incur, whereas Seventh-Day Adventists like Sherbert were not. So Sherbert has a *comparative* claim to be treated on fair, equal terms with others. But it is also plausible to say (as the Court in fact said) that to condition Sherbert's access to benefit on her willingness to violate a cardinal principle of her faith would be unduly to penalize and burden her rights of religious freedom. On this view, Sherbert has a *pro tanto* claim to practice her religion freely (absent a compelling state interest). To the fundamental wrong that Sherbert had suffered was added the further wrong of being treated unequally with those whose religious day of rest fell on Sundays.[48] So it might be the case that some citizens—whether of minority or majority faiths—are disproportionately burdened by a general secular law: this is a noncomparative claim that singles out a category of burden as ethically salient. Consider again the Newark Muslim officers: a regulation preventing them from wearing a beard on religious grounds might be unfair *even in the absence of comparable medical exemptions.*

So far I have shown that the theory of equal liberty, for all its elegant and economical simplicity, deploys not one but two normative criteria of comparability between religious and nonreligious claims: vulnerability to discrimination, and depth of commitment. Furthermore, it is not entirely clear how they are related—an issue to which I shall return in Part II. For now, our presentation of Eisgruber and Sager's theory of exemptions is not yet complete. I have explicated the two criteria they use to justify *individual* exemptions, but Eisgruber and Sager also address the issue of *collective* exemptions. The equal liberty approach ambitiously aims to account for what in U.S. law is known as the "ministerial exception": the right of religious entities to be exempt from regulation of their employment relation with their ministers, including when the latter bring suits of discrimination on grounds of gender or sexuality. The Catholic Church, for example, cannot be forced to employ female clergy. How can the theory of equal liberty account for this apparent anomaly? For a theory whose chief value is individual equality and nondiscrimination, it is particularly tricky to justify the rights of groups to offend equality and discriminate *against individuals*. It looks as though the ministerial exception might be a clear instance where religion is uniquely special: it is because of the special demands of religious autonomy that churches enjoy exorbitant rights to discriminate. Eisgruber and Sager, not surprisingly, reject this implication. In line with the equal liberty approach, they show that, whatever rights churches should have—including the ministerial exception—they should have them because of a feature they share with comparable groups. But which feature is this?

The third criterion, which Eisgruber and Sager deploy specifically to justify collective rights of exemption, is *close association*. They justify the ministerial exception as an implication of the more general liberal values of privacy, expression, and associational autonomy. The right of privacy is grounded in the Due Process Clause of the Fourteenth Amendment, and guarantees highly personal relationships a substantial measure of sanctuary from unjustified interference by the state. The privacy cases recognize that there are certain foundational human relationships that are irreducible structures of existence, and that participants are entitled to order them as they see fit without governmental intrusion, even when the choices made or conditions imposed on each other are inconsistent and even repugnant to conventional morality. Freedom of expression, for its part, follows from the Speech Clause of the First Amendment. As Eisgruber and Sager note, the rights of privacy and free expression have distinct, associational dimensions. Put together, they generate a distinct right of close association, which allows groups of people who form durable bonds to have discretion over who they associate with.

Religious organizations, for Eisgruber and Sager, are close associations: "Organised religious activity projects distinctively private behavior into public space and involves distinctly private relationships that are bound by contract and compensated by dollars. Religious leaders are moral advisers, confidantes, friends, and spiritual guides. The state cannot prescribe a non-discriminatory protocol for a group's choice of the person who is to bear this private responsibility to its members any more than the state could prescribe such a protocol for the selection of a psychiatrist, or of a neighbor in-home to confide one's hopes and concerns. The aspects of religious practice that are uncontroversially secure from the reach of some state commands are so secure because they are private in general and recognisable ways, not because they are religious."[49]

This ingenious theory has been further developed by Sager in a recent essay.[50] The right of close or intimate association held by churches derives from two sets of relationships: the relationship between leader and congregants (dyadic), and the relationship among members, from which, in turn, the autonomy in the choice of leaders derives (group). Put together, they explain why churches should be allowed to discriminate on the basis of race and sex: choosing a spiritual counselor is as private as choosing a spouse, therapist, or lawyer. Neither right, however, uniquely applies to religious associations. As the title of Sager's article indicates, he would also extend the discretionary associational right to select its leaders to the Tarpon Bay Women's Blue Water Fishing Club (which, presumably, should not be forced to accept men as members, let alone leaders). So the right of close association is not enjoyed only by churches. To make their case, Eisgruber and Sager have also drawn on a Supreme Court decision (*Boy Scouts of America v. Dale,* 2000) that allowed the Boy Scouts of America to be exempt from a New Jersey law that prohibited discrimination against homosexuals.[51]

What are we to make of the criterion of close association? It promisingly identifies a feature that religious and nonreligious associations share, and also explains what it is, in virtue of which this feature generates special rights. Eisgruber and Sager's approach suggests that, to understand the rights of religious associations, we do not need to appeal to freedom of religion at all. Rather, such rights can be derived from generic rights of association and privacy. Although in the case of individual exemptions, what matters is either the vulnerability of identities or the depth of commitments (or both), in the case of collective exemptions we should look elsewhere, in features that make certain types of *association* ethically salient—the intimate or close nature of the relationship between members. Eisgruber and Sager, therefore, offer the outlines of a strategy of *disaggregation* of the notion of religion, which allow the various ethically salient features of religion to be protected across a range of different liberal rights. I will pursue and deepen this strategy further in Part II.

Although I applaud this disaggregative approach, I wonder whether close association is the appropriate feature to pick out in order to justify collective rights of autonomy. To put it simply, it is not obvious that churches are close associations. Intimate or close associations, such as families or circles of friends, are typically small in scale, selective in their membership, and secluded in their relationship from others. Churches, by contrast, are often large, hierarchical, bureaucratic organizations. When large-scale organizations appoint professional therapists or lawyers, the intimate relationship is diffuse, if not broken altogether. While the process by which a small Baptist congregation (say) chooses its minister is analogous to other intimate choices of families or small groups, it is not clear that the argument applies equally well to the Catholic Church, where it is not congregants, but a centralized and top-down church hierarchy, that selects priests. The close association argument assumes, first, that individuals are bound together in constitutive relationships and, second, that the choice of leader is made by those who have close relations with that leader. Even if the former condition obtains in the Catholic Church, it is not clear that the latter does. Only those isolated sub-relationships within religious groups that involve few people and are both highly selective and generally private are likely to receive any protection under the right of close association. As Sager concedes, the "moral spark" of the right to discriminate is the dyadic right of close association; the additional group-centered version of that right is on "somewhat more fragile moral ground," because of the risk associated with the emergence of large pockets of resistance from well-justified antidiscrimination legislation.[52] The fact that the Catholic Church's claim takes more of a group-centered than a dyadic form is a problem for Eisgruber and Sager, because their theory is designed paradigmatically to apply to the Catholic Church. If the close association argument is the only one that can successfully defend a full ministerial exception (that is, discretion in associational decisions), and it does not apply to the churches that paradigmatically require it, it might be that the ministerial exception is not justifiable. I will bite this bullet in Chapter 5, where I will defend a more limited right of associational freedom that rules out the full ministerial exception.[53]

Narrowing Religion

The third strategy narrows down the category of protection-worthy commitments to a distinctive category: that of conscientious duties. It can be seen as an explication of Eisgruber and Sager's depth criterion. It has been developed by many liberal egalitarians in relation to secular conscientious objection—notably the U.S. Vietnam draft exemption cases. The thought here is that we have a higher-order interest in following the dictates of our *conscience*.[54] Conscientious duties are particularly weighty demands that constitute and maintain our integrity as moral persons. If we fail to act according to what our conscience demands, our lives are blighted in a particular way. Many nonreligious people can recognize the force of conscientious duties: having to do something "in conscience" is a familiar experience of our moral life. As Paul Bou-Habib has argued, while not everyone would agree that having a religion is itself good, many would agree that acting in light of one's deepest moral commitments—living with integrity—is good.[55] Indeed, freedom of conscience is often presented as the basic, most conclusively justified, and least controversial liberal freedom.[56]

But why should it be so weighty that it can be invoked in public reason as a justification for an exemption from the burden of general laws? After all, if laws do not directly violate freedom of conscience and are defended by appeal to good public reasons, they will inevitably have an uneven impact on people's ability to pursue their particular life plans, and they will inevitably conflict with the conscientious convictions of some. Why is this problematic at the bar of liberal justice? A plausible Rawls-inspired

answer invokes the notion of "strains of commitment."[57] When Rawls—
whose work had a long-standing and profound influence on liberal
egalitarianism—sought to justify what he calls the "lexical priority of the
basic liberties,"[58] he illustrated it by drawing attention to the particularly
burdensome strains of commitment attached to being forced to perform
some action that promises eternal damnation in the afterlife. What
grounded the special priority of freedom of conscience, for him, was
the particular burden attached to fear of extratemporal, divine punishment. On this view, the parties in the original position would not commit
themselves to a strict consequence-blind pursuit of justificatory neutrality. They would not want to put themselves in a position where the law
would place on them intolerable strains—typically, burdens on their conscience. Generalizing the point, in public reason it would be unreasonable
for us to ask conscientious objectors to bear burdens that we would not
ourselves be willing to bear. Provided we identify a higher-order interest
in living with integrity, and narrow religion down to conscience in this
way, it is possible to justify religious exemptions in public reason.[59]

We find an exemplary presentation of this position in a recent book
by Charles Taylor and Jocelyn Maclure, *Secularism and Freedom of Conscience*. In line with the liberal egalitarian starting point, Taylor and Maclure argue that religious belief, for purposes of legal exemptions, should
be seen as a subset of a broader category of beliefs that deserve protection: "moral beliefs which structure moral identity"—what they call
"meaning-giving beliefs and commitments."[60] And they envisage this to
cover a broad spectrum of nonreligious beliefs and practices—from secular pacifism to ecocentric vegetarianism, through duties of care to terminally ill family members. In what follows, I argue that their theory
has a number of advantages over the other theories surveyed in this
chapter. But it also has limitations.

Taylor and Maclure's narrowing strategy implies a double move. First,
they argue that meaning-giving commitments do not have to have the
structural features associated with traditional religion. For example, they
find Rawls's requirement that conceptions of the good be "comprehen-

sive" (that they cover most dimensions of life) too demanding. It is a feature of the secular age, they point out, that people's ethical commitments take the form of "fluid, eclectic sets of values" that are not integrated into a comprehensive, integrated whole, and that are not perceived as "unconditional rules for action."[61] At certain times, however—such as the illness of a loved one—the pursuit of certain core values becomes paramount and gives meaning and shape to one's life. Taylor and Maclure also reject Martha Nussbaum's appeal to "ultimate questions"—the meaning of life and death—as an excessively intellectualist vision of the virtues of the contemplative life: the life of reflection about the ends of life.[62] Drawing on Taylor's exploration of modernity in *Sources of the Self,* they point to the moral dimension of ordinary life—family, work, friendship—and their role in structuring people's moral identity.[63] In sum, we can say that Taylor and Maclure take the ethical pluralism of the secular age more seriously than other egalitarian philosophers. Rawls and Nussbaum still hold a traditionally religious understanding of the scope ("comprehensive") and content ("ultimate questions") of what counts as a morally weighty belief.

Yet while Taylor and Maclure reject both the *content* criterion and the *scope* criterion for a secular belief to be as morally weighty as a traditional religious belief, they retain a third criterion, which can be called the *categoricity* criterion. The second move in their theory, then, is this. Narrowing down religion allows them to extend protection to secular commitments that are similarly rooted in the categoricity of conscience. Promisingly, Taylor and Maclure detect pockets of moral depth in the fragmentation of ordinary life: in the sudden encounter with finitude and mortality in the event of the death of a loved one, or in ecocentric vegetarians' profound convictions about the wrongness of meat consumption—to take their two favorite examples. Secular beliefs must be respected, according to Taylor and Maclure, even when they have neither the same (metaphysical) content, nor the same (comprehensive) scope, as religious beliefs. Secular beliefs are morally weighty when they prescribe duties of conscience. What the caretaker for a terminally ill parent and the ecocentric vegetarian have in common is that they both seek to act with *integrity*—where integrity is defined as congruence between one's perceptions of one's duties and one's actual actions.[64] Recall Martin Luther's statement in defiance of the Church's injunctions: "Here I stand, and I cannot act otherwise."[65] Taylor and Maclure note that forcing someone to act against their deep conscientious convictions constitutes a "moral harm" equivalent to the kind of "physical harm" that justifies citizens with disabilities being specially accommodated. So, they conclude, citizens with intense conscientious meaning-giving secular beliefs have a *pro tanto* claim to be considered for exemptions from burdensome laws.

The advantages of the narrowing strategy for liberal egalitarians should by now be obvious. Conscience is an ecumenical value that can appeal both to religious and secular citizens. It is what is at work in the case of conscientious objection to military service—the paradigmatic case of secular exemption for liberal egalitarian theorists. The narrowing strategy also responds to Dworkin's concern that if protection is extended to nontheistic beliefs and commitments, then it is "difficult to see how it can be limited at all."[66] Taylor and Maclure do not shy away from limiting exemptions to commitments that have ethical salience. They distinguish between trivial and important commitments. Implicitly drawing on Taylor's early critique of "negative freedom,"[67] they argue that freedom of religion cannot dispense with a "strong evaluation" of the ends it is designed to pursue. By contrast to Dworkin, they do not dissolve these ends into any kind of preference or belief. Freedom of religion, in their view, cannot be described in a way that is purely negative and neutral toward the good. It is about the pursuit of ends that are "central and not trivial," that are about "core convictions," not "mere preferences." Freedom of religion, then, is intrinsically perfectionist, even at that high level of generality: it implies a judgment about ethically salient commitments and values.

Who, then, is to make the strong evaluations required to distinguish between meaning-giving and trivial commitments? Taylor and Maclure's empathic response to this is: the individual claimant herself. Here they anticipate the charge—often leveled at Taylor's conception of positive liberty—that the principle of strong evaluation could give the state the authority arbitrarily to discriminate between better and worse ways to exercise freedoms, and thereby violate the very idea of freedom as respecting the individual capacity to find the good *for herself*. Instead, Taylor and Maclure assert that "the special status of religious beliefs is derived from the role they play in people's moral lives, rather than from an assessment of their intrinsic validity." They defend what they call a *subjective* conception of freedom of religion, according to which only individuals—not the state, nor collective religious authorities—are entitled to determine what is the correct interpretation of religious, or more broadly moral, demands on them.[68] This tallies with Taylor's recent endorsement of a version of liberal neutrality as requiring that the state abstain from judgments about the good. The value of subjective freedom of religion, then, is weakly perfectionist (it draws on a thin theory of the liberal good) but its promotion is not paternalist (it does not entrust the state to make fine-grained judgments about how that freedom should be used).

Does this mean, however, that anything that a claimant calls "my religion" should *ipso facto* benefit from the protections afforded by freedom of religion? Not so. Recall that Taylor and Maclure do not seek to protect an ill-defined category of "religion" as such but, instead, a distinct class of beliefs: meaning-giving commitments and, in particular, acts of conscience that allow individuals to live with *integrity*. Integrity, then, functions as the weak public standard against which individual claims are evaluated. But only individuals are in a position to explain which particular beliefs and commitments are key to *their* sense of moral integrity.

Taylor and Maclure, it seems, have squared many circles at once. They understand the value of freedom of religion as an objective higher-order interest (living with integrity, according to the demands of one's conscience) that can be realized only if individuals live in accordance with what *they* take to be their conscientious duty. Their version of liberal egalitarianism protects traditional religious practices, and extends protection to secular commitments on the same basis, without assuming that such commitments have to be as comprehensive or ultimate as religious beliefs. By contrast to Dworkin, Taylor and Maclure do not dissolve religion into a broad, internally undifferentiated category of beliefs, preferences, values, and lifestyles. And by contrast to Eisgruber and Sager, they do not "mainstream" religion into a vague, internally incoherent category of things that are "serious" and "important" (such as family commitments and medical conditions). The narrowing strategy, then, is more determinate than other versions of liberal egalitarianism.

There is, however, one problem with this strategy: it is *too* narrow. The first point to note is that the theory does not quite protect everything that it claims to protect, and is inconsistent, by its own standards. Taylor and Maclure effectively collapse religion into conscience, and implicitly assume that the latter category is more inclusive than the former. In other words, their account of freedom of conscience is assumed to extend protection to nonreligious, secular conscientious acts, *while at the same time securing existing protections of traditional religious practices.* But we may wonder whether this is the case, or whether anything is lost in the redescription of freedom of religion as freedom of conscience. This, recall, was the upshot of what I call the Protestant critique in Chapter 1.

Assume I am a devout Muslim. I observe Ramadan, recite my prayers every day, wear hijab, give *zakat,* and send my children to Koranic school. Or assume I am a practicing Catholic. I observe Lent, do not eat meat on Fridays, celebrate Easter, go to church every Sunday, have my children baptized and confirmed. For many Catholics and Muslims (but also other Christians, Jews, Hindus, and Buddhist) the religious experience is fundamentally about exhibiting the virtues of the good believer, living in community with others, and shaping one's daily life in accordance with the rituals of the faith. These rituals are meaning-giving and connected to believers' sense of their moral integrity. Yet they are not strictly speaking duties of conscience, and therefore do not meet the criteria that Taylor and Maclure ultimately settle for. The good religious life is a life of constant, difficult, ritual affirmation of the faith against the corrupting influences of the secular world. It is not always—not often—one in which one single obligation (say, wearing the *hijab,* going to Mass) is so stringent as to promise eternal damnation if it is not fulfilled. Taylor and Maclure, then, reinterpret acts of habitual, collective religious devotion into Protestant duties of conscience.[69]

I have pointed to an internal tension in Taylor and Maclure's theory. The upshot is that, by protecting freedom of conscience, they do not protect all religious beliefs and practices, because religion cannot be reduced to conscience. One response is available to Taylor and Maclure. They could bite the bullet and argue—in line with an interpretive theory of religion—that when religion is not conscientious, then it should not be protected. As I suggested in Chapter 1, the semantic critique need not worry liberal egalitarians. It does not matter whether the law protects religion as such, provided it protects what is normatively worth protecting in religion.[70] And it might well be that what is worth protecting in religion is conscience.

But here too we may wonder whether Taylor and Maclure's approach is not too narrow. Even if religious practices are not rooted in duties of conscience, they might still express the ethically salient value of integrity. Individuals act with integrity when they are faithful to relationships of community—be they cultural, linguistic, or religious—that are of central importance to their lives. And they are sometimes *unfairly* deprived of such opportunities—for example, in cases where the state unequally accommodates some ways of life over others. Such a worry is central to the literature on multicultural equality, and is particularly resonant in the Canadian context, as well as in Taylor's own influential writings on the subject.[71] In *Secularism and Freedom of Conscience,* Taylor and Maclure too artificially separate concerns about freedom of religion from concerns about multicultural equality, by underplaying the ethically salient cultural dimensions of religion. Yet there are cases when a

minority religious practice should be exempted, not because it is a weighty
duty of conscience, but because it is unfairly accommodated in relation
to some comparable majority practice that is itself given privileged status
by the state. Liberal egalitarianism—I shall argue further in Chapter 6—
must engage more deeply with the ethically and politically salient connections between religion and culture.

There is one final omission in Taylor and Maclure's theory: they only
consider exemptions for largely benign religious practices—from the
wearing of religious signs to ritual devotion in the workplace. These practices are benign in the sense that they infringe neither on the rights of
others nor on the other rights of the claimant. The chief issue that such
"reasonable accommodations" raise is that of the fairness of the terms
of social cooperation, notably in the workplace, and the distribution of
its costs. This is of course no small issue. But it leaves aside harder cases
such as the accommodation of less benign practices, and exemptions from
more general laws—from vaccination requirements to nondiscrimination on grounds of gender or sexuality. To be fair, Taylor and Maclure's
book contains a section about the limits of accommodation. By contrast
to Dworkin, they do not assume that it is sufficient simply to delimit
the scope of religion adequately to define the extent of the rights of
freedom of religion. Taylor and Maclure, then, gesture at a two-pronged
theory of exemptions (Is it relevantly "religious"? Should it be accommodated?). I will build on this insight in Chapter 6, to show that an
interpretive theory of religion (even my preferred disaggregative approach)
is not sufficient to settle the deeper normative question of the justice of
exemptions. As we shall see, answering the interpretive question "Is
religion special?" does not settle the normative question "When should
it be exempted?"

3

꧁꧂

Liberal Egalitarianism
and the State Neutrality Puzzle

Liberal egalitarians argue that the old idea of religious nonestablishment should be generalized into state neutrality about the good. But why should the state be neutral about the good? Which dimensions of the good are unsuitable for state endorsement? And why should the state not establish religion in the first place? In Chapter 2, I explored the ethical salience problem by focusing on the question of exemptions, which asked which particular beliefs, commitments, and practices deserved special concern. In this chapter I ask whether liberal egalitarians can answer the ethical salience problem, as Dworkin suggests, by appealing to a more general principle of state justificatory neutrality. I explore the promise and difficulties of this strategy, and argue that the liberal state is not neutral toward religion or the good generally, but only toward a restricted subset of religion or the good.[1]

A close analysis of key liberal egalitarian texts about state neutrality, furthermore, reveals that different authors have in mind substantially distinct subsets. I identify three different strategies for generalizing non-establishment. Dworkin justifies state neutrality in the name of *ethical independence:* the state should not usurp people's conceptions of personal ethics. Eisgruber and Sager locate the wrong of establishment in the *civic disparagement* of vulnerable minorities: they connect nonestablishment to equal citizenship against a background of divisive and conflicting identities. Jonathan Quong defends neutrality by appeal to *foundational disagreement* about religion: he thinks it is because of the epistemic nature of certain kinds of disagreement that the state should not take a stance about them. I look at these three strategies (roughly: the ethical, sociological, and epistemic strategies) in turn and, by showing that each is incomplete, I suggest the need for a more thorough disaggregation of religion and the good. I also introduce the jurisdictional boundary problem. The general thought is that state neutrality, however it is conceived, requires that sovereign determinations be made about what the state is neutral about—that is, where the boundaries of the religious and the nonreligious, the political and the comprehensive, the public and the private are in the first place. Neutrality, I argue, gives no guidance about the meta-jurisdictional question of ultimate competence and sovereignty.

Ethical Independence

In Chapter 2, I analyzed Dworkin's dissolving strategy for free exercise purposes, and showed that it ran into the ethical salience problem. The attempt to dissolve religion into an undifferentiated class of beliefs, preferences, and commitments turned out to be incompatible with the special respect due to a class of ethically salient commitments (such as Native American rituals or Muslim religious dress). In this chapter I show that a similar dilemma runs through Dworkin's broader theory of state nonestablishment and state neutrality. Dworkin's starting intuition is that liberalism is a form of government where political decisions are, so far as possible, "independent of any particular conception of the good life or what gives value to life."[2] The state's attitude to religion, then, is only an application of a broader liberal principle of justificatory neutrality. The state fails to show equal concern toward all citizens if, when justifying its constitution and policy, it endorses or favors one conception of the good life over others. The state is neutral about religion, that is, because it is neutral about the good in general.

In this section, I ask what exactly the category of "any particular conception of the good life or what gives value to life" refers to. Although Dworkin seemed at times to endorse what I call *broad neutrality,* most of his writings point toward *restricted neutrality,* which applies only to a distinctive subset of views, conceptions, and commitments, what Dworkin called matters of ethical foundation.[3] This is not too surprising, because Dworkin justified state neutrality by appeal to the value of ethical independence—itself a substantive, if thin, notion of the good. I ask what this restricted neutrality implies for the claim that the state is neutral toward (traditional, theistic) religion. Is religion only—and always—a conception of personal ethics? If it is not, what follows for how we should decide where the boundaries of personal ethical independence lie?

Let me first explain how Dworkin derived his theory of liberal neutrality from the constitutional principle of nonestablishment. In line with his non-positivist, non-originalist, interpretive method, Dworkin sought to reformulate constitutional traditions in order to capture "what is really of value in our values."[4] What is still of value in the norm of the nonestablishment of religion? For Dworkin, religion should not be interpreted as the ordinary-sense notion associated with conventional theistic religions (such as Christianity).[5] Instead, Dworkin interprets religious nonestablishment as one instance of a broader, less parochial and less sectarian set of constraints on the justification of state action. As he put it in *Justice for Hedgehogs,* "If we insist that no particular religion be treated as special in politics, then we cannot treat religion itself as special in politics. . . . So we must not treat religious freedom as sui generis. It is only one consequence of the more general right to ethical independence in foundational matters."[6] The liberal state should not only be a state of religious nonestablishment: it should be a state of ethical neutrality. The state should not establish religion because the state should not usurp individuals' own ethical judgments: the state is neutral about the good out of respect for individual ethical independence. What Dworkin offers, therefore, is a non-neutral justification of neutrality, one based on a substantive commitment to ethical independence. The demand of neutrality acts is a constraint on the kind of arguments that are permissible as public or legal justification: Dworkin can be said to endorse a form of public reason in this sense, despite his theory of the continuity between ethics and politics.[7]

By analogizing religion with conceptions of the good or ethical views, Dworkin generalizes the old ideal of religious nonestablishment into a new model of liberal neutrality. Neutrality, as a constraint on state action, rules out reasons that mandate state regulation of the fundamental decisions people make about the ethical dimensions of their lives—not only decisions regarding whether to pray to God (religious nonestablishment) but also decisions about whether to have an abortion, or to marry one's loved one, of whatever sex (liberal neutrality). A ban on same-sex marriage, for Dworkin, is unavoidably grounded in an impermissible ethical judgment about others' ways of life. It fails to respect citizens' ethical independence, and therefore violates the norm of nonestablishment understood as liberal neutrality about reasons—that is, permissible justifications. Just as government should not take sides between orthodox theistic religions, similarly it should not take sides between different ways of living well—between alternative views of good sexuality, for example.

It is not only same-sex marriage but a range of substantively liberal causes that Dworkin thinks are entailed by liberal neutrality. If religious conservatives were willing to admit that their commitment to freedom of religion is rooted in a more general right of ethical independence, they would concede that the point of a liberal state is to let individuals take responsibility for their own lives, whether these are conventionally religious or not. Thus, the state has no business interfering with people's sexual and reproductive choices (as long as they do not infringe on others' rights), just as it has no business interfering with the way they practice their religion, and their private display of religious attire and signs. In turn, the state, to respect the ethical independence of all, should scrupulously avoid endorsing religion in its institutions and symbols: it should not teach the truth of religion in its schools, including theories of intelligent design; it should avoid endorsing openly Christian symbols and ceremonies, and so forth.[8] Substantively liberal policies, then, can be justified not through a first-order argument about the superiority of non-religious, progressive, individualistic lifestyles but through a second-order defense of the value of ethical independence for all citizens.

To understand how ethical independence differs from alternative conceptions of liberal neutrality, Table 1 might be useful. Dworkin's favored account of neutrality is labeled (1) in the table. It focuses on the *justification* rather than on the subject matter of policies and laws; and neutrality is *restricted* to ethical conceptions, not extended to all conceptions: this is the sense in which neutrality upholds ethical independence. It is worth briefly mapping how this relates to the other positions set out in the table.

Table 1 Four Conceptions of Neutrality

Scope ↓	Focus →		
		Justification	Subject Matter
Restricted		(1) Ethical independence	(3) Noninterference with personal ethics
Broad		(2) Neutrality toward the good	(4) Noninterference with all preferences, conceptions, commitments

Dworkin rejects (4). Noninterference or mere "freedom" is not a value in itself. The liberal state can rightfully, for sound reasons (such as the pursuit of distributive justice), limit people's freedom to pursue their projects. "Liberty"—a moralized notion for Dworkin—is the protected right to do what one is rightfully entitled to do within a system of just laws, and entails no presumptive right not to be interfered with. As we saw in Chapter 2, Dworkin is more ambivalent about (3). In *Religion without God,* he argues that freedom of religion does not entail a special right of protection; like any other preference or commitment, it can be interfered with out of sound, neutral reasons. However, Dworkin also conceded that the fact that a practice is considered a "sacred duty" makes it worthy of special concern, and in *Justice for Hedgehogs* he took the view that liberty is violated when people are denied the "power to make their own decisions about *matters of ethical foundation.*"[9] There he seemed to imply that a liberal state should avoid interfering in certain ethically salient matters, regardless of its justifications for doing so.[10]

In this section I concentrate on justification and the question of its scope (restricted / broad). At times Dworkin seems to endorse a broad view of justificatory neutrality (2). This is usually taken to be an implication of the general anti-perfectionist defense of liberal neutrality that he set out in his early, influential statement of neutrality. Dworkin noted that we all orient our lives around our own conception of what makes life good. For Dworkin, this applies as much to the "scholar who values a life of contemplation" as it does to the "television-watching, beer-drinking citizen" who has "never given the matter much thought."[11] And in *Religion without God,* even though he developed an expansively ethical view of "religion,"[12] which encompassed both traditionally theistic and atheistic conceptions, he insisted that such ethical evaluations should not be validated or endorsed by the state. Neutrality demands that no individual should be devalued because they do not have a religion, even in this expansive ethical sense. As he points out, a "worshipper of Mammon" can be "as devoted to his life of hedonistic consumerism as a traditional religious believer is to her duties to God."[13] The liberal state should not be given the power "to choose among sincere convictions to decide which are worthy of special protection and which not."[14] From the point of view of the state, there should be no compelling distinction between a religion and some other general kind of attitude toward life. This radical anti-perfectionism underpins what I call *broad neutrality*.

One implication of broad neutrality is that a neutral liberal state, just as it cannot establish or support any conventionally religious conception of the good, should not support culture or the arts because of their intrinsic value. As Dworkin himself noted, "orthodox liberalism . . . holds that no government should rely, to justify its use of public funds, on the assumption that some ways of leading one's life are more worthy than others, *that it is more worthwhile to look at a Titian on the wall, than watch a football game on television*."[15] For Rawls, this fundamental anti-perfectionist liberal commitment rules out "subsidizing universities and institutes, operas and the theatre, on the grounds that these institutions are intrinsically valuable."[16] This would imply that current, large-scale state subsidies for higher education, the fine arts, and the humanities are impermissible at the bar of liberal neutrality. But Dworkin demurred from this. And this, I contend, is because broad neutrality is in tension with his preferred position, which restricted neutrality to a subset of ethically salient conceptions.

Restricted neutrality (1) is rooted in the value of ethical independence. This is the protected right not to have one's own ethical evaluations coercively usurped by the state. But this does not mean that the state cannot justify its laws by appeal to other conceptions about the good, which are not ethical conceptions in Dworkin's sense. So what is this category of ethical conceptions, which are impermissible as grounds of state action? Not surprisingly, Dworkin elaborated this category as a reflection about the notion of *religion*. In his 1992 writings on abortion and euthanasia, he put forward his favored interpretive definition of "religious" as being bound up with personal ethical conceptions of the meaning and value of life.[17] Dworkin thinks of both pro-abortion and anti-abortion views as paradigmatically religious convictions: "convictions about why and how human life has intrinsic objective importance."[18] It is because abortion is about personal ethics in this sense that the state must adopt a neutral (or agnostic) position toward it. As Dworkin forcefully put it, "Any government that prohibits abortion commits itself to a controversial interpretation of the sanctity of life and therefore limits liberty by commanding one essentially religious position over others, which the First Amendment forbids."[19] The state must not take sides in what is essentially a religious dispute, and must leave it to women to take responsibility for their own ethical choices, whether or not to have an abortion. So once an argument or ideal is defined as substantively "religious" (that is, as being about personal ethics), it falls under the scope of a conception of the good that the state cannot permissibly appeal to without violating the ethical independence of individuals. For Dworkin, impermissible conceptions of the good are those that usurp individual judgment in the realm of personal ethics. Ethical independence demands that the state not endorse any particular view about the good of sexuality, euthanasia, and abortion: it should, out of justificatory neutrality, leave them to the free choice of individuals.

But ethical independence does not demand neutrality toward other kinds of goods—the good of culture, the arts, or the environment, for example—because they do not fall into this domain of personal ethics. Liberal states may provide certain cultural goods on a subsidized or free basis without falling foul of liberal neutrality. How so? Dworkin offers two arguments. The first one is an argument about justice. The argument is not unproblematic; even if it is true that the liberal state can permissibly appeal to reasons of justice, it is difficult to explain why justice demands the provision of specific cultural goods without drawing on controversial views about the good.[20] But I leave this aside here to focus on Dworkin's second argument, which is that the state in fact only needs be neutral about a specific subset of the good. This relies on an account of "detached," impersonal values, such as natural or man-made beauty, that transcends the interests of particular rights-bearing persons and therefore are not relevant to justice. Dworkin presented cultural policy as having to do with "intrinsic" values, and he illustrated this by reference to "art, . . . historic buildings, . . . endangered animal species or future generations."[21] As an illustration, Dworkin alluded to the protection of the environment—not (only) because of the "derived" value it has for the interests of present and future persons, but also out of "detached," impersonal respect for its natural beauty. In later work, he forcefully argued that individuals should not enjoy "immunity from laws that protect impersonal values like natural or artistic treasures."[22] This is because, he makes plain, such laws do not infringe on ethical independence rightly conceived—independence in matters touching the meaning of life.

He argues that state commitment to the protection of forests does not infringe on the ethical independence of "the logging executive [who thinks] that ancient forests are of no particular interest or value" because (in Dworkin's view) "it is not an ethical conviction. . . . It is neither derived from nor formative of convictions about the importance of human life or of achievement in a human life."[23] So, just as in his discussion of exemptions, Dworkin conceded that one set of beliefs—those concerning "sacred duties"—might deserve special respect, so, in his discussion of nonestablishment and state neutrality, he also singles out some conceptions of the good as impermissible justifications for state policy. The implication is that the state may appeal to some conceptions of the good, provided these are suitably impersonal and do not touch on matters of personal ethics. So, for Dworkin, liberal neutrality is compatible with state support for the arts, culture, and environmental protection. Nonestablishment is not generalized into neutrality toward the good-in-general but instead is restricted to neutrality toward personal ethics. A neutral liberal state leaves people free to live by their ethical convictions about the sacredness of human life, but not necessarily those concerning the preservation of biodiversity.[24] This is the sense in which Dworkinian neutrality is restricted.

What are we to make of this argument? I want to follow Dworkin's interpretive strategy through to its logical conclusion. I argue that, if the state must be neutral toward religion because religion is a system of personal ethics, it follows that the state need not be neutral toward religion *when it is not.* This is an unavoidable implication of Dworkin's theory, one that he did not fully recognize himself. This is because, as we saw, he *started* from the assumption that the nonestablishment of religion is the paradigm for neutrality about the good. But once he has defined the relevant good as that of personal ethics, we can ask legitimate questions about how best to interpret the original paradigm of religious nonestablishment. In what follows, I consider two cases in which religion is not a conception of personal ethics, and suggest that, in such cases, it is not clear that the state can or must be neutral about religion—even on the justificatory notion of neutrality that I focus on here.

The first case is when religion is not a conception of personal ethics but instead an impersonal good such as culture or the environment.[25] As we saw, Dworkin accepted that the state can permissibly appeal to the value of such goods. It is striking that the Dworkinian cultural structure excludes religious traditions. Dworkin at one point suggests that there can be cultural arguments for the promotion of religion.[26] But he dismisses them as infringing on ethical independence: a majority, he says, should not have "the power to shape my convictions according to its standards of how to live well."[27] The problem is that this assumes what has to be proven, namely, that any recognition of religion "shapes convictions" in a way that infringes on ethical independence.

Arguing against those Christian conservatives who seek to see the state actively endorse and promote the religious culture of the majority, Dworkin retorts that "our collective religious culture should be created not through the collective power of the state but organically, through the separate acts of conviction, commitment and faith of people drawn to such acts."[28] This, of course, tallies with a long-standing liberal reticence publicly to sponsor and endorse conventional religion—one crucial implication of the U.S. Establishment Clause. But how about noncoercive, educational, ecumenical policies—aiming, say, at promoting awareness of the diversity of religions, and their cultural heritage? Do such policies not structurally resemble the permissible liberal policies of support for secular culture? As Dworkin is willing to see the state support culture and the arts, we need an account of why exactly religion cannot be part of the cultural structure. For example, Dworkin does not consider the possibility that religions may contribute to the richness and complexity of the cultural structure. Might our cultural structure be less rich if whole religions disappear?[29] Or—a harder case— would it be radically impoverished if people lack the basic religious knowledge required to understand works of art (such as Titian's painting of the sacrifice of Isaac)?

In other places Dworkin is more willing to accept the permissibility of some forms of religious establishment. He suggests that symbolic en-dorsement of the majority religion by the state is wrong to the extent that it is controversial and divisive. So liberal neutrality is incompatible with the use of "state funds or property to celebrate one godly religion, or godly religion in preference to godless religion or no religion."[30] Conversely, he is willing to concede that ecumenical signs, symbols, and institutions (such as the establishment of the Anglican Church) are permissible when they "have been genuinely drained of all but ecu-menical cultural significance" and there is "no discriminatory life left in them."[31] The assumption here is that Anglican establishment does not usurp people's ethical judgment—it does not infringe on their personal ethics. But note that Anglican establishment displays an additional fea-ture that makes it permissible: it endorses the symbols of a diluted, patrimonial, culturalized Christianity, such that the message it conveys is not divisive and controversial. So we can add another feature to Dworkin's interpretive notion of religion: Religion should not be estab-lished when (insofar as) it is controversial and divisive. We will see later that such feature plays a key role in other liberal theories.

This feature already appeared in Dworkin's early writings on abor-tion and religion. Dworkin's justification of state neutrality about the morality of abortion ran as follows: "A state may not curtail liberty, in order to protect an intrinsic value, when the effect on one group would be special and grave, when the community is seriously divided about what respect for that value requires, and when people's opinions about the nature of that value reflect essentially religious convictions that are fundamental to personality." This crucial sentence highlights three different features in virtue of which establishment of religion is problematic, and it is useful to disentangle them (as I will do more fully in my disaggregation strategy in Part II). The first is that the impact of the law on one group would be "special and grave": this picks up on the especially salient nature of the interest that the state is interfering with—as per (3) in Table 1.[32] The second is that the policy is divisive and controversial—an idea also found in the theories of Eisgruber, Sager, and Jonathan Quong, as we shall see below. The third is that the law directly relates to conceptions of personal ethics that are "fundamental to personality," and therefore infringe on personal independence—as per (1). Neutrality about the good, then, turns out to be a much more complex and layered ideal than many liberals have assumed.

The second case in which these complexities appear relates to the difficulty of specifying when and where personal ethics applies. To see this, and to introduce what I call the jurisdictional boundary problem, let me focus on the issue of abortion. Recall that Dworkin argues that because abortion touches on deeply controversial matters of personal ethics, the state must adopt a neutral position about it. The state must not take sides in what is essentially a religious (in Dworkin's sense) dispute, and must leave it to women to take responsibility for their own ethical choices, whether or not to have an abortion. Yet note that to think of abortion in this way in the first place, Dworkin must have excluded two other logical possibilities. First, he must have denied that fetuses have interests—of the kind that a theory of justice as equal concern for the interests of all must protect. Second, he must have denied that the protection of the detached, impersonal, sacred value of human life should trump the personal choices of women. To be sure, Dworkin provides powerful arguments in support of both positions in his extensive writings on the subject.[33] Yet he argues that such arguments are neutral toward the good, and that they can be endorsed both from nonreligious and conventionally religious perspectives (at least those that converge on the value of ethical independence).

The problem is that Dworkin's arguments are not neutral in his sense: they are substantive arguments that take a distinctive stance on what he *himself* describes as religious matters. As many critics have pointed out, Dworkin does not explain how we should weigh intrinsic values (here, the value of human life) against personal interests (of the fetus or the woman).[34] In particular, it is not clear why intrinsic values should give way in the case of abortion. A religious believer who holds that the sacredness of human life essentially derives from divine (rather than human) investment in it will not be convinced by any argument that fetal life can be destroyed in the pursuit of other (however admirable) values, such as women's ethical independence. Or a believer who sincerely thinks that abortion is tantamount to murder—and therefore as much about basic justice as anything can be—will plausibly reject the characterization of her view as being merely about personal ethics. At crucial points, therefore, Dworkin draws the boundary of religion— of personal ethics as opposed to more impersonal values—in a place that can be challenged *even by those who are committed to ethical independence.* Ethical independence, it turns out, is indeterminate about its own domain of application. It can deliver a determinate solution to the abortion controversy only if it is supplemented by a substantive judgment about the moral status of fetuses—precisely the kind of judgment that (even restricted) neutrality bars.[35]

There is something, therefore, to the critical religion charge against liberalism, to the effect that liberals "privatize religion," provided the point is carefully set out. The privatization of religion is often a good thing. As systems of personal ethics, religious conceptions should be not endorsed and promoted by the state, lest they infringe on individual independence. The intuition behind Dworkin's generalization of religious establishment into liberal neutrality toward matters of personal ethics tracks a well-grounded liberal principle. Insofar as critical religion theorists reject ethical independence, their criticisms should not worry us. A more pertinent criticism, I think, is that religion is not only or always a system of personal ethics. When religious believers present views about the permissibility of abortion or euthanasia, they are not only presenting views about how *they* should live their lives. Nor are they only expressing what Dworkin dismissingly called "external preferences"— preferences about how *others* should live their lives. Their conceptions might be compatible with neutrality and ethical independence, when they are presented as claims about justice and what is owed to others (including the unborn, the dying, and future generations) or as claims about the protection of impersonal values (such as religious culture or the value of life itself).

Therefore, it is not good enough for Dworkin to appeal to the value of ethical independence to dismiss these claims. It looks as though Dworkinian liberalism relies on a more substantive view of the liberal good than he acknowledged. Ethical independence is a very valuable ideal— provided, I will argue, it is combined with an account of the salient interests that can be permissibly burdened, as per (3). But it is indeterminate about its own scope of application. Commitment to the value of ethical independence does not in itself determine the boundary between personal and impersonal ethics, between the personal and the political, and between the religious and the nonreligious. To address the jurisdictional boundary problem in ways that show equal concern for all, we will have to resort to the defense of a more substantive liberalism, as well as to procedural—democratic—solutions to reasonable disagreement about boundaries. I shall return to these questions in Chapters 4 and 5.

Civic Disparagement

In this section I return to Eisgruber and Sager's book *Religious Freedom and the Constitution* to distill the animating principles of their interpretation of the Establishment Clause of the U.S. Constitution.[36] Like

Dworkin, Eisgruber and Sager interpret the Establishment Clause as an implication of liberal principles of neutrality and equality. What the clause prohibits, in their view, is "the advantaging or disadvantaging [of] persons or groups because of the spiritual foundations of their deeply held beliefs and commitments."[37] That the state should not promote or advantage religion, however, does not imply that the state should be strictly separate from religion. Eisgruber and Sager are critical of conventional notions of church-state separation: they point out that religious institutions and people depend on the state for the common rights, opportunities, and obligations of shared social and civic life, and so are not immune from state interference—be it police and fire protection, legal instruments of incorporation, banking, and contract, and duties to respect the rights of others.[38] But traditional theories of separation also err in singling out religious institutions for unique disabilities: they are cut off from opportunities of funding and expression, opportunities that are available to their secular counterparts. This, in Eisgruber and Sager's view, is not compatible with equal liberty.

Their theory is deployed along two dimensions: funding and expression. I shall concentrate on expression, which raises fundamental questions about liberalism's religion, but let me first say a few words about funding. According to Eisgruber and Sager, religious groups pursuing public-interest activities must not be treated differently from nonreligious groups just because they are religious. Eisgruber and Sager reject both the separationist blanket ban on state support of religious activities and services and the accommodationist partiality toward faith-based, religiously motivated teaching and charity.[39] They argue that if two organizations, one nonreligious and one religious, provide public goods on an equal basis, it would be discriminatory for the state to fund the latter and not the former. For example, they broadly agree with the U.S. Supreme Court's reasoning in the landmark *Zelman v. Simmons-Harris* 2002 decision that authorized the Cleveland school authorities to distribute educational vouchers to parents, who can use them either in religious or in public (secular) schools.[40] Insofar as associations are free to organize to promote the deep commitments of their members, be they religious or secular in nature, *and* insofar as government is permitted to offer financial support for the provision of public services (education, welfare, and so on) by nonprofit associations, it would seem discriminatory to deny funding to a religious organization providing a public service on the same terms as a nonreligious one. Arguably, it is in relation to such cases of fair distribution of public benefits that the theory of equal liberty between religion and nonreligion is most plausible.[41] I shall say no more about this, except to note that the theory cannot be self-standing: it must rely on a substantive theory of which services must be statutorily provided, whether they must be provided directly or indirectly,[42] by which organizations, and under which conditions. We need to know more about what justice requires in terms of education, health care, and so forth, before we can make sense of the idea of equal treatment between secular and nonreligious providers. I leave aside this important issue here, although I will return to the question of equality in the secular state, and the boundaries of associational autonomy, in Chapters 4 and 5.

In the rest of this section, I focus on the issue of state expression. The Establishment Clause is often interpreted as ruling out state endorsement of religion. It prohibits religious government speech to the citizenry at large, as well as religious messages in public schools. But why should religion be singled out in this way? And does this not contradict the principle of equal liberty—which, presumably, also entails equal burdens and prohibitions? To reconcile non-endorsement with equal liberty, Eisgruber and Sager rely on an expressive theory of law and the state.[43] Against the libertarian view that the Establishment Clause only prohibits *coercive* entanglement of government with religion, they point to the unavoidably *expressive* dimension of law and the state—the fact that non-coercive messages and actions can have an impact on the civic status of citizens.[44] Eisgruber and Sager conceptualize the normatively relevant features of establishment as the institutional expression of symbolic inequality. So religious establishment is found to raise "a different kind of equality-concern: the worry that by sponsoring religious displays or ceremonies, the government affiliates itself with or endorses a particular theological perspective and implicitly disparages other ones."[45]

Here they follow Justice O'Connor's influential "endorsement test," which postulates that the state's symbolic entanglement with religion is wrong insofar as it undermines the equal civic status of citizens.[46] The test was elaborated in relation to the Supreme Court's first case involving holiday displays, *Lynch v. Donnelly* (1984). This involved the display by the city of Pawtucket, Rhode Island, of a nativity scene or crèche. The crucial question for O'Connor turned on whether symbolic endorsement of one religion undermined the equal status of all citizens. As she put it, "The Establishment Clause prohibits government from making adherence to a religion relevant in any way to a person's standing in the political community. . . . Endorsement sends a message to nonadherents that they are outsiders, not full members of the political community, and an accompanying message to adherents that they are insiders, favored members of the political community."[47]

Eisgruber and Sager likewise argue that governmental expressive action is impermissible if it creates a perception in the mind of a "reasonable observer" that the government is either endorsing or disapproving of religion.[48] What matters is not the subjective feeling of alienation but, rather, whether the social meaning of particular displays can be objectively construed as disparaging.[49] Objective social meaning is context-dependent but not individual-dependent; it turns on how a reasonable (and reasonably well-informed) member of a community would understand the actions of public officials who undertake to display material that has religious content.[50] In a country such as the United States, Eisgruber and Sager suggest, the structure of religious belief and affiliation is such that religious endorsements carry with them the taint of disparagement. It is because of the sociological and cultural features of religions—"their comprehensiveness; their tendency to treat people as either 'in' or 'out'; their use of symbol and rituals to signal who is 'in'; and, finally, the profound stakes they attach to the status of 'in' or 'out' "[51]—that religions are especially vulnerable to invidious discrimination or neglect by majorities.

So Eisgruber and Sager object to the phrase "under God" in the Pledge of Allegiance, arguing that nondenominational references to God are disparaging to nonbelievers and nontheistic believers. They also argue that Nativity scenes, however secular many of their trappings have become, have religious—that is, socially salient—valence: they depict the birth of Christ, one of the most profound events in Christian theology. The "three-plastic-animals rule" does not neuter the religious nature of a Nativity display; but only serves as a *fig leaf* for it.[52] Yet Eisgruber and Sager are prepared to accept the permissibility of some cultural *framing* of religion. They give the example of a town's display of a Fra Angelico painting of the Annunciation as part of an exhibition on the treasures of the Italian Renaissance. Here, although the meaning of the object is religious, the meaning of the display is not: the cultural framing of the object holds its religious meaning at arm's length. In general, though, Eisgruber and Sager argue for certainty and predictability: given the social meaning of religion in the United States, it is best to avoid public endorsements.[53] The state should generally avoid any endorsement of religion, in order not to convey messages of second-class citizenship or disparagement to minority believers or nonbelievers.

While religious endorsement is especially suspect of disparaging effects, it is not uniquely so. The anti-disparagement norm does not attach only to religious expression. Eisgruber and Sager invoke Justice Harlan's famous dissent in the segregation case *Plessy v. Ferguson,* in which he decried the defamatory and stigmatizing social meaning of racial segregation. "Separate but equal" railway cars carried the invidious social meaning that contributed to the perpetuation of social caste, and were therefore unconstitutional.[54] Likewise, the suspect constitutional status of religious practices and beliefs must be related to their "social meaning" in American culture, where "important constituents of identity—most notably, race and religion— . . . function as *especially significant markers of social division.*"[55] The Establishment Clause should be read in light of the Equal Protection paradigm. Just as the officially sanctioned separation between the races carried a message of inferiority and disparagement to African Americans, the public endorsement of religion carries a special charge or valence, given the role of religion in defining civic identity in the United States.[56]

Critics have objected that governments often appeal to divisive views and symbols, with equally disparaging effects. Governments exhort citizens to follow ideals such as patriotism; endorse controversial political ideals in implementing their policies; and teach children specific values in public schools—from patriotism to sex education, from Darwinian evolution to feminism. Is it not the case that religion is the subject of unique prohibitions that have no secular analogues—and therefore that the norm of civic disparagement cannot do all the work in justifying nonestablishment?[57] Eisgruber and Sager naturally seek to resist this implication. Instead they bite the bullet and, taking their cue from the anti-orthodoxy principle articulated in the flag-salute decision *Barnette,* suggest that government should not endorse *any* orthodoxy that might have disparaging effects on some citizens.[58]

So they find themselves disposed to extend the ban on state endorsement of religion to patriotic pledges, to pro-heterosexual slogans,[59] and more generally to the teaching of controversial partisan orthodoxies in schools, because they might convey a disparaging or exclusionary message to those who do not share them.[60] Secular education in itself, they note, is not a problem; it does not come attached to disparaging secular rituals, and it does not force children to profess allegiance to, say, Darwinian evolution or feminism. Discussing Michael McConnell's example of a coach offering feminist words of encouragement to his team—which would be permitted, while religious words of inspiration would not—Eisgruber and Sager note that any feminist encouragement would be "so bland as not to offend anyone." What would be unconstitutional would be to require them to pledge allegiance to the values of the American feminist movement.[61] Likewise they criticize a biology teacher who refused to provide reference letters for students who would not affirm that they believe the theory of evolution—in Eisgruber and Sager's view, he could demand only that they *understand* it, not that they *endorse* it.[62] In sum, "the Constitution protects schoolchildren from the imposition of orthodoxy, religious or not."[63]

This is a compelling theory. Before I raise one critical remark, let me summarize the virtues of Eisgruber and Sager's equal liberty account. First, like Dworkin, they adopt an interpretive approach. They pick out those distinctive features of religion that explain and justify the norm of nonestablishment, instead of assuming that religion is uniquely special. Nonestablishment only applies to a subset of symbols, ideals, and identities: like Dworkin's neutrality, it is a restricted, not a broad, notion. Second, Eisgruber and Sager pick out a distinct feature of religion— confirming the heuristic potential of the disaggregation of religion into different salient dimensions. For them, when we think of religion in non-establishment of religion, religion is not a matter of personal ethics (as it is for Dworkin), nor does it have anything to do with the depth of commitments (as Eisgruber and Sager had argued in their theory of exemptions). Here they suggest a different answer to the ethical salience problem: what is prohibited is official endorsement of *significant markers of social division*.

What emerges from their analysis is that when we seek to interpret the wrong of religious establishment, religion does not need to be a deep commitment or a matter of personal ethics. What is relevant about religion is that it is a marker of socially divisive identity. The reason the state should not endorse religion is that, much like race, religion has historically functioned as a social category structurally vulnerable to hostility, discrimination, disparagement, and neglect. The implication of Eisgruber and Sager's insights is profound. It means that, for some purposes, religion is treated like race in law—it is defined in relation to the historically sedimented social meanings associated with certain practices and rituals, whereby dominant groups use state power to affirm and entrench hegemonic identities (white, male, Protestant) as normal, and to construe and disparage minority identities as deviant. Witness the process of structural racialization of religious minorities—Jews, Mormons, Catholics, Muslims—in U.S. history. The analogy between race and religion allows Eisgruber and Sager to construe the wrong of state religious endorsement, from an egalitarian standpoint, as an expressive wrong—a wrong connected to the communication of messages of disparagement or exclusion of minorities. From a nonestablishment perspective, religion functions as a third-person, externally defined category of social classification—whereas the value of free exercise picks out the first-person, subjective dimensions of religious experience. A state that proudly proclaims its Christian identity commits an expressive wrong, by signifying to minorities that they are outsiders, that they do not belong on the same terms to the political community. Regardless of whether members of those minorities themselves see their religion as a source of deep, serious, moral commitments, official endorsement of the majority religion makes their non-Christian identity relevant—negatively—to their civic status.

So, it is exclusionary for a state school to adorn classrooms with Christian crucifixes *even if* members of non-Christian groups do not see membership of non-Christian groups as a source of deep ethical commitment for them. By analogy, U.S. segregation laws disparaged African Americans, not because they offended African American culture and ways of life, but because they construed blackness as a negative ascriptive identity, a marker of subordination and inferiority. What the ban on civic disparagement focuses on are those dimensions of the socially constructed meanings of religion that structurally resemble other suspect categories of oppression and domination, such as race.

It seems, therefore, that Eisgruber and Sager's theory contains two intriguingly different answers to the "equality of what?" question. On the one hand, people's ability to act in accordance with their deep commitments should not be subjected to unequal state burdens; on the other hand, the state should not endorse the symbols and rituals of dominant religions because they could be disparaging to racial-like minorities. The difference between the two conceptions is obscured by the authors' equal liberty principle: "No-one should be disparaged on grounds of the spiritual foundations of their deep commitments." Yet they point to different benchmarks for the fair treatment of religion: for some purposes, religious beliefs, identities, and rituals should be treated like racial and gender identities, from a collective, structural, and third-person perspective; for other purposes, they should be treated like deep ethical, comprehensive commitments, from an individualized, case-by-case and first-person perspective. This is a potentially fertile disaggregative approach, which I shall develop in Part II.

There is, however, one problem with Eisgruber and Sager's theory of civic disparagement.[64] In brief, it is unconvincing to argue that the only reason schools can teach gender equality but not Christianity, and Darwinian evolution but not creationism, is the risk of disparagement. What can be said to the religious fundamentalist who object to such teachings?[65] As we saw, Eisgruber and Sager suggest there is a difference between a "pledge" and mere "understanding." They argue that it would be unconstitutional to "require students to pledge their support for evolution, feminism, or other doctrines inconsistent with their fundamentalist religion."[66] The problem is that, in the educational context, it is difficult to see how this distinction can be sustained: biology students must be taught that the theory of evolution is true (at least scientifically true, that is, refutable by science).

Eisgruber and Sager further appeal to the wrongness of disparagement to explain why the teaching of creationism or intelligent design would be wrong. It would "affiliate . . . the government with a particular religious view and so violate . . . the Equal Liberty reading of the Establishment clause."[67] This is because the undisputed social meaning of these theories involves endorsement of the book of Genesis as truth: this is a case of state-imposed religious orthodoxy.[68] But Eisgruber and Sager do not explain why the teaching of mainstream science, and Darwinian evolution, is not an "orthodoxy" in the same sense. To be sure, Eisgruber and Sager refer to evolution as being "established by science," "foundational in all of modern biology," a "rigorous and respected body of knowledge." Here they hint at an *epistemic* distinction between two kinds of knowledge, which suggests that scientific knowledge is epistemically superior (in the *biology* classroom, albeit not in the ethics curriculum) and that it can be promoted by the state on this ground. But by analogy, the problem with teaching creationism is not a disparagement problem: it is not that it demeans nonbelievers, but rather that it teaches bad science. It is not a problem of religious establishment as civic disparagement, but a problem of religious establishment as the inculcation of incorrect factual beliefs.[69]

In sum, Eisgruber and Sager's theory of equal liberty does not fully explain why secular education (and its commitment to controversial science) should be enforced against *Mozert* fundamentalists. They argue that "government cannot, through its teachers or other officials, throw its weight on the side of religion, or on the side of particular religions, any more than it can take a position against religion."[70] But when the state promotes particular conceptions of liberal justice (gender equality), or teaches science (Darwinian evolution), it does communicate its rejection of (some features of) religion. In this context, religion should not be interpreted as a socially divisive marker of identity (and if it is, this is *not* what justifies its nonestablishment). "Religion" can also refer to comprehensive conceptions of justice, as well to self-contained bodies of knowledge or epistemic *doxa*. In such cases, the state is under no obligation of nonestablishment or neutrality, even if the ideals it endorses contradict traditionally religious teachings. The norm of nonestablishment *in this sense* need not infringe on equal liberty and restricted neutrality.

More generally, the mere fact of divisiveness or controversy cannot be the sole reason the state should not endorse some commitments and beliefs. The fact that some views are endorsed by the state does not necessarily disparage those who hold them—as in the case of gender equality or Darwinian evolution. This suggests another way of justifying liberal neutrality: by appeal, not to the mere *fact* of disagreement, but to its *nature*. This epistemic strategy has recently been developed by Jonathan Quong, to whom I turn next.

Foundational Disagreement

In the previous section, we examined the sociological and historical argument for state neutrality. It is because some salient social identities—racial and religious, paradigmatically—have historically been the source of acute conflict that the liberal state should not endorse any of them. Many liberal philosophers, however, argue that the legitimacy of the liberal state should not be rooted in such contingent historical facts about diversity and conflict. Rather, it should draw on a normative argument about the most appropriate response to what Rawls calls the fact of pluralism—the fact that citizens endorse a plurality of religious, moral, and philosophical doctrines.[71] Assuming—as we should—that the fact of pluralism is not a contingent but a permanent, structural feature of modern society, how can the exercise of political power be justified?

One influential answer is provided by public reason liberals.[72] Public reason liberalism seeks to ground the legitimacy of the liberal state on its ability to justify coercive laws in terms that those affected by them can reasonably be expected to accept. And because citizens profoundly disagree about the good, they cannot reasonably accept reasons that draw on their diverse, conflicting, and incompatible conceptions of the good. Instead, they should find reasons that are public, that is, that appeal to shared, freestanding political principles, notably basic principles of justice and the right. But in virtue of what, exactly, are conceptions of the good impermissible in public reason? How can we "separate the public wheat from the private chaff," to borrow Christopher Eberle's memorable phrase?[73]

In this section I show how public reason liberals rely on an *epistemic* criterion to reject conceptions of the good from the set of permissible public reasons. I use "epistemic" in a broad sense, to refer to conditions of knowledge, belief, and deliberation, and to notions such as rationality, reasonableness, acceptability, accessibility, intelligibility, and so forth. I first show why epistemic criteria are required in public reason, and I then explore the epistemic argument for neutrality recently put forward by Jonathan Quong.[74] Quong's is the most sophisticated attempt to draw out the implications of Rawls's interpretation of religion as one conception of the good among others. In brief, Quong assumes, with Rawls, that religious beliefs are only a subset of a broader family of conceptions of the good, which contain perfectionist judgment about what constitutes human flourishing.[75] What distinguishes conceptions of the good from conceptions of the right is that reasonable disagreement about the former is particularly deep and intractable: *foundational,* in Quong's phrase. The epistemic argument for neutrality, therefore, is that the state should be neutral about the good because disagreement about the good is foundational: it appeals to no premise that all citizens can reasonably expect to share.[76]

To see why public reason liberals such as Quong have been drawn to an epistemic interpretation of disagreements about the good, I start by setting out an influential and persuasive objection to public reason liberalism. The objection says, roughly, that public reason liberalism is untenable because there is as much disagreement about justice as there is about the good. According to this *asymmetry objection,* it is not clear why religious beliefs, ideals of character and virtue, aesthetic and cultural values, and norms of sexual behavior are excluded from playing a role in public reason, while controversial arguments about justice and individual rights are not similarly excluded. Historically, conflicts about power and rights—revolutions, decolonization, the workers' movement— have been as violent and divisive as conflicts about the good life. And people continue to disagree profoundly about what justice entails in the areas of wealth distribution, criminal law and punishment, war, abortion, same-sex marriage, and the place of religion in society. Such disagreements about justice arise and persist, not because of contingent unfavorable circumstances, nor because people fail to reason about justice properly. They arise because people, in their practical reasoning, are affected by what Rawls called the burdens of judgment. What Rawls meant by this was that even if people make a sincere, good-faith effort to apply their reason to moral, religious, and philosophical questions under conditions of freedom, they will encounter epistemic obstacles to ethical agreement. Among those burdens of judgment, Rawls, for example, noted that the evidence bearing on a question may be conflicting and complex; there may be disagreement over the amount of weight to attach to different considerations; concepts are vague and are subject to hard cases of application; values are plural and conflict with one another; there are difficulties with settling priorities; and so on.[77]

The asymmetry objection states, *contra* Rawls, that the burdens of judgment apply to matters of justice (such as distributive justice, abortion, and war) just as they apply to conceptions of the good.[78] Several responses can be made to the asymmetry objection. Some public reason liberals have been tempted to drop the epistemic feature altogether. Stephen Lecce, for example, has argued that state neutrality can be justified purely through a contractualist procedure, without reference to the Rawlsian notion of the burdens of judgment.[79] In his view, previous neutralists have unnecessarily relied on a notion of epistemic asymmetry between knowledge of contractually produced justice and knowledge of comprehensive conceptions of the good. He argues that the fact of pluralism, the ideal of moral equality, and a contractualist procedure are sufficient to generate fair principles of justice—that is, principles that do not draw on particular conceptions of the good. But as Quong has pointed out, the argument is fatally question-begging.[80] We would still need to know why "fairly situated hypothetical contractors"[81] would not appeal to their conceptions of the good (why, for example, parties in Rawls's original position are deprived of such knowledge). The answer cannot be simply that it would be wrong to coercively enforce controversial principles on others: principles of justice are controversial, too, and yet are legitimately enforced by the liberal state. Lecce's non-epistemic solution, then, is no answer to the asymmetry objection.

I now turn to Quong's sophisticated rebuttal of the asymmetry objection. It is two-pronged. Quong begins by agreeing with critics that the burdens of judgment apply to both justice and the good. The abortion debate, for example, is a reasonable disagreement about justice: both pro-life and pro-choice advocates appeal to a reasonable balance of political values. This simply means that public reason is inconclusive: it sets out broad normative parameters for public reasoning, but it need not generate a single, fixed conception of justice. Rawls himself allowed that there could be "a family of liberal conceptions of justice." Quong concedes, therefore, that there can be reasonable disagreement about justice as well as about the good.[82]

Yet it does not follow that disagreement about justice is on the same plane, epistemically speaking, as disagreement about the good. There are two different types of disagreement at stake, both of which are directly relevant to the legitimacy of state coercion. Quong presents an ingenious reformulation of the basic neutralist intuition: that there must be a feature of conceptions of the good that rules out any possibility of them being agreed to by all. What could that be? The answer, according to Quong, is that when we disagree about the good, this disagreement is "almost certainly" foundational in the sense that it goes "all the way down."[83] We share no premise from which to disagree, no justificatory framework that would allow us to weigh the merits and flaws of one another's views. As an example, Quong asks us to consider a disagreement between two hypothetical characters, Mike and Sara, about the morality of recreational drug use. Mike thinks that drug use is immoral because it is a hedonistic dereliction of our God-given responsibilities toward our lives. Sara thinks that drug use is not immoral so long as it does not affect others: morality applies only to the category of what we owe to other persons. Mike and Sara are having a foundational disagreement about morality because they hold incompatible standards of justification (what we owe to God versus what we owe to other persons). If the state drew on Mike's views as the rationale for its drug laws, it would appeal to a premise that Sarah cannot reasonably accept, and would thereby fall foul of justificatory neutrality.[84]

Disagreements about justice, according to Quong, are quite different: they are "necessarily justificatory and not foundational."[85] In his version of Rawlsian political liberalism, Quong assumes from the outset that reasonable persons share a set of liberal political values: freedom, equality, fairness, and so forth. And they are further reasonable in the sense that they seek to achieve fair terms of cooperation with others, and accept that, because of the burdens of judgment, no agreement will be forthcoming about foundational values. Consequently, in public reason, such persons will appeal only to what can be expected to be shared—namely (and *ex hypothesi*) the political values of liberalism.[86]

As an example, Quong asks us to consider a dispute between Sara (whom we have already encountered) and Tony (another hypothetical character) about the justice of allowing the Catholic Church to discriminate on the basis of gender when employing priests—the "ministerial exception." In this dispute, Tony and Sara share a currency of common reasons. Tony, who defends the ministerial exception, invokes the political ideals of freedom of association and freedom of religion. Sara, who rejects the ministerial exception, appeals to equality of opportunity and nondiscrimination. They disagree about how to rank and weigh these values, and therefore reach divergent substantive conclusions about the case at hand. But as long as they appeal to freestanding political principles that do not draw on sectarian doctrines, they respect the ideal of public reason. If the state were to draw on Tony's view as the rationale for its policies concerning the reach of antidiscrimination legislation, it would appeal to a premise that Sara can reasonably accept, and would thereby not fall foul of justificatory neutrality.[87] According to Quong, the same reasoning applies to *prima facie* harder cases such as abortion. As long as citizens limit their disagreement to disputes about the optimal balance of *political* values (in this case, the right to life versus women's right to control their bodies), their disagreement is justificatory and firmly located in public reason. Only absolutist pro-life or pro-choice positions are unreasonable, insofar as they do not present a reasonable balance of political values.[88]

Quong offers liberal egalitarians a sophisticated argument for the generalization of the nonestablishment of religion into neutrality toward the good in general. What religion and conceptions of the good share—what makes religion a "conception of the good" in the relevant sense—is the depth and intractability of disagreement about them. Even though *historically* religious conflict might have been particularly bloody and intractable, *normatively* it is foundational disagreement about the good that justifies the state's refraining from "establishing" any such conception. Note that this is a normative and epistemic, not an empirical, point.[89] Quong is prepared to concede to perfectionist critics that, in practice, people may share certain ideals of the good: most of us, for example, think that a life of addiction (to toxic substances) is not a good life, by contrast to a life enriched by family, friends, and beauty.[90] Yet Quong argues that political liberalism should not be hostage to the actual views of existing citizens, as there may be empirical convergence on illiberal or otherwise unjust views.[91] His account, therefore, is epistemic in the sense that he does not rely on *actual* disagreement but on *necessary* disagreement about the good, given its structural features—notably, that ideals about the good run "all the way down," to premises that others cannot share. The salient feature of ideals about the good is not that they are (empirically) nonshared, but that they are (epistemically) nonshareable.

In a pioneering critique of liberal neutralism, Eberle persuasively demonstrated that, whether they recognize it or not, theorists of public reason must avail themselves of epistemic considerations.[92] This is because they need to identify a feature that (in Eberle's terminology) private reasons lack and public reasons possess, and they inevitably draw on epistemic notions such as rationality, reasonableness, accessibility, mutual acceptability, and such. Some neutralists seek to avoid the epistemic route by asserting that public reason is about the right, and private reason about the good. But as we saw, this merely stipulates what has to be demonstrated: that public reason should not draw on conceptions of the good. I have shown that Quong bites this bullet and provides a sophisticated, noncircular, epistemic account of the distinction between the right and the good. Appeal to conceptions of the good is impermissible in public reason because such conceptions are the object of foundational disagreement. It is the epistemic nature of the disagreement, then, that justifies liberal neutrality about the good.

An additional virtue of Quong's approach is that it allows us to formulate a robust response to Eberle's main charge. The charge is that public reason liberals single out religious convictions, *qua* religious, as epistemically suspect. It is because religious reasons are presumptively inaccessible, unintelligible, nonfallible, nonshareable, or not externally criticizable that public reasons liberals such as Thomas Nagel, Bruce Ackerman, Charles Larmore, and Brian Barry exclude them from public reason. Quong's revision of Rawlsian public reason liberalism is not vulnerable to this charge of anti-religious bias. In line with liberal egalitarianism as I have defined it, Quong argues that there is nothing special about religious convictions, such that they are uniquely inaccessible or nonshareable. Disagreements about conceptions of, and ideals about, the good share this epistemic feature. In the next section, I return to these two claims and assess whether liberal neutralists such as Quong can fully escape a more nuanced version of Eberle's charge.

Quong argues that the reason the state should be neutral about the good is that "reasonable disagreements over the good life will frequently be foundational in the sense that there will be no shared justificatory framework regulating the debate."[93] It is because reasonable people profoundly disagree about the good—because they do not have a "common currency" for their disagreement—that the state should refrain from enforcing any conception of the good life. By contrast, the state can and should enforce conceptions of justice. Even though people disagree on how they should weigh, rank, and apply the political values of justice, such political values provide a shared framework for their disagreement.

In the rest of this section, I raise two objections to Quong's theory. The first is that it does not successfully rule out moderate perfectionism—and is therefore an instance of restricted rather than broad neutrality. The second is that it does not take seriously enough the problem of jurisdictional boundary—the political challenge of fixing the boundary between the right and the good.

First, although Quong does not single out religious conceptions as special, neither does he fully succeed in explaining why *ideas about* the good—as opposed to *comprehensive conceptions of* the good—cannot be appealed to in public debate. In particular, he does not decisively rule out the possibility that what Joseph Chan calls "moderate perfectionism" may be compatible with liberal neutrality.[94] If my argument is correct, the implication is that the set of impermissible reasons is narrower than Quong intends. It cannot be conflated with conventionally religious reasons, but neither does it encompass all ideas about the good. In the end, Quong remains indecisive about what makes a set of beliefs "sectarian" in the relevant sense.

Quong makes it clear that the distinction between justificatory and foundational disagreements does not fully overlap with the distinction between the right and the good. This makes sense. Because the nature of disagreements is supposed to provide an independent explanation for neutrality about the good, it should not collapse into a definitional restatement of the right / good distinction (which, we saw, marred approaches such as Lecce's). Quong, therefore, concedes that "*some* reasonable disagreements about the good life will be justificatory."[95] He agrees with Chan's observation that "one does not need to achieve any kind of full agreement on a comprehensive doctrine in order to reach more modest agreements on particular issues that reflect perfectionist values."[96] One example Quong gives of such a shared, partial ideal about the good is, as we have seen, the idea that a life of addiction (to toxic substances) is not a good life. Call this the *badness of addiction* argument.

If people broadly agree about the badness of addiction, it would seem to follow (on Quong's theory) that the state can permissibly appeal to this reason to justify its tax and health policies, without being in breach of liberal neutrality. Yet Quong resists this moderately perfectionist conclusion, and it is important to survey the reasons he provides. Quong alludes to three objections, none of which is compelling, but all of which are revealing of deeper tensions with his approach. I call them: the *empirical objection,* the *restricted set objection,* and the *restricted subject matter* objection. I look at them in turn.

The *empirical objection* points out that agreement on the badness of addiction is merely an empirical fact, and that political liberalism should not be founded on empirical claims about the nature of disagreement in existing societies. Why not? Quong's answer is that this would "open the door to perfectionism in a way that is incompatible with political liberalism."[97] The problem with this is that it begs the question as to the status of Quong's own statement that some disagreements about the good are justificatory. Here Quong faces a dilemma. If it is an empirical observation, it should be ruled out from the outset as irrelevant: people might think that they can have justificatory disputes about the good but—it can be shown—they are mistaken. But in this case, the justificatory / foundational distinction collapses into the right / good distinction and does not provide the required independent criterion of impermissibility. If, by contrast, the statement is an analytical truth—some debates about the good are justificatory, say, because of the structural features of the moral reasons that pertain to them—then the empirical objection has no force against it. The empirical objection, therefore, does not rule out moderate perfectionism.[98]

The *restricted set* objection points out that arguments about the good are justificatory only for a subset of persons who share a particular view of morality. Recall Quong's example of a disagreement about the morality of recreational drug use. One of his hypothetical characters, Sara, holds what Quong calls a "Scanlonian view of morality," in reference to

Tim Scanlon's view that the concepts right and wrong do not apply to purely private acts (those that do not affect others) but apply only to the category of what we owe to other persons.[99] Sara might disagree with another Scanlonian about whether drug use does affect others, and they will reach different conclusions about its morality. Their disagreement is justificatory because they share the same view of morality. Presumably, they could not have a justificatory debate with a non-Scanlonian citizen who thinks that drug use is immoral *per se,* regardless of its effects on others.

This objection has undeniable force. Seen from the perspective of all reasonable people and not only a subset of them, citizens are unlikely to agree on the morality or immorality of drug use. But would the same argument apply to the badness of addiction argument? As we saw, Quong conceded that the view that a life of drug addiction or alcoholism is not a good life is widely shared. Admittedly, we have different reasons for holding this view: some hold that addiction inevitably imposes costs and harms on others; others, that it is a disrespectful or wasteful dereliction of our human capacities; yet others that it deprives individuals of basic control over their own lives. But while we disagree about what would make life good, we agree that addiction makes all lives bad.

At this point Quong would object that it is precisely because individuals have different moral reasons for thinking addiction bad that their agreement is not a justificatory agreement.[100] More precisely, they do not share a framework for making sense of their disagreements about what exactly makes addiction bad. This raises the fundamental question of whether citizens in liberal societies need to share the "reasons for their reasons"—the deeper, foundational reasons that justify their commitment to certain values. One way to think about this problem is to ask whether it would apply in the same way to our views about justice. Presumably, citizens who endorse liberal principles of justice also have different reasons for doing so. Quong, after all, does not argue that our shared commitment to ideals of justice is framed by a deeper agreement on the reasons we are committed to them. What distinguishes political from comprehensive liberalism is precisely that the former does not demand that people share the same comprehensive moral framework. By analogy, we cannot exclude the possibility that some thin values about the good are structurally similar to thin values about the right—values over which there is enough agreement to allow proper public debate and disagreement, without the need to go into deeper "reasons for reasons."[101] So the restricted set objection fails to show that disagreement about the good operates with a structurally more restricted constituency than disagreement about the right.

The *restricted subject matter* objection takes a different tack. It suggests that the badness of addiction is too substantive an ideal to be the subject of public justification, but there are other ideas about the good that are more suited for public justification. Thus Quong focuses on special cases where disputes about the good can be justificatory "in exactly the same way" as disputes about justice.[102] What Quong has in mind is Rawls's thin liberal theory of the good, whose scope is limited. In Rawls's theory, it serves to identify the basic moral powers (rationality, reasonableness) for the exercise of which all individuals require a bundle of primary goods (rights, income, opportunities, and so on) as a matter of justice.[103] Quong says that disagreement about this thin theory of the good is regulated by a shared justificatory framework.[104] But we may wonder how abstract the thin theory of the good must be. One could construct a valid argument, for example, according to which people are capable of exercising their basic rational moral powers (the faculty they have to form and revise their conceptions of the good) only if they are not in the grip of an addiction. The badness of addiction argument, therefore, can be derived from a reasonable interpretation of the thin liberal theory of the good. Were such an argument to succeed, it would easily meet Quong's restricted subject matter objection.

Although Quong does not discuss the thin theory of the good in *Liberalism without Perfection,* he sought to give more definite content to it in an earlier article.[105] In his attempt to articulate an egalitarian theory of cultural exemptions, he argues that society should be arranged so that people have equivalent opportunities to pursue their conceptions of the good. But which conceptions of the good, in particular, are so fundamental that their pursuit should be located in the opportunity set that should be equalized? Quong answers that religious obligations, as well as a family life, are not Rawlsian primary goods *strict sensu*, but are "generally seen as fundamental opportunities in a human life."[106] The thin liberal theory of the good, therefore, incorporates ethically salient goods such as family commitments and religious pursuits. This may be a plausible and attractive ideal about the good. But one thing is clear: it is no less substantive than the badness of addiction argument. If anything, it is at least as controversial, and it is doubtful that a broader, justificatory moral theory will provide the common currency through which disagreements about it can be conducted. Admittedly, Quong's specification of the thin theory of the good is general, rather than detailed and specific; and it is positive (highlighting essential elements of the good life) rather than negative (focusing on one aspect of a bad life). But it is unclear what normative conclusions should follow from these differences. What appears is that if, on Quong's own theory, family commitments and religious pursuits are included in the set of basic opportunities that should be equalized, his commitment to liberal neutrality does not dispense with judgments of ethical salience, insofar as it relies on a (more or less) thin theory of the good.

Let me sum up. The point of my engagement with Quong's sophisticated analysis has not been to defend either moderate perfectionism in general or the badness of addiction argument in particular. Instead, I have attempted to show that Quong's theory of neutrality does not successfully rule out all appeals to ideals about the good. Indeed, Quong himself offers a cautious conclusion on this point: "While moderate perfectionism within political liberalism is not necessarily ruled out by my argument, we have good reasons to doubt its validity."[107] But the reason

for this, he thinks, is because perfectionists will fail to construct a notion of reasonableness that will be compatible with political liberalism
(or with their own commitments).[108] So Quong thinks that the onus is
on perfectionists to establish the compatibility. I have tried to suggest,
instead, that the problem is internal to his political liberalism. At several
points Quong posits that reasonable people, *qua* reasonable, will avoid
appealing to reasons drawn from "sectarian doctrines," "particular conceptions of the good or other controversial doctrines."[109] But why should
those impermissible reasons overlap with "the good" (or with "religion")?
Quong's answer is that disputes about the good are more likely to be
foundational—to go "all the way down"—than disputes about the
right. Yet I have shown that, on closer analysis, partial ideas about the
good are not necessarily characterized by foundational disagreement in
the sense that matters to justification, and that if they do, they do so in
exactly the same way as ideas about the right. Focus on the epistemic
nature of disagreement, therefore, does not justify state neutrality toward
the good.

The second objection I want to raise to Quong's theory is a version
of the jurisdictional boundary problem. Recall that the realist critique
(examined in Chapter 1) is that state power is essentially arbitrary. The
liberal answer is that it is not arbitrary for the state to enforce liberal
principles of justice. Quong accepts that there is reasonable disagreement
about justice, in which case there must be democratic deliberation, in
public reason, about justice. Then it is legitimate for the state to enforce
the democratically arrived-at conception. Liberal democratic sovereignty
is therefore not arbitrary. What this assumes, however, is that even though
there is reasonable disagreement between conceptions of liberal justice, there is reasonable agreement about what the domain of justice is—
which social practices are justice-apt, so to speak. In what follows, I
cast some doubts on this assumption. I show that drawing the boundary
between justice and the good often requires drawing on contested ideas
about the good. If this is correct, it raises a new challenge for Quong's
theory of liberal legitimacy.

For Quong, as we saw, the liberal state should not take sides in foundational disagreements about morality. This is because such disagreements go all the way down, to questions about the meaning and value of life, and other metaphysical beliefs and perfectionist values. Recall the disagreement between Quong's two characters, Mike and Sara, about the morality of recreational drug use. Mike believes drug use is immoral because individuals have divinely ordained obligations not to waste their lives in hedonistic pursuits. Sara, a Scanlonian, thinks that the concepts right and wrong apply, not to purely private acts (those that do not affect others), but instead to the category of what we owe to other persons.[110] Mike and Sara hold incompatible standards of justification (what we owe to God versus what we owe to other persons) and therefore they should not draw on those standards in public reason. Quong writes: "Suppose that Mike is asked, not whether he believes recreational drug use is morally wrong, but whether he believes recreational drug use is unjust. If Mike states that recreational drug use is unjust, and he advances the same set of reasons for this view about justice as he did about morality, then he is clearly being unreasonable in the political liberal sense. . . . There are other reasonable citizens who do not share his religious beliefs, thus those beliefs cannot ground a reasonable political claim."[111]

But how about Sara? Quong assumes that Mike and Sara are in an exactly symmetrical position but—I shall argue—they are not. Sara thinks that morality is about what we owe to other persons, not to entities such as God or the good. Clearly, as a full theory of what morality is, this cannot form the basis of an argument about justice. But there is the rub. Liberal justice is also—paradigmatically—about what people owe to other persons. Admittedly, the scope of justice is narrower than the scope of morality: it only applies to the basic structure of legal, social, and political institutions. Yet while its *scope* is narrower than Scanlonian morality, its *regulating principle* is, at bottom, the same: liberal justice, much like Scanlonian morality, is a matter of interpersonal relations. We find this view of liberal justice in the writings of all canonical liberal philosophers, even though it has been expressed in different ways.[112] The basic thought is that the liberal state deals with *interpersonal* morality—what we owe to each other, politically speaking—and not with the pursuit of impersonal, extratemporal, and other goods. So in Quong's example, the liberal state can permissibly side with Sara's line of reasoning, but not with Mike's. Mike and Sara are not symmetrically situated. Liberal justice turns out to coincide with Sara's preferred view of morality—Scanlonian morality—as applied to social and political institutions. Insofar as an action does not harm others, or infringe on their rights, to that extent it should not be regulated by the state in the name of liberal justice.

Should this conclusion worry Quong? In one sense it need not. After all, Quong assumes, at the start of the justificatory process that he adopts, that reasonable people already share a set of liberal principles—liberty, equality, and so forth. By taking liberty, fairness, and equality (rather than, say, divine command, utility, virtue, or tradition) as their core values, Quongian citizens already endorse the basic blocks of a Scanlonian view of (political) morality. They are reasonable insofar as they refrain from enforcing their own conception of the good on others, and seek mutually justifiable, fair terms of political cooperation between free and equal citizens pursuing their good in their own way. On the "internal" theory of political liberalism that he defends, Quong thinks he does not need to provide a justification for this starting assumption.[113] This view is contested: other philosophers reject such a deflationary account of the justificatory ambitions of liberalism.[114] I do not aim to settle this debate here. Whether or not a full philosophical justification of liberalism is available, the view that the liberal state should concern itself with justice, conceived as a matter of interpersonal relations between free and equal persons, is compelling. So the fact that the liberal state, in the name of justice, is *not* neutral between Scanlonian Sara and theistic Mike need not, in itself, undermine the coherence, or lessen the appeal, of Quong's theory.

The problem, I think, lies elsewhere. Assume we agree that it is proper (on whichever theory of liberal justification we favor) that the state only concern itself with justice, conceived as a matter of interpersonal relations between free and equal persons. The further question arises: Who is to say what belongs to the relevant category of interpersonal relations? And can this decision be made without appeal to foundational questions—precisely of the kind that is barred by liberal neutrality? This is what I call the jurisdictional boundary problem. In what follows, I suggest that liberal neutrality lacks resources to solve the boundary problem. Even assuming that liberals can justify that the state should concern itself with interpersonal justice, they need to justify the state's prerogative to set the boundaries of where interpersonal justice lies in the first place, in the context of foundational disagreement about the boundary of justice itself.

To see the blind spot in Quong's theory, let me refine his example. Assume that Sara and Mike disagree not only about recreational drug use, but about several other issues, as follows:

> Sara is in favor of first-trimester abortion because she thinks that any reasonable balance of values should prioritize the rights of women over those of an unborn child. Mike thinks that because the fetus is a person, abortion is equivalent to murder and is therefore an injustice, if anything is.
>
> Sara thinks that insofar as nonhuman animals have more human-like features than fetuses, they should have rights. Mike thinks that, although we have a duty of care to the natural environment, of which animals are part, only beings with distinctively human capacities and potential have rights, properly conceived.
>
> Sara thinks that on grounds of equality, same-sex couples should have the right to marry. Mike thinks that the scope of equality can only be defined on the basis of a substantive assessment of the purpose and value of marriage.

In all these cases, it is not obvious that the state can side with Scanlonian Sara without taking a substantive stance about the status of fetuses, animals, and marriage. The state would thereby draw on much thicker conceptions of the good than Quong's thin theory of the good allows. One possible response may be that these cases are "limit cases"—cases where what is at stake, for example, is the status of fetuses.[115] We should not be surprised to find that inter*personal* justice is dependent on a prior definition of what a *person* is. Here disagreement about justice is foundational. The state cannot allow, or oppose, abortion without taking a stance on prenatal status. Liberal neutralists have to concede the indeterminacy of public reason in these limit cases.[116]

Yet the problem, I argue, goes deeper than this.[117] It is not simply that interpersonal justice is parasitic on a substantive account of what a person is. It is also parasitic on an account of where the boundaries of the personal and the interpersonal, the public and the private sphere, are to be drawn. Consider areas such as health, the family, sexuality, and education. Are they public or private? Are they about the good or about the right? Clearly, there has been a momentous shift, from the nineteenth century onward, whereby these areas, traditionally regulated by the norms and institutions of traditional religion, have progressively been brought under the ambit of the interventionist state. On a Foucauldian analysis, this can be seen as a long-term structural process of the emergence of a particular type of governmentality—the political governance of bodies and souls. A progressive liberal reading of these developments would point out that these areas have progressively been defined as key sites for the pursuit of interpersonal justice. Education, the family, and sexuality are no longer immune to the liberal agendas of personal freedom, racial and gender equality, children's rights, and minorities' rights.

For a contemporary example, witness the current debate over the reach of egalitarian norms of nondiscrimination—notably on grounds of gender or sexuality—within the internal life of religious associations. As we have seen, Quong argues that this debate can and must be conducted in public reason. He refers to a disagreement between Sara and Tony, about the legitimacy of the ministerial exception (the right for churches to be exempted from norms of antidiscrimination in clergy appointment), and argues that there can be legitimate disagreement about how best to balance the relevant political claims of freedom of association and rights to nondiscrimination. This is correct. But to claim that the church should be construed as an association—and therefore subject to the relevant norms of liberal justice—is itself a controversial position about where the boundary between the right and the good lies.[118] The very fact that the debate is conducted in public reason implies that the state—or, more precisely, the process of democratic deliberation that gives it legitimacy—has the prerogative of deciding that the issue of clergy appointment falls under matters of "the right," and not simply "the good."

The problem is, no theory of neutral justification can justify *this* prerogative—that of adjudicating the boundary problem in the first place. The prerogative consists in being authorized to define which social spheres are apt to be subjected to the scrutiny of liberal justice—in other words, *where* the boundary between the right and the good lies. Theorists of liberal neutrality tend to assume that the right and the good are self-evident categories of moral reasoning; yet, clearly, they have evolved historically and are themselves the sites of foundational political disagreement. Disagreement about justice goes deeper than Quong admits. It is not only about what is the correct or best conception of liberal justice. It depends on a prior identification of which areas of social life are justice-apt. And this determination cannot be made without judgments of substantive, metaphysical, and ontological questions— judgments that, ultimately (I shall argue in Chapter 4) it is the province of the state to make. This raises a challenge for Quong's theory, because it entails that the state does not meet his own criterion of liberal legitimacy: it draws on matters about which reasonable citizens have a foundational, not merely a justificatory, disagreement.

In sum, it looks as though critical religion theorists have a point when they say that liberal neutrality assumes a prior conception of the legitimacy of the state as a "meta-jurisdictional" authority. The sovereign state patrols the boundaries of justice—it decide what pertains to the private sphere of conceptions of the good (of which religion is paradigmatic) and to the public sphere of liberal justice. Liberal egalitarians, I shall argue in Part II, must address the jurisdictional boundary question head-on. They must provide an account of the legitimacy of state sovereignty—in particular, the legitimacy of democratic resolutions of foundational disagreements about liberal justice.

II

DISAGGREGATING RELIGION

4

⍏⍉⍏

Disaggregating Religion
in Nonestablishment of Religion

Defending Minimal Secularism

In Part II, I build on, and improve, the liberal egalitarian account of religion and the state. Existing liberal egalitarians theories, I have argued, work with too loose an analogy between religion and "the good." It is reductive, and often misleading, to say that the liberal state should be neutral toward religion or the good, *simpliciter*. Instead, I propose to disaggregate the concept of religion. In this chapter, I explore those dimensions of religion that are relevant to understanding the secular nature of the state—what U.S. constitutionalists refer to as the Establishment Clause of the First Amendment.[1] In what sense, if any, should the liberal state be *secular?* I introduce secularism as a minimal normative requirement of liberal legitimacy. It is not a comprehensive nonreligious conception of the good but, rather, a political doctrine specifying the rightful place of religion in the state. Secularism focuses, not on the duties and dispositions of citizens, but instead on the institutions of the state and the obligations of its officials. It asks whether liberal democracy requires some form of separation between state and religion, which form, and why.[2]

It should be obvious that the question is important and pressing. As Ran Hirschl has illustrated, the great majority of people in the world live under either regimes that are what he calls constitutional theocracies—where religion is formally enshrined in the state—or regimes in which religious affiliation is a pillar of collective political identity.[3] In countries otherwise as different as Egypt, Israel, Turkey, India, Indonesia, Poland, and many others, politics and religion are interconnected in ways that belie any simplified model of secular separation.[4] Many such states, for example, appeal to a religious tradition in making the law, provide material and symbolic advantages to members of the majority religion, and enforce conservative laws in matters of bioethics, sexuality, and the family.[5] Are they *ipso facto* in breach of liberal legitimacy? Is there a minimal secularism—or separation between state and religion—that is required by liberal legitimacy?[6]

Some are inclined to think this is the wrong question to ask. As we saw, liberal egalitarians have suggested that liberal states should not be secular: they should instead be neutral. That is, states should not endorse a particular religion, but only because states should not endorse any conception of the good, religious or not. On this view, religion is not special: it is only a subset of a broader category of conceptions of the good; and secularism is only a subset of liberal neutrality. The implication is that insofar as the states of Egypt, Israel, and Poland favor or recognize a particular conception of the good *via* their constitution and laws, and provide material and symbolic advantages to those holding that conception, they are—straightforwardly—non-neutral, and therefore in breach of basic liberal legitimacy.

As I have argued in Part I, however, the ideal of state neutrality about the good is more complex than this account suggests. Liberal egalitarians are not in fact committed to what I called *broad* neutrality. They have articulated different theories of *restricted* neutrality, which only applies to a subset of beliefs, identities, and conceptions of the good. Dworkin argued that the state should be neutral toward conceptions of personal ethics. Eisgruber and Sager argued that the state should not endorse socially vulnerable identities. Quong argued that the state should not enforce policies about which reasonable people have a foundational disagreement. Liberal egalitarian theorists, then, have singled out different relevant features of the good: ethical, sociopolitical, and epistemic. As I shall show, they all have a place in the normative architecture of liberalism. Liberalism picks out different features of religion and the good, which should be carefully disaggregated, and which are connected to distinct liberal ideals. Secularism and neutrality should not be reduced to one value, but explicated in relation to a constellation of liberal values.[7]

My reworking of liberal theory takes the disaggregation project a step further. Recall that the restricted neutrality of Dworkin, Eisgruber, Sager, and Quong implies that the state may endorse some features and dimensions of the good. When some conception or practice does not infringe personal ethics (Dworkin), is not socially vulnerable (Eisgruber and Sager), or is not the object of foundational disagreement (Quong), then it is permissible for the state to endorse it. I argue that the same is true of religion. When religion does not exhibit the features that make it impermissible as an object of state endorsement, then there is nothing wrong with the state endorsing it. This is a logical implication of the interpretive method adopted by liberal egalitarians, yet this is not a bullet that they have willingly bitten. Because they start from the assumption that the separation of state and religion provides the *paradigm* for liberal neutrality, they have generally assumed that liberal neutrality, whatever else it applies to, applies to religion. But, of course, much depends on how the original paradigm of religious nonestablishment is itself interpreted.

In what follows, I argue that when religious ideas and practices do not have the features that make state establishment impermissible, then the state may endorse and affirm them. Not all features of Hirschl's constitutional theocracy are impermissible, and Western-style separation between state and religion is not the only legitimate liberal model. My argument, then, goes some way toward answering the charge that liberal secularism and neutrality are ethnocentric because they are rooted in a specifically Western history of parochial intra-Christian conflict in the seventeenth century. Instead of asking the question, "can secularism travel?" (which invites answers measuring how well non-Western countries fare in relation to Western secularism), I prefer to start from liberal democratic ideals, assume that they are not themselves ethnocentric, and then ask how much, and what kind of, state separation from religion is required to secure these ideals.[8]

Liberal egalitarians have put forward their own preferred model of neutrality and secularism but have not recognized that—*by their own interpretive and normative standards*—other models are permissibly liberal. There is more variation in legitimate state-religion relationships than liberal egalitarians have recognized. Just as neutrality is restricted, so secularism is minimal: it only applies to certain dimensions and features of religion. To defend secularism as minimal does not mean that secularism has a shifting, uncertain, or reduced place in liberalism. It applies in restricted areas, but it applies robustly there.

I identify the different liberal values that minimal secularism helps to sustain, and I suggest that each relates to one specific dimension of religion, not to religion (or the good) *simpliciter*. The aim is to articulate a universal minimal secularism, one not tied to a particular Western history of secularization, yet one that meets basic liberal democratic desiderata. My enquiry is internal to liberalism. I do not deny that secularism—the idea of separation between politics and religion—is not always or intrinsically liberal. I am solely interested in the sense in which liberalism must be secular. Assuming (as I do) that liberal democratic ideals are not purely Western inventions but have transcultural value, to what extent do they carry secularism with them? I attempt to extract the minimal secular core of liberal democracy. I argue, in particular, that liberal democracy does not require a strict wall of separation.

Standards of liberal neutrality allow a greater variety of state-religion arrangements than liberals have realized. Symbolic recognition of religion, conservative laws in matters of bioethics, religious accommodations from general laws, and religious references in public debate are not incompatible with minimal secularism and liberal legitimacy. Much depends on which dimension of what we call religion is at stake.

In this chapter, I propose three normative criteria of minimal secularism, which offer finer distinctions between types of regime than Hirschl's simple category of constitutional theocracy is able to provide. Drawing on (and modifying) insights from Quong's epistemic theory, Eisgruber and Sager's sociopolitical theory, and Dworkin's ethical theory, I identify three components of minimal secularism: the *justifiable state*, the *inclusive state*, and the *limited state*. Each picks out a different feature of disaggregated religion: religion as *inaccessible*, religion as *vulnerable*, and religion as *comprehensive*.[9] What this genealogically minded conceptual exercise brings out is that, when particular instances of religion do not exhibit the relevant disaggregated feature (that is, when religious ideas, institutions, or practices are not inaccessible, vulnerable, or comprehensive), then liberal states may permissibly establish, recognize, or endorse them. Once we disaggregate religion into its constituent parts, we can also disaggregate secularism. The secular state, I argue, relates to three dimensions of religion (and of the good) in different ways, and therefore the liberal state is secular in three distinct senses.[10] The main argument I intend to map in this chapter can be seen in Table 2.

The Justifiable State

In the aftermath of the post-Reformation European religious wars, early modern and Enlightenment philosophers grappled with the question of how to secure political legitimacy in societies violently divided by religious conflict. Their solution, in a nutshell, was to "take God out of politics": states should not enforce any of the diverse conceptions of the

Table 2   Minimal Secularism, Neutrality, and Disaggregated Religion

	Liberal State	Liberal Value	Dimension of Religion	Nonreligious Analogues	Neutrality toward the Good?
1	Justifiable	Justification to actual citizens	Nonaccessible	Nonaccessible reasons E.g., Personal experience.	Epistemic abstinence
2	Inclusive	Civic equality	Vulnerable	Vulnerable and divisive identities E.g., Race.	Equality of treatment
3	Limited	Personal liberty	Comprehensive	Comprehensive secular ideologies E.g., Ecocentrism.	Thin theory of the liberal good

true faith onto the whole citizenry, and should draw their legitimacy from a stock of less controversial, commonly shared ideas.[11] It is this fundamental intuition that is at the root of modern theories of public reason and state neutrality about the good. Rawls's political liberalism generalizes from early modern toleration to ground the legitimacy of the liberal state in a political conception of liberal justice that is not derived from any of the reasonable comprehensive conceptions of the good held by citizens.[12]

Yet the Rawlsian picture, evocative as it is, conflates the three distinct wrongs involved in the establishment of religion by the state. The first, epistemic wrong is that when the state appeals to the authority of a particular God, nonadherents are coerced in the name of reasons that they do not understand and cannot engage with: they are not respected as *democratic reasoners*. The second, substantive wrong is that minority citizens are accorded unjustifiably unfavorable treatment by the state: they are not respected as *equal citizens*. The third, substantive wrong is that when citizens are coerced into living in accordance with a comprehensive doctrine of the good life, this intrudes on their personal integrity, conscience, and sense of self: they are not respected as *self-determining* agents. The three wrongs are distinct. They relate to different dimensions of both religion and the good, and suggest that these should be carefully disaggregated.

In the case of state-backed religious coercion, the state commits a distinctive epistemic wrong (it does not provide citizens with reasons accessible to them) and it commits a double substantive wrong (it infringes both liberty and equality between citizens). These dimensions are confused and conflated in Rawlsian theories of liberal public reason, yet they point in different directions. A law or constitution can be inaccessible (in its *justification*) yet not comprehensive (in its *scope*): consider, for example, a state that ratifies an impeccably liberal constitution by appeal to Christian scripture. Symmetrically, a law can be comprehensive, yet accessible: consider, for example, an ecocentric state enforcing a strict comprehensive way of life on citizens.[13] In this first section, I outline a thinly epistemic theory of public reason. I shall return to the substantive values of equality and liberty in the next two sections.

I propose to reserve the term "public reason" *(stricto sensu)* to refer to a thin epistemic filter, rather than a thick substantive condition, of political deliberation. Public reason is the collective reason of democratic publics. The basic thought is that state-proffered *reasons* for laws must be articulated in a language that members of the public can understand and engage with. There are epistemic constraints on the *inputs* into public debate—what I call constraints of public reason *stricto sensu*. Official justification by the state should not appeal to reasons that actual citizens find inaccessible: that they cannot understand and discuss as reasons. The epistemic theory of public reason explains the widely shared intuition that state officials should not appeal to divine will or to personal revelation to justify exercising coercion on all.[14] This is not, I submit, simply because people *disagree* about whether such sources are authoritative or not. People, after all, reasonably disagree about many things and, as I showed in my critique of Quong, the distinction between different kinds of disagreements—justificatory or foundational—is difficult to sustain. Instead, I submit, some reasons are problematic in public justification because they lack some basic epistemic quality: they are not accessible to common reason.

Theorists of public reason have tended to resist this move. They suspect that it implies skepticism about the truth of religion or—worse— that it entails the view that religious views are somewhat irrational. My theory of public justification is not burdened by any such assumption. We can accept that people using their reason under conditions of pluralism will come to endorse different religious and ethical convictions. We need only posit that certain considerations are more amenable to *public* justifiability than others. So Principle 1 of minimal liberal secularism can be stated as follows: *When a reason is not generally accessible, it should not be appealed to by state officials to justify state coercion.*

Here it is useful to distinguish between intelligibility, accessibility, and shareability. Roughly, *intelligible* reasons can be understood only in relation to the specific doctrine or epistemic standards of the speaker. *Shareable* reasons are endorsed according to common standards. *Accessible* reasons can be understood and assessed, but need not be endorsed according to common standards.[15] Table 3 shows these three types of reason arrayed by their basic characteristics.

Accessibility is an epistemic desideratum, in the sense that it sets out conditions of knowledge and understanding: more specifically, the conditions of possibility of public debate. My approach departs from Quong's and other versions of Rawlsian public reason in the sense that,

Table 3 Accessibility, Intelligibility, and Shareability

	Agent's Own Standards	Common Standards
Understanding	Intelligibility	Accessibility
Endorsement	X	Shareability

for me, public reasons are reasons that actual (not idealized) publics find accessible.[16] Public reasons, on this view, are analogous to official languages: they are the vocabulary, grammar, and references of the shared political language of particular societies. Accessibility articulates what citizens need to share, in particular societies, in order for public deliberation to be possible at all, while remaining indeterminate about the substantive content and outcome of public reasoning.

Consider, to illustrate, two different types of reasons against laws allowing assisted suicide in a pluralistic society. The first reason is that, because life is a gift of God, no person has the right to put an end to it, even the person whose life it is. The second reason is that, because the sick and the dying are fragile and vulnerable, their conscious determination to die cannot be ascertained with full certainty, and their vulnerability will easily be exploited by others. Although the former reason is intelligible, only the latter reason is publicly accessible, because it appeals to no premise, such as "life is a gift of God," that is neither shared nor subjectable to common standards.[17] My proposal here bears some similarity to Robert Audi's epistemic defense of secular reasons. Audi suggests that "a secular reason for an action (or belief) is roughly one whose status as a justifier of action (or belief) does not evidentially depend on (but also does not deny) the existence of God; nor does it depend on theological considerations, or on the pronouncements of a person or institution as a *religious* authority."[18] For my part, I do not postulate that secular reasons are public reasons, but instead explain the sense in which they are, when they are. The relevant epistemic principle that separates out public reasons from nonpublic reasons is not the secular content of reasons, but their accessibility.

At this point one may question the normative relevance of the distinction between accessibility and shareability, between understanding and endorsement. If I do not *agree* with a reason presented to me (I do not agree that it has force in the case at hand), does it matter that I can *understand* and *assess* it (that I can evaluate its force according to common standards)? It does. It is important to provide citizens with accessible reasons, because these are the currency of democratic debate. Those citizens who are outvoted in a particular debate—say, those who favor laws allowing assisted suicide—can see that the reason motivating the law is a reason they can engage with and continue to criticize. This way, even though they are outvoted, they are respected as democratic reasoners. Accessible reasons make possible and facilitate continuing democratic deliberation about the reasons for laws. Quong's conception of justificatory disagreement was based on the plausible intuition that when people disagree about something, the disagreement is less profound when they share a currency of disagreement. My point is a related one. It is one thing to be coerced in the name of reasons one does not understand (such as that life is a gift of God) and quite another to be coerced in the name of reasons that one does not agree with but can engage with (such that the idea that consent in assisted suicide requests cannot be reliably ascertained). The accessibility condition allows us to explain the asymmetry between the two following statements: "God wishes us to treat all as free and equal" and "We should treat all as free and equal." The substantive, normative content of both statements is identical. The difference is that the former is not accessible in public reason, whereas the latter is. Public reason *stricto sensu* is a principle of epistemic abstinence: of restraint about questions of deeper foundation and authority.[19]

How does public reason *stricto sensu* differ from the more substantive liberal public reason outlined by Quong and other liberal theorists? The main difference is that, while liberal values are part of public reason *stricto sensu,* they are not coextensive with it. First, my theory allows that the pool of public reasons is wider than the pool of liberal norms of liberty and equality. Liberal norms, plainly, do not exhaust the whole of actual political debate. Public reason does not only contain appeal to liberal norms such as the freedom and equality of all, but also appeals to broader political values, partial ideas about the good, and public goods (security, public order, clean air, the value of science, welfare, and so on). There is a wide range and diversity of reasons that count as public, and even in well-ordered liberal states they are not all liberal in inspiration and content. What matters is that they are accessible, that their force and import can be assessed and evaluated publicly.

Second, my theory suggests—*contra* Quong—that substantive judgment about the liberal permissibility of laws cannot be entirely derived from the liberal pedigree of the reasons that are brought to justify them. To be sure, some reasons are so illiberal that they irremediably taint the liberal quality of the law. Reasons that directly deny the moral equality of persons (such as the basic inegalitarian premise of Nazis or religious theocrats) can never justify liberal laws. But a host of permissible public reasons are not illiberal in this straightforward sense. For example, religious conservative appeals to the public good of social order, to the good of the institution of marriage, to the right to life, and so forth, cannot be ruled out as incompatible with public reason (as long as they are publicly accessible and do not directly appeal to scriptural or theological authority). It follows that public reason *stricto sensu* (*qua* accessibility) is a necessary but not a sufficient condition for the law's liberal quality. The latter involves an all-things-considered judgment about whether the law, on balance, is compatible with the pursuit of liberal justice.

To illustrate: Appeal to law and order is a *prima facie* good public reason, but the liberal permissibility of particular security laws depends on all-things-considered judgments about whether they are compatible with substantive protection of liberal values, such as personal liberty and other human rights. I suggest, therefore, that the liberal credentials of particular laws are a function of their substantive content, not only of the reasons that justify them. Reasons must be accessible, and they must not directly contradict basic liberal norms of freedom and equality. Beyond these two minimal requirements, all kinds of reasons are permissible inputs into public debate. Substantive liberal principles act as an external constraint on the *outputs* of political debate (Is the policy adopted all-things-considered compatible with liberal values, regardless of the reasons that have been put forward in its favor?). In the sections below, I shall give more content to the substantive principles of liberty and equality. On my theory, these operate as *ex post* checks of the liberal permissibility of law, rather than as intrinsic qualities of reasons *per se*.

A full defense of the accessibility condition cannot be provided here.[20] Let me, instead, draw attention to the advantages of my version of the accessibility view over two chief alternatives: the intelligibility view defended by inclusivist theorists of public reason, and the shareability view defended by exclusivist theorists. The intelligibility view is endorsed by theorists such as Gerald Gaus and Kevin Vallier, who argue that existing theories of public reason unfairly and arbitrarily exclude religious views from the public sphere. For them, it is sufficient (and necessary) that views articulated in public be intelligible: that they be justified to the persons who hold them according to their own standards.[21] Any more stringent demand of public accessibility is unfair because it imposes an extra burden on religious citizens, by forcing them to translate their religious reasons into public reasons, gravely infringing on their integrity and undermining the free expression of religious beliefs. And it is arbitrary because it fails to identify an epistemic feature that religious, but not secular, views, display.[22] I agree that a theory that would be unfair and arbitrary in this way would be, for these reasons, an unattractive theory.

Fortunately, my version of accessibility is not vulnerable to either criticism: first, because the demand of accessibility applies only to a narrow class of state officials and, second, because accessibility does not map onto the secular/religious divide.[23] First, then, minimal secularism does not impose any special burden on ordinary citizens, only on state officials. Recall that minimal secularism does not specify any civil or legal duty of citizens but, instead, articulates the special constraints that the state and its officials are under. It follows that there is no restriction on views and arguments that ordinary citizens can put forward in public debate. Minimal secularism does not create additional or unfair burdens on religious citizens. Only state officials, such as judges and lawmakers, are required to put forward accessible arguments as justification for their decisions and policies.

Because they have representative obligations—they speak in the name of all—and because state acts are particularly coercive, public officials (MPs, ministers, judges, civil servants, and so on) are under an obligation of restraint when they publicly justify their actions and policies. No such obligation falls on ordinary citizens. For example, the demand, made in the name of French *laïcité*, that state school pupils, or users of public services, show restraint in the expression of their religious beliefs, is an illegitimate extension of the demands of secularism from the state to citizens. The state should be secular so that citizens do not have to be secular—nonestablishment of religion by the state is what allows the latter freely to exercise the rights associated with freedom of conscience.[24] In civil society and in what Jürgen Habermas calls the informal public sphere, where citizens exchange ideas and deliberate with others within churches, civil associations, universities, and other public forums, they are not bound by public reason.[25] So we should guarantee full rights of free expression to ordinary citizens in the opinion-making sphere, while imposing stringent obligations for state officials in the decision-making sphere. This deceptively simple distinction, however, obscures an important intermediate sphere, where citizens act both as private citizens and as putative holders of political office. The question then arises: To what extent should citizens taking part in politics—say, as candidates for office, or as party leaders—be expected to appeal only to accessible reasons? Elsewhere, I have suggested that citizens have differentiated, scalar duties depending on their position on the opinion-making / decision-making continuum.[26] More work needs to be done, however, on how the demands of accountability, partisanship, and representation affect the site of public reason.[27]

The second rejoinder to the inclusivist critique is that, on my theory, religious views are not arbitrarily singled out, because they are not uniquely special from the point of view of accessibility. It is clear that some nonreligious ideas are inaccessible in my sense. As Christopher Eberle has shown, there is no relevant epistemic difference between a personal testimony and a religious revelation—they may be intelligible to others, but they are not accessible to others—so it would be arbitrary to exclude the latter but not the former.[28] On my theory, however, state officials cannot permissibly appeal to purely personal experience any more than they can appeal to religious revelation (although ordinary citizens may appeal to either).[29] So even if religiously based views have a tendency to be more inaccessible than nonreligious views, the relevant interpretive feature applies to nonreligious views in exactly the same way as it does to religious views.

In addition, crucially, not all religious views are inaccessible. As Jeremy Waldron observes, "secular theorists often assume they know what a religious argument is like: they present it as a crude prescription from God, backed up by threat of hellfire, derived from general or particular revelation, and they contrast it with the elegant simplicity of a philosophical argument. . . . But those who have bothered to make themselves familiar with existing religiously-based argument in modern political theory know that this is mostly a travesty."[30] One reason for this is that many religiously inspired ideas can be *detached* from the doctrine from which they originate. Their epistemic source does not determine their ethical or political content. For example, the normative import of religiously inspired views and ideals need not exclusively rely on contested appeals to divine authority: like other systems of thought, religious doctrines contain detachable and self-standing reasons. In this respect, Christianity or Islam are no different from utilitarianism or ethical humanism. Their deeper foundations and claims to authority may not be accessible to all; but they all generate (in exactly the same way) detachable, accessible public reasons that can be the object of public discussion.[31] These appeal to a variety of moral principles, ethical insights, social practices, and cultural traditions, whose plausibility and appeal can be understood and discussed in pluralistic societies, even by those who are nonadherents. These are ideas whose validity does not depend on acceptance of the authority of a particular God, text, or religious hierarchy. As Patrick Neal has noted, "religious believers do not have different standards of inference, logic, deduction or grammar than do non-believers."[32] Take, for example, Catholic natural theology. New Natural Law reasoning is based on inferences that require no appeal to special knowledge such as divine revelation. Given their beliefs about God's nature, it is said, Christians should expect to find nonreligious grounds for moral truth, and can present these as public reasons.[33] Likewise, as Mohammed Fadel has shown, accessible public reasons—reasons whose validity does not depend on pronouncements about the will of God—are available within the Islamic tradition of legal reasoning.[34] The continuing process of rational criticism *(ijtihad)* is central to nonfundamentalist Islam. More generally, the non-fideist strands of Judaism, Christianity, and Islam insist that the workings of the divine mind are such that they can also be apprehended, without mediation or faith, by human reason. The Torah, the Bible, and the Quran are rich depositories of shared references and stories, which are (culturally, socially) accessible even to nonbelievers. As Jürgen Habermas has noted, religious insights can be "translated from the vocabulary of a particular religious community into a genuinely accessible language."[35]

So it is not correct to suggest, with Richard Rorty, that religious reasons are unsuitable to democratic deliberation because they are "conversation-stoppers."[36] This is the case only if religious reasons are intelligible exclusively by reference to the source of their authority—if they only appeal to a personal experience of revelation, or to extra-human sources of authority, neither of which is shared. This applies, paradigmatically, to reasons of the type "God wants us to do X," which assume that those to whom the reason is addressed share a commitment to do what God prescribes, but which are inaccessible to those who do not share that commitment. Beyond these cases—religious reasons *stricto sensu*—religious language is not different from secular language.[37]

Furthermore, it is a fact seldom noticed by political theorists that religious ideas have a vestigial presence in the political culture of even pluralistic and secularized societies: much secular language is secularized religious language. Jeremy Waldron's scholarship has shown how our theories of basic rights, of property and justice, of the respect due to the human person, are all rooted historically in theories of natural law and in conceptions that were specifically theistic and, indeed, Christian in approach.[38] And Jeffrey Stout rightly notes, "The speeches of Abolitionists taught their compatriots how to use the terms 'slavery' and 'justice' as we now use them."[39] Many religiously inspired concepts, stripped of their theological, communal, and authority-based claims, survive in the public reason of liberal democratic societies. Marriage has religious origins, and secular justifications. Human dignity has religious origins, and secular justifications. Just war doctrine has religious origins, and secular justifications. And so forth. These secular justifications, of course, can be good or bad justifications. But it is not sufficient to point to the religious origin of these ideas to discredit them. The multilayered notions and concepts that make up our public language are "secular" only to the extent that they have become accessible to the public reason of actual citizens, not because they have been moved to a different, more reliable epistemological plane. Moral and religious beliefs are on epistemic continuum: it is not the case that the former are rooted in "reason" and the latter in "faith."[40] So it is misleading to contrast "religious" and "secular" reasons, as many political theorists do, in discussions about the content of public reason where—I have suggested—the relevant criterion is accessibility.

An intriguing implication follows. In pervasively religious communities, religious reasons *stricto sensu*—reasons that are grounded in a religious doctrine and have normative force only for those who accept that doctrine—may well provide the only currency of public reason. On my empirical theory of public reason, we cannot exclude the possibility that religious reasons are accessible—that they are understood by members of the public, and that they provide a common currency of argument and debate. Such societies are not *ipso facto* illiberal. Their liberal credentials, I argued above, are a function of the content of their laws and policies, not directly of the reasons that justify them. Of course, in practice few societies today are so homogeneous that shared religious reference can provide a genuinely public language. As soon as there is religious pluralism and/or societal secularization, religious reasons lose their status as public reasons. Public reason becomes secular *because of pluralism*—this, I think, is the kernel of truth in the liberal story of modernity "taking God out of politics." Once citizens no longer share unquestioned allegiance to the authority of one doctrine, appeal to that doctrine no longer functions as a public reason. Christianity provided the public language in which the abolition of slavery was debated in the early nineteenth century, but it should not provide the public language in which today's equality campaigns are fought in legislatures and courts (which is not to say, of course, that individual citizens and civil society associations cannot draw on Christian language themselves).

In sum, if we disaggregate religious reasons properly—between accessible and inaccessible ideas—we can see that public reason can permissibly contain more religion than liberals have countenanced, and therefore is not vulnerable to the inclusivist critique.[41] Let me now turn to the critique of accessibility of exclusivist philosophers, who worry that appeals to religious ideas in public discourse are incompatible with liberal values, and prefer to request that citizens appeal only to shared or shareable ideas (such as liberal conceptions of justice).

The problem with the accessibility condition, on that view, is that it lets in so many values and commitments that it will not automatically guarantee liberal policies and laws. Here the worry is that a merely epistemic constraint on justifiability is too permissive and lets in perfectionist and nonliberal reasons for state coercion.[42] This is correct, but it does not invalidate the accessibility condition. The accessibility condition, as an epistemic constraint on the inputs of public debate, is not a sufficient condition of liberal legitimacy. It is necessary: for the range of laws whose liberal content is indeterminate and subject to reasonable disagreement, it is crucial that officials provide citizens with reasons that the latter can understand and engage with. Yet it is insufficient: the accessibility condition rules out a very limited class of reasons, and does not generate determinate or conclusive public justifications. Admittedly, it prohibits appeal to reasons that are intelligible only by reference to personal experience or divine will—but few reasons, including religious reasons, are inaccessible in this sense. But the accessibility condition is intended not as a *final* test but as a *prior* test of permissibility. It identifies what kinds of reasons can enter the "permissibility pool" but does not specify which reasons are conclusive enough to provide a full justification for public policy and law.[43]

What can we say, more specifically, about the anti-perfectionist worry? Anti-perfectionist liberals worry that appeals to the good, when they are accessible in my sense, become part of public reason, and that this is *in itself* incompatible with the liberal injunction to treat all citizens as free and equal. As I have suggested in several places in this book, however, I am not convinced that liberals should be committed to strict anti-perfectionism in the first place. Undeniably, some appeals to the good—to the illiberal foundations of inegalitarian and authoritarian comprehensive doctrines—are *ipso facto* incompatible with liberalism. But beyond these cases, liberals need to explain how and why appeals to the good as such infringe on freedom and equality. This, recall, was in fact the strategy pursued by the liberal egalitarian theories studied in Chapter 3. All, I argued, ended up defending restricted neutrality rather than broad neutrality. The implication was that when promotion of some good is not the subject of foundational disagreement (Quong), when it is supportive of individual ethical independence (Dworkin), or when it is not socially disparaging (Eisgruber and Sager), it becomes permissible. Strict anti-perfectionists draw too quick analogies between the wrong of religious establishment and state-backed religious coercion, on the one hand, and public appeals to the good, on the other. Yet to suggest that public support for culture and the arts is analogous to egregious laws, such as sodomy or heresy laws, radically trivializes the wrong of religious establishment.[44]

Disaggregating religion, and the good, in turn, allows us better to identify what exactly is wrong with certain forms of perfectionism—paradigmatic of which is state-backed religious coercion. The liberal outcomes of public reasoning, in my view, are not *ipso facto* compromised by appeals to the good.[45] Here are a few illustrations we have already encountered. First, and least controversial, are appeal to public goods, such as security, defense, and clean air. Second, the promotion of cultural goods such as universities and the arts is not necessarily incompatible with liberal ideals of nonpaternalism and equal respect.[46] Third, liberalism itself contains a thin theory of the good, which explains which primary goods any rational person would desire, and explicates the moral powers of the person. As I suggested, this thin theory of the good draws attention to the ethical salience of particular commitments and values. Fourth, appeals to the good and to other substantive matters are unavoidable when deciding on the contested boundaries of justice, in matters such as the status of personhood, or animals, or of social institutions such as marriage and churches. I shall say more about some of these issues in the course of my argument.

For now, I turn, in the next two sections, to explicating further the two substantive standards that account for the wrongness of perfectionist policies. I suggest that state endorsements of religion (and the good) are impermissible when they infringe on civic equality or on personal liberty. When the state affirms the truth of one religion, enforces its precepts, and favors its adherents, this is straightforwardly incompatible with liberal neutrality on precisely these two grounds. The civic equality complaint is often phrased as a demand of equal respect: the state should not take sides between citizens in ways that infringe on their equal status. The personal liberty complaint is often phrased as a complaint against paternalism: the state should not usurp citizens' capacities to make decisions about their own lives. Liberal neutralists are right that the core cases of non-neutral justification—the substantive and coercive establishment of a religion by the state—are illiberal *qua* non-neutral. But in the next two sections, I draw attention to penumbra cases: cases where religious establishment is not, *per se,* illiberal.

But this is a substantive, not an epistemic, condition. Nothing is gained, in my view, by running together the epistemic (inaccessibility) and the substantive dimensions of religion or conceptions of the good.

At most, what the principle of epistemic justification will generate is a wide set of publicly accessible reasons. Such reasons will not necessarily be neutral about the good; nor will they necessarily be substantively liberal. But this simply means that the accessibility condition is necessary, but not sufficient, for liberal legitimacy. As I suggested, this is because it picks out only one dimension of the original paradigm of "religion": epistemic inaccessibility.

The Inclusive State

The first condition of liberal legitimacy, then, concerns the accessibility of the reasons offered by the state to justify its laws and policies. However, this is not sufficient, as a state may offer an accessible justification in support of an illiberal law or policy. Consider, for example, a state that formally establishes a religion and promotes its doctrine on grounds of social peace or national tradition. Insofar as this implies the denial of equal rights to members of a minority religion, it is a straightforward violation of liberal equality, regardless of the soundness of the justification provided. This suggests that neutrality of *justification* is not sufficient for liberal legitimacy: we also need something like equality of *treatment*.[47] No constitutional theocracy or "religious democracy" that fails to grant equal rights to minority citizens meets basic criteria of liberal legitimacy. If we carefully distinguish between the justification of laws and politics and the actual treatment of citizens, we can explain why many forms of religious establishments are wrong—even if they appeal to sound public reasons.

This, however, is an easy case. It is quite uncontroversial that a policy of establishment that denies equal treatment to majority and minority *religious* citizens is not liberal. A more daunting challenge for liberals is to explain how to treat *religious* and *secular* citizens equally. Consider the following controversies about the extent to which the state can permissibly establish and recognize religion. Should the state deny subsidies to religious groups that provide social services such as health care on the same basis as nonreligious groups? Can it provide special religious services, such as chaplaincies, in enclosed spaces such as prisons and the military? Should it fund faith schools as well as secular schools? Should secular schools provide any teaching of religion, or about religion? Can the state grant exemptions from general laws to nonreligious as well as religious citizens? Should the state apply to churches the same legal regime (of control and taxation) that it applies to businesses and other private groups? In all these cases it is difficult to ascertain what equality requires, and familiar liberal principles of separation and neutrality are not particularly helpful, as I now briefly illustrate.

Consider, first, the principle of separation. Plainly, erecting a "wall of separation" between religion and state is not always the best way to honor equality between citizens. As is now well established in the normative literature on secularism, strict separation between state and religion is not a foundational liberal principle; it is, at best, a secondary, derivative principle. Securing equal liberty and equal treatment may require, or be compatible with, state interference with, control of, and support for religion.[48] As Tariq Modood and others have illustrated, all European states, for example, are states of "moderate secularism," which extend to religious groups and institutions various forms of support and assistance.[49] Even countries, such as France, where a strict principle of separation is the official public ideology, there is well-justified interference and intervention of the state in religious affairs: from state funding and control of religious schools, to provision of religious services in enclosed spaces, through to official support for representative institutions for religious communities.[50] None of these policies appeals to the good of religion: instead, they are rooted in all-things-considered judgments about how to guarantee equal rights to citizens holding diverse beliefs and commitments.

It is tempting, therefore, to substitute an ideal of liberal neutrality for that of separation. Yet neutrality is also of limited help in conceptualizing equality between "religion" and "nonreligion." To be sure, the ideal of neutrality is not empty: it rules out partiality or *animus* toward religion, as well as appeal to its truth or untruth, and it rules out accommodating one religion over another religion. But it tells us little about what it means to treat religious and nonreligious citizens equally. Fair resolution of controversies such as those above requires "zooming out" and locating them within a broader account of social justice, welfare entitlements, the aims of liberal education, the fairness of burdens on conscience, the scope of freedom of association, and so forth. The principle of neutrality as equal treatment between "religion" and "nonreligion" does little work, because neither category is precise enough: the relevant interpretive dimensions of both need to be carefully disaggregated and explicated in relation to the liberal ideals in question.[51] Clearly, there is large reasonable disagreement about which set of rights and policies—which specific mix of "establishment" and "separation"—best guarantees an inclusive state.[52] I shall say more about some of these controversies, focusing in particular on how equality can be reconciled with special exemptions for religious individuals and religious associations, in Chapters 5 and 6.

For now, let me focus on one area of controversy that is at the heart of debates about nonestablishment and secularism. This concerns, not the actual rights and opportunities of citizens, but instead their *symbolic* treatment by the state. An intensely debated issue in the separation-establishment debate is whether the liberal state can legitimately attach itself to the majority religion—via, for example, religious symbols in public institutions, the recognition of religious holidays, and nonmandatory oaths and prayers in public. What, if anything, is wrong with symbolic religious establishment? A number of familiar answers will not do. It is not that such establishment infringes basic rights of religious freedom: I postulate that symbolic establishment does not infringe such rights—this is the sense in which it is symbolic. It is not that such establishment is incompatible with public reason because it does not provide accessible reasons to nonadherents: it can do, often in the form of appeal to historical continuity or national tradition. It is not, either, that such establishment violates the liberal requirement to treat all citizens neutrally, with equal respect. Again, the neutrality requirement is too vague: liberal states endorse—including in their symbolic communications—many non-neutral commitments, such as patriotism, gender equality, the teaching of Darwinian evolution, and subsidies for the arts and universities. Non-neutral communications do not necessarily express disrespect. So there must be something more specific to symbolic *religious* establishment that is problematic for liberal democracy.

It is, I think, this. Symbolic religious establishment is wrong when it communicates that religious identity is a component of civic identity—of what it means to be a citizen of that state—and thereby denies civic status to those who do not endorse that identity, who are then treated as second-class citizens. Equal civic status requires, not simply a legal guarantee of equal rights and distributive fairness, but also appropriate expressive treatment as civic equals by state institutions. This account relies on an expressive account of government actions: what matters is not what government intends to communicate, nor how citizens subjectively perceive it but, rather, whether governmental messages express objectively appropriate attitudes toward people.[53]

On this expressivist conception of citizenship, a state that closely associates itself with one religion risks alienating members of minorities in ways that infringe on their equal civic status, just as a state that would closely associate itself with an ethnic or racial identity would.[54] The wrong of symbolic establishment, importantly, does not hinge on the presence of subjective feelings of alienation from the state.[55] Not all and every kind of subjectively felt alienation is problematic at the bar of inclusive citizenship: racist citizens' alienation toward an anti-racist state, for example, is not rightful alienation. Of course, subjective alienation may be one of the appropriate *indicators* of status inequality. But status inequality requires an objective test—in the spirit of Justice O'Connor's "reasonable observer" test, which asks whether particular endorsements of religion by the state (say, the display of a nativity scene in a municipal hall) can reasonably be construed as "sending a message" of civic exclusion.[56]

The thought is that when the state associates itself too closely with the symbols of the majority, nonadherents are rejected outside the imagined community of citizens. Symbolic establishment is wrong, on this account, when it constitutes and perpetuates social relations of hierarchy, subordination, and domination. What matters here is a form of social equality—defined by David Miller as "a form of life in which people in a very important sense treat one another as equals," one that is "not marked by status divisions such that one can place different people in hierarchically ranked categories."[57] On the expressivist theory of nonendorsement, political institutions have a crucial role to play in securing the equal status of citizens. One prominent advocate, Martha Nussbaum, defends nonestablishment by appeal to liberal neutrality, but the rhetoric she draws on is distinctively republican, echoing very similar language by political philosopher Philip Pettit.[58] Symbolic establishment, Nussbaum writes, is a "slap in the face of the sort that a noble gives a vassal," one that "both expresses and constitutes a hierarchy of ranks."[59] The motivating ideal here is not neutrality toward the good in general, but a social idea of nonsubordination and nondomination.[60]

Why is religion suspect in relation to nondomination? I suggest that symbolic establishment is wrong if religious identity independently functions as a marker of social vulnerability and domination in the society in question, or if such establishment can reliably be predicted to increase the social salience of religious identity. Religious identities have clearly been salient in the Western world, where religion has provided one of the most enduring fault lines of social conflict and exclusion—one at least as salient as divisions of class, caste, race, and gender. The medieval expulsions of Jews from Europe, the persecution of heretics, the convulsions of the Reformation, the confessionalization of Western states, the marginalization of religious minorities throughout the eighteenth and nineteenth centuries, the colonial subjugation of non-Western religions: all testify to the exclusive dynamic of religious conflict. It is not surprising, therefore, that the struggle for the liberalization and democratization of Western states often took the form of their disestablishment.

In the nineteenth century, Catholics, Jews, and Protestants fought for the disestablishment of majority religions in England, the United States, and France, in the name of egalitarian citizenship. Today this is exactly how constitutional theorists (such as Eisgruber and Sager) interpret the Establishment Clause of the First Amendment of the U.S. Constitution: as an inclusive framework of equal protection and fair inclusion of vulnerable and marginalized identities. On this view, symbolic nonestablishment—the secular state—is the best framework for guaranteeing the equal civic status of members of religious minorities. We have, then, Principle 2 of liberal minimal secularism: *When a social identity is a marker of vulnerability and domination, it should not be symbolically endorsed and promoted by the state.*

So is religion uniquely special here? It is not—but the relevant analogy is very different from those we considered in the previous section. Here, religion has nothing to do with personal experience or inaccessible belief, or even doctrines or conceptions of the good. It is, rather, structurally similar to *other socially vulnerable identities,* such as race, and sometimes culture or ethnic identity. Here, religion refers not to a first-person belief but to a third-person identity: it is principally a matter of how others classify and relate to one's perceived identity and membership.[61] Religion at times functions exactly like race—an assigned identity serving to affirm and consolidate boundaries between dominant and dominated groups. As we saw in our analysis of Eisgruber and Sager's equal liberty theory of nonestablishment, it does not matter whether members of minorities see their religion as a source of deep, serious, moral commitment for them. The wrong of official endorsement of the majority religion is that it makes their minority status relevant—negatively—to their civic status. In a society, such as the United States, where religion is a socially salient category of membership and exclusion, it is exclusionary for a state school to adorn classrooms with Christian crucifixes, even if members of non-Christian groups (atheists, Jews, or Muslims) do not see membership in such groups as a source of deep commitment for them. *Ceteris paribus,* an analogy can be drawn with the evil of racial segregation. U.S. segregation laws denied African Americans equal status, not because they disparaged African American culture and ways of life, but because they construed blackness as a negative ascriptive identity, a marker of subordination and inferiority. Expressive accounts of symbolic equality have been criticized for their vagueness and arbitrariness.[62] To an extent this criticism is legitimate, because the criterion of civic inclusiveness is singularly context-dependent. But this does not make it fatally indeterminate. The key is to specify which identities are, in particular societies, vulnerable from the point of view of equal citizenship; and which official symbols perpetuate and consolidate these vulnerabilities. The fact that religion is a marker of social vulnerability does not mean that all state-endorsed religious signs, buildings, and symbols are suspect. The expressive power of religion-in-general must be disaggregated at the level of individual symbols too.[63] As Eisgruber and Sager rightly noted, Renaissance paintings of biblical scenes are acceptable in public places because the cultural framing of the object holds its religious meaning at arms' length. Likewise, not all publicly displayed crucifixes and crosses carry the same exclusionary valence: a cross displayed in a public square or cemetery does not have the same expressive power as a cross in a school, parliament, or courtroom.

Not *all* religious symbols, then, have exclusionary valence. But it is also the case that not *only* religious symbols have such valence. Any collective identity—be it racial, ethnic, religious, or cultural—can be harnessed to state power in ways that consolidate and perpetuate the domination and marginalization of minorities. Consider, for example, the recent promotion by European states of a "culturalized" Christianity—the reappropriation of religious symbols and references as markers of national identity, shorn of their specific theological content. Does the shift from religion to culture allay the secular worry about inclusiveness? It does not, as national and cultural identities can be just as exclusive as religious identities.

Let me illustrate this point by reference to a recent controversy about the ban of Muslim minarets in Switzerland.[64] Defenders of the ban have relied on two crucial premises. First, such a ban *would* be impermissible if minarets were central to Islamic practice; but they are not, so the ban does not infringe on Muslims' rights of religious freedom. Second, because the preference for Christianity over Islam is cultural rather than religious, the ban does not violate liberal values of religious nonestablishment and neutrality. Both premises, however, are contestable. First, admittedly, defenders of the ban are right to point out that the chief issue with the ban is not that it infringes Muslims' interest in *religious freedom*. Few Muslims in Switzerland practice Islam; and for those who do, minarets are not essential dimensions of their practice. But here is the rub: when official endorsements (or prohibitions) of religious symbols are concerned, it is irrelevant whether the prohibited symbol is positively endorsed by those associated with it. Whether or not Muslims value minarets, a public ban on minarets unambiguously sends a message of exclusion to Muslims. What is wrong with the ban is that it places minarets—and, by analogy, Muslims—at the outer border of the imagined national community.

The second premise of the argument for the ban is that the presence of church buildings, or crucifixes, is merely an expression of Western Christian heritage. Here Christianity is redefined as compatible with, even supportive of, secular democratic values such as tolerance, the separation of church and state, and gender equality. Christianity is readily available for reinterpretation in cultural or civilizational terms, with no reference to matters of theology, belief, or ritual. This is what has recently been called the new "Christianist" secularism of Europe.[65] But it does not follow that because Christianity in Switzerland is a cultural rather than a religious identity, it is permissible to give it privileged status in the public sphere. It is true that the Swiss majority do not practice the Christian religion, and they see churches and crucifixes not as symbols of faith but as cultural symbols. On my expressivist theory, however, the semantics of "faith" and "culture" are not in themselves indicative of the expressive message of symbols. Clearly, both faith and culture can be used as markers of exclusion and vulnerability, as ways of signifying inequalities of status between those who belong and those who do not.

Insofar as vestigial symbols of historical establishment perpetuate, consolidate, or newly trigger the domination of minorities, in a context of politicization of both majority and minority religions, they are problematic at the bar of equal citizenship.[66] It will not do, as the European Court of Human Rights did in the much-discussed *Lautsi* decision, to redescribe crucifixes in Italian schools as cultural instead of religious symbols.[67] What matters is whether state-enforced symbols are markers of social vulnerability; and culture is not intrinsically more inclusive than religion. This, I think, is what is wrong with symbolic establishment, and it applies to a particular dimension of religion, which religion shares with germane social categories such as race or culture—a context-dependent, social marker of vulnerability and subordination.

In sum, the wrongness of state-endorsed religious symbols should be assessed in relation to the following criteria. First, it is not religion-dependent: it does not hinge on the semantic meaning of religion, but instead relies on an interpretation of its social meaning as one possible suspect category for purposes of social discrimination and domination. Second, it is not person-dependent: it does not hinge on individuals' perceptions of exclusion or domination; nor does it hinge on whether individuals positively associate with the group or identity that is excluded from state endorsement. Third, it is context-dependent: social meanings vary from society to society. Fourth, it is symbol-dependent: different symbols can have different social meanings in different locations.

Because religion is a fault line of social vulnerability and exclusion in contemporary Europe, most forms of state-endorsed symbolic establishment of Christianity—even through seemingly "cultural" signs such as crucifixes in state schools—are suspect at the bar of liberal inclusiveness. Beyond Europe, likewise, a liberal democratic state should not define itself as a Hindu state or a Jewish state or a Muslim state, in contexts where such identities have become socially divisive and vulnerable identities, as is the case, for example, in contemporary India,

Israel, or Egypt. This, however, does not mean that religion should play no role in the construction of national identity. It does not mean, in particular, that all countries should adopt a U.S.- or French-style model of strict symbolic separation. In societies that are pervasively religious, or in societies profoundly divided over the role of religion in the state, secular symbols and signs are not necessarily symbols of inclusiveness: they are as likely to be seen, alternatively, as alien or as divisive. Theorists of secularism such as Charles Taylor and Saba Mahmood (in different ways) are right to point out that secularism is as much a lived culture and discipline as a set of abstract ideals and principles.[68] One advantage of my disaggregative strategy is to keep the two separate: to distinguish the political values of secularism (justifiability, equality, and liberty) from their historical embeddedness in a particular Western culture.

When we think about the cultural and symbolic dimension of secularism, therefore, the relevant normative value is not *separation* of religion and state but, rather, *inclusiveness* of all identities. Evidently, in many countries, particularly in the Western world, the default mode of inclusion is nonreligious: citizens of diverse and mostly secularized societies are more likely to identify with symbols that have been shorn of particular and parochial religious connotations. But the U.S.- or French-style separation model of the "naked public sphere" does not travel well to other societies, where the relationship between civic inclusiveness and public recognition of religious identities is complex.[69] Indian secularism, for example, draws on the ecumenical, overlapping political secularism of the state's founders and its explicit culture of inclusion of, and even-handedness toward, Muslim minorities.[70] In Israel, the only conceivably shared national identity is a broad pan-Israeli identity inclusive of non-Jewish Arabs, which also recognizes the status of Israel as a Jewish homeland.[71] In the Arab world and the Middle East, the challenges of articulating an inclusive liberal national identity are daunting, between the Scylla of a tainted secularism associated with the colonial and post-colonial project of enforced Western modernization, and the Charybdis of the emergence of Islamism as a radically antiliberal and antisecular alternative political identity.

Shifting our gaze to other parts of the world, however, things look different. Religion is not always and everywhere a politically incendiary, socially vulnerable mode of identification: it is not a universally stable, universally toxic mode of political identity. Many religious traditions, such as those of polytheistic cosmologies in Africa and Asia, do not generate socially salient and exclusive political identities. Anthropologist Michael Lambeck observes from his ethnographic work in Madagascar: "Among Malagasy speakers in Mayotte and in northwest Madagascar, religion during the last quarter of the twentieth century has been inclusive. People regularly observed that God was the same everywhere and hence it mattered little which avenue one used to approach Him. . . . In some families one child was assigned to ancestral tradition, another to Christianity, a third to Islam."[72] Or consider the case of contemporary Senegal. This is a Muslim democracy, where the state associates itself loosely with a religious identity, but not in a way that relegates minority members to second-class citizenship. It was shaped by the French legacy of *laïcité*, but *laïcité* has been interpreted as compatible with active official engagement with, and recognition of, the powerful cultural and social power of the *Sufi* brotherhoods. This model of "Sufi-secular mutual respect" has been hailed by comparativists, such as Alfred Stepan, not only as proof that Islam is not incompatible with democracy (Indonesia and India are other examples of democratic countries with large Muslim populations) but also as evidence that secularism should not be conflated with the French-U.S. model of strict separation.[73] We should, instead, talk of the "multiple secularisms of modern democracies."[74]

The inclusiveness criterion, then, is of necessity context-dependent. It draws attention to the powerfully toxic fusion of religion and national chauvinism, and its potentially deleterious impact on the prospects of egalitarian citizenship. But it does not single out religion as a universally and intrinsically divisive identity. Western liberals often take it for granted that religion is the kind of identity that is paradigmatically not suitable as an object of state recognition. Will Kymlicka, for example, has argued that although the state cannot avoid recognizing culture in some form or another, there should be a strict separation between the state and religion.[75] This, however, is too quick. Kymlicka implicitly assumes that religion always exhibits the feature that makes establishment problematic at the bar of equal citizenship. In particular, he must be assuming that religion is always politically divisive and socially vulnerable—a warranted generalization from a specific Western (and colonial and postcolonial) history, but by no means a definitional truth.[76]

The Limited State

This section examines the third wrong connected to religious establishment: that it does not respect citizens as self-determining agents. One of the fixed points of the liberal tradition of political thought is its commitment to the ideal of personal liberty. Liberalism, from Locke to Dworkin, relies on a distinctive view of the scope and limit of state authority, and of the liberty-based claims of citizens against it. The most succinct and radical formulation of this idea was advanced by John Stuart Mill. According to Mill's harm principle, a liberal state is a state that does not interfere with the ways in which individuals live their lives, unless they harm others.[77] Religious states, by contrast, violate the harm principle by regulating and intruding on the self-regarding dimensions of individuals' lives, by enforcing a comprehensive view of the right and the good on them. Yet, as Mill insisted, the promotion of someone's good, against his wishes, is never a good reason to interfere with his liberty. Such paternalism is wrong because it usurps people's judgment about how they should live their lives. It is because minimal secularism is committed to the substantive ideals of personal liberty that it rejects the enforcement of comprehensive doctrines, such as religious doctrines, by the state.

The dimension of religion that this liberal value picks out is that of religion as *comprehensive ethics,* in the sense that it integrates within a meaningful framework a whole range of matters—family arrangements, sexuality, education, eating codes, work, dress, and so forth. In many societies, religious moralities have been coercively entrenched through state policies, codified in personal and family law, and backed by the social power of religious authorities. As a result, liberal rights were often products of hard-won struggles, against the authority of traditional religious authorities, to construct and preserve a sphere of individual self-determination in private life. Consider the range of liberal laws in the nineteenth and twentieth centuries, such as laws about marriage and divorce, education, women's rights, and sexuality, and contemporary conflicts about abortion and LGBTQ rights in America and Africa.

In these conflicts, liberal secularism abstains from enforcing a particular conception of the good, but only because it prioritizes individual rights of self-determination in ethical matters. These take precedence over other goods such as tradition, social stability, the good of the family, the value of human life, and so forth (these goods can be appealed to in the mix of public debate, but their collective pursuit is limited by the liberal constraint of personal liberty). In a liberal society, individuals may live their private lives by their religion's lights. But the liberal state, in eschewing the enforcement of any comprehensive view, inevitably sides with permissive conceptions of the good (conceptions that, by definition, are not comprehensive) over moralizing (often religious) conceptions of the good. A secular liberal state is a limited state in the specific sense that it does not intrusively regulate what Michel Foucault called the ethics of the self.[78] In sum, liberal secularism is committed to Principle 3: *When a practice relates to comprehensive ethics, it should not be coercively enforced on individuals.*

The ideal of the limited state, then, draws attention to the ethical individualism that lies at the heart of liberalism. In Rawls's thin theory of the liberal good, individuals have a higher-order interest in developing their moral powers—including the capacity to form, develop, and pursue their own conception of the good life. Individuals must be free from state enforcement of comprehensive religion, because only they have authority in how they conduct their lives. Is religion special here? Arguably, religions have historically been the most prominent comprehensive, coercively enforced systems of ethics. This explains the protracted and profound nature of the conflicts over the relationships between civil-secular and religious law, notably in matters of sexuality and the family.[79] Liberal rights—the right to choose one's sexual partner, who to marry, whether to divorce—were secured against religious prescriptions. Nonetheless, religions do not provide *the only* impermissible conceptions of personal ethics. A state that enforces a secular comprehensive conception of the good—Rawls's favorite example was a philosophy of Kantian autonomy, but we could think of other comprehensive worldviews, such as ecocentrism—would fall foul of liberal legitimacy on exactly the same ground as would a comprehensively religious state.[80]

Nor is religion *only* a comprehensive conception of the good, and when it is not, its recommendations can be legitimately enforced by the state. This is because the neutrality that personal liberty demands is only required in relation to the state's treatment of *comprehensive* conceptions of the good. To elucidate this crucial point, a few clarifications are in order. In Chapter 3, in my discussion of Dworkin, I introduced two relevant distinctions. The first, between *broad* and *restricted* neutrality, concerns the scope of neutrality; the second, between the *justification* and the *subject-matter* of a policy, concerns the focus of neutrality.[81] In what follows, I examine the connection between neutrality about the good and personal liberty—the connection is not, as many liberal neutralists assume, a definitional or tautological connection.

Dworkin's core intuition about state neutrality about the good is that the state usurps individual ethical independence if it appeals to a conception of the good in justifying its actions. Dworkin defined ethical independence as the protected right not to have one's ethical evaluations usurped by the state. As systems of personal ethics, religious conceptions should not be endorsed and promoted by the state, lest they infringe on individual independence. But on the Dworkinian logic, while the state must be neutral toward religion when religion is a system of personal ethics, it need not be neutral toward religion *when it is not*. In what follows, I pursue and develop a connected thought.[82] I suggest that the value of personal liberty explains why neutrality should be doubly restricted: At the level of justification, neutrality applies to *comprehensive* conceptions of the good; and concerning its subject matter, it applies primarily to what I call *integrity-related* liberties. The suggestion is that my liberty is egregiously violated by a freedom-restricting law if (1) the law is justified by appeal to a comprehensive worldview; or if (2) however the law is justified, it limits my liberty to live with integrity. Both demands are rooted in the particular importance of personal ethics, at the heart of liberalism's commitment to ethical individualism.

Consider first the justification of laws. As Dworkin argued, if a state declares a religion to be true, this limits my ethical independence, regardless of the salience of the particular interests it burdens. Consider, for example, a state that enforces particular dietary rules, modesty in dress, and restrictions of free movement (for instance, on Shabbat) on the ground that these allow citizens to live virtuously, according to an authentic and true conception of the good life. This state is infringing citizens' ethical independence, regardless of whether the freedom to eat particular foods, to wear particular dress, and to move freely in a neighborhood are salient freedoms or not. To this extent, it is quite not correct to suggest, as some authors have, that there is no freedom *from* religion when the freedoms in question are trivial and unimportant.[83] Ethical independence implies that I must not be forced to live according to some conception of comprehensive ethics (but it does not imply that I must live according to my own salient or determinate conception of ethics). In that case, the mere fact that my ethical judgment is usurped violates my personal liberty, regardless of the particular freedoms it burdens.

Matters are different when the state does not make an ethical judgment but instead grounds its decision to favor or promote a religion in accessible public reasons. Two cases are pertinent: partial ideas about the good (such as badness of addiction, attachment to tradition) and public goods (social cohesion, public health, rules of social coordination, and so forth). Here the worry about usurpation dissolves: the state is not imposing its own comprehensive ethical evaluations but instead is appealing to noncomprehensive public justifications. In this case, is there a residual liberty-related concern? There is. I suggest that such a policy is problematic if (on balance) it unjustifiably limits citizens' integrity-related liberties. In this case, the salience of the particular freedoms and the interests they protect becomes relevant.

What are integrity-related liberties? I shall say more about integrity in Chapter 6. For now, let me simply define integrity-related liberties as liberties that are essential to the exercise of citizens' core moral powers: notably, their capacity to formulate and live by their own ethical commitments and projects. Such liberties paradigmatically (but not exclusively) concern core areas of intimate, expressive activity, such as religion, sexuality, family, and friendship. These liberties have ethical salience because they are closely connected to individuals' basic moral powers and their ability to make "strong evaluations" about how to lead their lives. Other liberties are not so tightly connected to basic moral powers: let us call them ordinary freedoms. The freedom to pursue leisure preferences, the freedom to wear this or that form of dress, the freedom to move unimpeded by traffic regulations, are not as tightly connected to integrity, and therefore not as salient. Two qualifications are necessary, however. First, the fact that ordinary freedoms are not as salient as integrity-related liberties does not mean that they are not important. The liberal state protects generic, basic liberties (of thought, conscience, association, movement, and so on), and these liberties are valuable regardless of the particular uses they are put to.[84] The thought, however, is that the reasons certain liberties are restricted matter. Ordinary freedoms can be limited more readily than integrity-related liberties: by a sound reason, rather than a compelling state interest (to use the language of the Religious Freedom Restoration Act).

Second, ordinary freedoms, when mediated by a comprehensive conception, can morph into integrity-related freedoms. Let me illustrate. While I might have an ordinary freedom to wear a clown hat at my workplace, my Muslim colleague has an integrity-related claim to wear her hijab. Similarly, while I might have an ordinary freedom to refuse to take an unnecessary long-haul flight, my ecocentric colleague might have an integrity-related claim to do so.[85] What matters is not the content of the freedom (the activity that it permits) so much as how people relate to it—the importance of that activity in their comprehensive conception of how their life should go. While integrity-related liberties paradigmatically apply to areas such as family, religion, and sexuality—the core of the liberal idea of privacy and intimacy—they can also apply to the broader ethical, philosophical, and political commitments that define people's sense of their own identity.[86]

I have fleshed out the liberal ideal of the limited state and elucidated the connection between state neutrality and personal liberty. The basic intuition is that the liberties to practice one's religion, to express one's sexuality, to pursue loving commitments, and so forth, are the paradigmatic liberties that the liberal state should respect. But I have suggested that there are two distinct normative desiderata in this basic liberal intuition. Personal liberty implies both restraint on the *justification* that the state can appeal to, and a focus on particular *interests* that the law sets back.[87] Although the state should not appeal to the truth of any comprehensive doctrine, even to burden ordinary freedoms, it should take care not unreasonably to burden integrity-related liberties, even in the name of noncomprehensive reasons.

If we combine both requirements, we can isolate a (small) class of religiously inspired policies that do not impermissibly infringe on personal liberty. These are policies that are not justified by appeal to the truth of a comprehensive doctrine, and that do not unreasonably burden integrity-related liberties. Take, for example, Sunday laws. It is permissible for the state to enforce a shared day of rest that suits a Christian majority, if two conditions apply. First, the justification for having Sunday as a shared day of rest is neither the inaccessible one that it is a God-anointed day nor the comprehensive one that Christianity is the true faith. Rather, officials may appeal to the need for the temporal coordination of leisure time,[88] coupled with the judgment that choosing an alternative, religiously neutral day would face leveling-down objections: it would benefit no one, while burdening the majority.[89] Second, even though Sunday laws unequally affect the ordinary freedoms of different members, they do not affect their personal liberty in equally serious ways. Clearly, Sunday laws, if they prevent religious minorities from celebrating their own holidays, are compatible with, or even require, accommodation for them. This is because minority integrity-related liberties have been unequally burdened in relation to those of the majority. I shall come back to the issue of the fairness of exemptions in Chapter 6. For now, the point I want to press is that Sunday laws do not burden the integrity-related liberties *of nonreligious citizens.* Given that a shared day of rest is preferable, and the choice of one day over another does not limit any integrity-related liberty (although it limits ordinary freedoms), it is permissible.

There are other dimensions of religion that do not relate to comprehensive ethics, and the demand of state secularism should be far less stringent there. It is not obvious, for example, that *Shari'a* (Islamic law) regulations concerning banking rates or charity *(zakat)* cannot be permissibly enforced by a liberal state—assuming they do not infringe on the personal dimension of the ethical life. Or, to take another example, a state that prohibits the sale of non-ritually slaughtered meat is not *ipso facto* in breach of minimal secularism. Imagine that the standard objection to ritual religious slaughter—the impersonal reason that it causes unnecessary pain to animals—is removed. (This is not fanciful, as techniques for reconciling the stunning of animals with *shechita* and *halal* slaughter are currently being developed.)[90] In that case, would non-Muslims or non-Jews have valid objections to a ban on non-ritually slaughtered meat? I think not, because being forced to eat such meat does not infringe on their integrity-related liberties. It might limit their ordinary freedom, but it does not limit their (ethically salient) liberty: it does not force them to do something that is ethically unconscionable for them. In this case, Gideon Sapir and Daniel Statman are right to suggest that there is no right to freedom from religion: when integrity-related liberties are not burdened and (I would add) when the state does not proclaim that there is just one way to live the good life.[91] There is no general right to freedom *from* religion, when religion is not a comprehensive system of personal ethics.

Minimal Secularism and Liberal Religious States

I have argued that the liberal state need not be separate from religion when religion is not inaccessible, divisive, or comprehensive. This follows from the restricted conception of state neutrality that I identified in the work of Dworkin, Eisgruber and Sager, and Quong, and from the interpretive project of disaggregation of religion in light of key liberal values. I have explicated three principles of minimal secularism. Principle 1 states that when a reason is not generally accessible, it should not be appealed to by state officials to justify state coercion. Principle 2 states that when a social identity is a marker of vulnerability and domination, it should not be symbolically endorsed and promoted by the state. Principle 3 states that when a practice relates to comprehensive ethics, it should not be coercively enforced on individuals.

Evidently, minimal secularism rules out egregious forms of religious establishment, of the kind that liberal egalitarians justifiably think are incompatible with liberal legitimacy. A state that makes laws on the basis of the ethical truths contained in a sacred text is in breach of the accessibility condition (nonbelievers and dissidents cannot debate the reasons for the laws), infringes on personal liberty (nonadherents are forced to live by a comprehensive conception of the good that conflicts with their own ethical views), and violates equal citizenship (if religion is a salient mode of sociopolitical belonging and conflict in that society).

But as I have insisted, liberal ideas do not rule out all appeals to the good in politics. I showed in Chapter 3 that ideas about the good can be accessible and even shared (badness of addiction, for instance), and can be compatible with personal ethics (such as protection of environ-mental diversity) and with equal citizenship (as in state promotion of cultural policies). By analogy, I have suggested, liberal ideals do not rule all appeals to religion in politics. One interesting implication is that some features of Hirschl's "constitutional theocracy" turn out to be compatible with liberal egalitarianism. There is more permissible variation in state-religion arrangements than many liberals have recognized. Here are two fictional states that broadly meet the demands of minimal secularism.

Secularia	*Divinitia*
• The state is strictly nonreligious. Officially endorsed religious symbols and messages are forbidden in the public sphere. The state is not substantively anti-religious, and religious citizens are not otherwise victims of civic exclusion or disparagement.	• The state symbolically recognizes one religion, but not in a way that infringes on the equal citizenship of nonadherents.
• All laws have nonreligious grounding and justification.	• Some laws are religiously inspired, but justification for them is accessible and the laws do not infringe on the personal liberty of nonadherents.
• There are permissive laws about abortion, euthanasia, and other practices in bioethics.	• There are restrictive laws about abortion, euthanasia, and other practices in bioethics.
• Schools are secular. Religious education is left to parents.	• There is wide range of provision for both secular and religious education within the school system.
• Antidiscrimination norms constrain the autonomy of religious groups.	• Religious groups enjoy extended rights of collective autonomy in the name of freedom of association.

(*continued*)

• There are no special exemptions or accommodations for religious citizens, but they do not suffer from unfair discrimination.	• There are numerous exemptions and accommodations for religiously motivated behavior, both individual and collective.

Both Secularia and Divinitia are legitimate liberal states. Like other "liberal egalitarians," my preferred conception of justice is closer to the progressive arrangements of Secularia. But liberal egalitarians should recognize that the more conservative Divinitia is a reasonably liberal state too. This is because it broadly honors and respects citizens as free and equal. To wit: it provides them with accessible reasons for its actions; it respects their personal liberty; and it secures their equal citizenship.[92] We could say, following Rawls, that the conception of justice that Divinitia implements belongs to the family of reasonable liberal conceptions of justice.

Note that Secularia and Divinitia are ideal types rather than descriptions of existing states. In practice, liberal democratic states exhibit features of both. Consider, as an illustration, Great Britain. In many U.S. commentaries about religion and state, Great Britain is typically presented as deficient in relation to the more perfectly secular state of the United States. The establishment of the Anglican Church is seen as incompatible with liberal equality—a tolerable state perhaps, but one that remains weighed down by the antiquated and inegalitarian legacy of religious establishment. Yet if we apply the disaggregated features of secularism to the main features of the British political settlement, we can reach a more nuanced conclusion—and one that also sheds light on many inadequately analyzed features of the U.S. system.

Concerning first the *justifiability* of laws and institutions. The United Kingdom is a parliamentary democracy where the monarch (and head of the Church) has no executive role, and where all laws have strictly secular grounding (and committees on bioethics and other extraparliamentary bodies tend to have only secular representatives). One could argue that religious references in public debate are more prevalent in the

United States. Moving next to *equality*. Formal establishment of the Anglican Church does not provide its members with special privileges or rights (with the exception of reserved seats in the House of Lords); nor does it deny members of minorities any right (with the minor exception of rules of succession to the throne). In institutional terms, establishment has provided the template or matrix out of which the British state has negotiated multicultural and multireligious differences.[93] Turning to symbolic establishment, the head of state is "Defender of the faith" (possibly soon "Defender of the faiths"). In a secularized society where religious differences are perceived to be socially salient, this might be seen to relegate nonbelievers to second-class status. But the monarchy is not the focal point of national identity, and the operative content of British civic identity is avowedly secular (without being secularist). Generally, British political culture is more welcoming to atheists than is the case in the United States—public officials in the UK do not "in God trust." As in the United States, the growing place of faith schools and faith initiatives raises profound questions about the best way to create a cohesive, egalitarian society—but no general comparison can be made on the basis of formal religious establishment versus separation. Finally, turning to *personal liberty*, the picture is also mixed, depending on where you look. For example, Great Britain (though not the UK, as Northern Ireland is less liberal) has liberal laws in the areas of abortion and same-sex marriage, as well as in experiments with bioethics. In sum, Great Britain is not a real-world example of Divinitia, just as the United States is not an example of Secularia. Minimal secularism sets out a set of normative benchmarks relating to accessibility, equality, and liberty, and Divinitia and Secularia are ideal types of permissibly liberal states, rather than descriptions of actual states.

The normative import of the contrast should now be clear: it draws attention to the range and scope of reasonable disagreement about liberal justice. The institutions and policies of both Secularia and Divinitia are based on permissible conceptions of justice. They draw on reasonable interpretations of the three ideals of the justifiable state, the limited state, and the inclusive state. The range of permissible conceptions is wider than liberal egalitarians have recognized. As Micah Schwartzman has recently argued, "although liberals have been reticent to accept it, . . . reasonable disagreement based on inconclusiveness is something to be expected within the normal politics of a liberal democratic society."[94] This entails that political liberalism is a dualist political theory. As a constitutionalist doctrine, political liberalism provides some content to public reason by conclusively justifying basic liberal norms and constitutional essentials. As a democratic doctrine, it more modestly provides a framework for reasoned deliberations between citizens: a framework for the resolution of their disagreements about justice. Rawls's political liberalism exhibits a dualist structure. On the one hand, it identifies broad conditions of constitutional legitimacy; and on the other, it allows for a high level of context-dependent political inconclusiveness, even about principles of justice.

Now in what sense is disagreement about justice *reasonable?* It is reasonable because disagreeing parties share a broad commitment to the liberal ideal of the basic moral equality of all. Citizens of Secularia and Divinitia are reasonable if they do not seek to enforce their religious or comprehensive conception of the good on others, and if they are ready to search for terms of cooperation that can be justifiable to all—that is, that do not violate basic liberal norms. But beyond this broad agreement, citizens substantially disagree about the proper role of religion, the rights of religious citizens, and what equality between citizens requires. The scope of this disagreement about justice is more extensive than liberal philosophers such as Quong have envisaged. To recap, we have encountered three different sources of reasonable disagreement (of these, only the first is discussed by Quong).

i. Different weight of liberal principles: freedom of association versus nondiscrimination; parental rights versus children's rights. Here liberal public reason is inconclusive and compatible with different permissible outcomes.

2. Rightful limits to the legitimate pursuit of societal goods: public goods, social cohesion, recognition of marriage, badness of addiction, and so forth. Just the fact that the state appeals to a good does not make it incompatible with public reason *stricto sensu;* nor does it *ipso facto* violate norms of freedom and equality. What is required is an on-balance judgment of the overall compatibility of the policy with liberal principles.

3. Indeterminacy of the boundary between justice and the good: bioethics, status of the person, status of social institutions (marriage, churches). This concerns the determination of which spheres of social life are justice-apt. Here liberal public reason is indeterminate: it cannot avoid drawing on controversial (albeit partial) ideas about the good and other substantive questions.

Public reasoners in Secularia and Divinitia do not appeal to their comprehensive conceptions of the good when they justify state coercion—this would be a straightforward violation of minimal secularism. But nor do they appeal only to shared principles of justice. They appeal to broad liberal norms, as well as to partial ideas about the good, and they reasonably disagree about which all-things-considered balance of reasons best expresses liberal justice. An important consequence follows. Because of the depth of disagreement about justice, citizens have to live under laws with which they foundationally disagree. Type 1 disagreements are nonfoundational in Quong's sense, Type 2 disagreements can be foundational, and Type 3 disagreements are almost always foundational. As reasonable people foundationally disagree about what justice demands, the Quongian neutrality solution to disagreement is not reliably available.

This raises a problem for liberal neutrality. Why should dissenters accept the legitimacy of a conception of justice that they do not endorse, when it justifies laws with which they foundationally disagree? Consider a few examples. In Divinitia, secular citizens must tolerate the religious inspiration of some legislation and arrangements and a robust presence of religion in the public sphere, as well as in education; women's rights advocates must tolerate exemptions of religious organizations from anti-discrimination legislation, and so forth. In Secularia, religious citizens must tolerate the intrusion of antidiscrimination laws into their churches, mosques and synagogues; pacifists must put up with their state going to war; Catholics must accept laws permitting assisted suicide, capital punishment, or experiments in bioethics. And so on. None of these dissenters is unreasonable—yet these laws cannot be justified to them at the bar of liberal neutrality.

It is not sufficient to say that laws are legitimate insofar as dissenters have been presented with public reasons for them—accessible reasons such as freedom of association, equality of opportunity, national security, or medical progress. The mere presence of public reasons, while necessary, is not sufficient to render these laws legitimate to those who think the laws are unjust. Dissenters can reasonably hold that public reason supports a balance of political values that is all-things-considered unjust (as in the case of war); or that public reason is inconclusive (as in the standoff between freedom of association and nondiscrimination); or that public reason is indeterminate (as in the case of bioethics, where the moral status of personhood is at stake). Disagreement about justice can be as foundational as disagreement about the good, and resolving it often involves adjudicating the boundary between justice and the good itself.[95]

We need to explain, then, how citizens who reasonably think that certain laws of Secularia or Divinitia are unjust can still hold Secularia and Divinitia legitimate. The answer is that decision making in that society meets some standard of procedural fairness. More specifically, publicly enforced laws must meet a standard of *democratic* fairness. It is because all citizens were included within a fair and inclusive process of democratic deliberation that they can accept the legitimacy of the laws.[96] Democratic deliberation offers the fairest procedural solution to reasonable disagreements about justice—especially as these cut across the boundary between the right and the good. Democratic deliberation, then, is legitimacy-conferring in a stronger sense than public reason liberals such as Rawls or Quong have admitted. The principle of democratic legitimacy explains why citizens can accept the imposition of laws that are (from their point of view) unjust.

Nor is this all. The principle of democratic legitimacy also explains why different states are justified in opting for one or another reasonable conception of justice. Specifically, it is not illegitimate for countries with secularized majorities to have laws that reflect their preferences; nor is it illegitimate for countries with religious majorities to do the same. State-religion arrangements can permissibly be sensitive to the religious make up of societies, without breach of liberal legitimacy. While many liberals have argued that citizens of faith must accept the secular state as reasonable, they have not symmetrically conceded that nonreligious citizens must also accept the legitimacy of religious liberal states such as Divinitia. Yet because appeal to public reasons is inconclusive or indeterminate about key political issues, it is compatible with a range of permissibly just state-religion arrangements.[97] Because liberal values are inconclusive and indeterminate, and compatible with a wide range of laws, policies, and institutions, democratic deliberation about them is essential to their legitimacy. A democratic constitution is what allows the legitimate resolution of foundational yet reasonable disagreements about justice.[98]

Taking seriously reasonable disagreement about justice does not entail that there is no fact of the matter about the true demands of justice. And the fact that justice is contextual does not commit one to ethical relativism or skepticism. There might well be a fact of the matter about what justice actually requires in a state like Divinitia, or a state like Secularia. My point is a point about political legitimacy, which closely mirrors what Rawls says in *Political Liberalism*. Rawls argues that the burdens of judgment entail that people have to accept that they will reasonably disagree about the good—even if they harbor no skepticism about the validity of the conception of the good they themselves hold. By analogy, even if there is a fact of the matter about what justice requires in a given society, there are epistemic obstacles to identifying it, as the burdens of judgment apply to disagreement about justice as much as disagreement about the good. Like Rawls, however, I isolate a set of liberal basic norms from the burdens of judgment: it is not morally acceptable to deny the basic moral equality of all and the validity of basic liberal rights.[99] Also like Rawls, I leave aside the deeper question of the justification of these liberal norms.[100] The point I merely want to press is that the set of justified liberal norms is narrower and more incomplete on my theory than on Rawls's and Quong's. As a result, there is a wider gap between liberal legitimacy and (different theories of) liberal justice. Citizens are likely to disagree foundationally about justice. And because reasonable disagreements about justice are foundational in Quong's sense, we need to articulate procedural—in my case, democratic—resolutions to them.[101]

On my theory, then, reasonable disagreements about liberal justice are wide, profound, and intractable. In Chapters 5 and 6, I shall set out my preferred conception of liberal justice. This conception, as will become clear, is closer to the progressive arrangements of Secularia than to the conservative arrangements of Divinitia. Though I offer substantive arguments in its defense, I do not postulate that it is the only reasonable position on matters of liberal justice. This means that it is not offered as a statement of basic political truths that should be entrenched (perhaps in a countermajoritarian way) in the constitution and laws of all liberal states. It is, rather, presented as a contribution to democratic political debate.[102] This, I hope, provides a response to Gerald Gaus's worry that liberal egalitarians have a tendency to frame their preferred progressive conception of justice as the only acceptable conception of justice, and to dismiss dissenters as unreasonable.[103]

I, for one, am ready to concede that my preferred conception of justice is *one,* rather than *the,* liberal conception of justice. Liberal legitimacy rules out basic violations of liberal norms, but is compatible (for example) with less egregious breaches of equality legislation, in the name of other liberal values such as freedom of association or freedom of speech. (As I shall suggest in Chapter 6, this matters when we think about issues such as the permissibility of religious exemptions from general laws.) The general implication is that my conception of liberal justice is both more *substantive* and more *democratic* than many neutralist liberal egalitarian theories. It is more substantive in the sense that it recognizes that it is rooted in commitments that even citizens also committed to basic liberal norms can reasonably reject. And it is more democratic because it accepts that foundational decisions about justice itself can legitimately be made through fair democratic procedures. As a result, my theory is, I hope, better equipped to grapple with deep reasonable disagreements about politics and religion, within the framework of the minimal secularism I have set out in this chapter.

5

ℰ🜨ℜ

State Sovereignty
and Freedom of Association

In this chapter I address the jurisdictional boundary problem head-on. I do so by engaging with recent theories of religious institutionalism, such as those of Richard Garnett, Steven D. Smith, and Victor Muniz-Fraticelli.[1] I argue that liberal egalitarianism relies on a presumption of sovereignty of the secular democratic state in deciding contested questions of the boundary and scope of religious autonomy. State sovereignty is a precondition for legitimate settlements about justice, including for religious groups.

I then go on to show that even though the state does not share sovereignty with other institutions, it must respect freedom of association as a core liberal value. I set out my preferred theory of just terms of association, applying my theory of disaggregation to the general puzzle of collective religious exemptions from antidiscrimination laws. I agree with liberal egalitarians such as Lawrence Sager, Jean Cohen, Richard

Schragger, and Micah Schwartzman that whatever exemption rights religious associations should have are derived from the liberal value of freedom of association.[2] However, I reject any reductionist view of freedom of association—any view that explains the rights of association by reference to just one feature of association. I disaggregate the different values freedom of association protects, so as to justify some of the collective rights claimed by religious groups.

I set out two salient associational interests: what I call *coherence* interests and *competence* interests. I argue that while many associations may appeal to coherence interests to defeat the application of some general laws, only some may, in addition, appeal to competence interests. Disaggregating associational interests into coherence interests and competence interests allows me to explain why religious associations (but not only they) can have some latitude in their employment and membership decisions. Once again, religious associations are not uniquely special *qua* religious, but an interpretive approach to their normatively relevant features allows us to justify some of the rights and entitlements they should have, as should other comparable associations.

State Sovereignty and Religious Institutionalism

Liberal democratic legitimacy presupposes the final authority of the state in solving what I have called the jurisdictional boundary question. The state is a politically organized community with exclusive and final jurisdiction over a given territory. There is no space here to offer a full justification of state sovereignty (and its limits). Let me simply point out two *pro tanto* reasons in its favor. The first is that the authoritative and stable resolution of conflicts about justice requires a final, ultimate source of sovereignty. Unless we are equally subjected to a legitimate authority that is able to authoritatively give content to, delimit, and enforce our equal rights of freedom, we remain structurally vulnerable to the arbitrary will of others. As the moral ideal of equal freedom is indeterminate as to the content of our precise natural duties, it is only with reference to the laws of a legitimate state that it can be fully defined and guaranteed. The democratic and republican social contract tradition, particularly drawing on Rousseau and Kant, has made this point eloquently.[3] The second consideration is that democratic states are fitting sources of sovereignty because they represent the interests of individuals *qua* individuals, regardless of their contingent features, identities, and memberships. Individuals are members of a plurality of groups and associations—from families to churches to trade unions—but their paramount interests as free and equal citizens must be represented by a universal-membership association.[4] Consequently, the liberal democratic state enjoys sovereignty over all other groups and associations on their territory.[5]

One of its rightful prerogatives is what constitutional theorists call *Kompetenz-Kompetenz:* the liberal democratic state has the competence to decide the respective areas of competence of associations within it. To use my preferred terminology, the state has the competence to adjudicate jurisdictional boundary questions. In particular, it adjudicates conflicts of jurisdiction between church and state, between what pertains to the religious and the secular, the political and the personal, the public and the private.[6] Even if, with Locke, we postulate that the state should deal merely with civil interests, and that spiritual matters must be left to religious groups, it is not obvious that the boundary between the "civil" and the "religious" is a clear one. It is, in fact, fuzzy and contested—and, ultimately, must be set authoritatively by the final sovereign authority.

If this suggestion is correct, liberal egalitarians must accept that there is some truth in the Protestant and realist accounts of the relationship between liberalism and sovereignty, discussed in Chapter 1. As Hussein Agrama, Marcus Dressler, Marvind Arvaid, Saba Mahmood, Stanley Fish, William Cavanaugh, and others have pointed out, the liberal state is a sovereign secular state.[7] What they mean by "secular" is that it is a state that has the prerogative to authoritatively determine the respective spheres of the political and the religious—it enjoys meta-jurisdictional sovereignty. Liberal egalitarians, as I showed in Chapter 3, have not been sufficiently forthcoming about this. They postulate that the state is neutral about religion and the good, but this presupposes that the state has already delimited what pertains to religion and the good—hardly self-evident categories of ethical or social practice. The move toward liberal neutrality, therefore, does not dissolve the need to define the sphere where neutrality applies in the first place. Citizens reasonably disagree about where jurisdictional boundaries are drawn—and to solve their disagreements, they must accept the legitimacy of democratic state sovereignty. Critical religion theorists are right to suggest that state secularism—here, the meta-prerogative to distinguish the religious from the nonreligious—supervenes on neutrality, both historically and conceptually.[8]

Secularism historically entailed a large-scale transfer and concentration of coercive power: from the church, and divinely appointed authorities, to an absolute sovereign, which later grounded its sovereignty in democratic authorization. One momentous implication was that, henceforth, the identity of individuals as citizens was to prevail over the identity of individuals as believers, when the two conflict. Citizenship trumps religious commitment. The most radical challenge to religion posed by secular liberalism is not its account of the role of religion in the public sphere, or its theory of public reason: as I have argued, secular liberalism is compatible with far-reaching presence of religion in the public sphere, as in Divinitia. The radicalism of liberalism, instead, lies in the fact that it assumes state sovereignty: the state's prerogative to decisively fix and enforce the terms of the social contract.[9] Secular liberalism assumes that reasonable individuals have a higher-order interest in living under political justice on this earth (in Rawls's terms, to find mutually acceptable terms of social cooperation) rather than in living by the word of God—the full truth as they see it. This is not a trivial assumption. Secularism affirms the autonomy and sovereignty of the political and, in its liberal and democratic mode, locates the source of this sovereignty in a social contract—the will of individuals to live together under terms they can reciprocally justify and accept. Secularism presupposes some autonomy of human power from divine power (an idea familiar to the majority of religious traditions, the greatest challenge being posed by polytheistic, immanent cosmologies). Secularism further assumes the legitimacy and sovereignty of self-constituted political communities: modern secular sovereign states. It is intimately connected to the modern state form, and insofar as some religious traditions reject state sovereignty (as Wael Hallaq has controversially claimed is the case of the Islamic tradition)[10] they will naturally resist secularism. Resistance to the secular state, of course, must also be traced to the fact that the state form was exported as the hegemonic matrix of modernity *via* Western imperialism, postcolonial interference, and market globalization.

In Europe, secular states emerged against a specific configuration of struggles between Christian churches and emerging civil powers. European states primarily asserted their sovereignty against the claims of powerful churches, in the aftermath of the Reformation. As British pluralist theorist and Anglican clergyman J. N. Figgis mournfully noted, "by the destruction of the independence of the Church and its hold on an extra-territorial public opinion, the last obstacle to unity within the State was removed."[11] The sovereign state broke with medievalist conceptions of political authority, which allowed overlapping and at times competing authorities, albeit within an overarching framework of Christian unity.[12] From the Reformation onward, states asserted their sovereignty over those forces—clerical and theocratic—that resisted their ambition to rule on behalf of the whole citizenry.

Here the dimension of religion that is targeted by the liberal secular state is the *theocratic* dimension of religion: the claim by churches to rule not only the private but also the public sphere—to enact coercive rules and norms for society as a whole. Instead, the modern state worked to locate religion within the private sphere of individual conscience, voluntary association, and the family—but the precise contours of the boundary between public and private have been fluid and historically contested. As critical religion theorists have rightly pointed out, religion is not a natural category of social and ethical experience. Rather, the categories of public and private, and the modern category of religion itself, were invented and formalized in the process of consolidation of modern states.[13]

It is not the case that before the so-called Great Separation between state and religion, something called "religion" ruled the public and the private sphere and blurred their natural boundaries.[14] In its modern sense, religion became the name given to what is "private." John Locke argued that the state should deal with civil interests, and leave spiritual matters of the salvation of the soul to individuals in their private lives. But who is to decide what pertains to the "civil" and what pertains to the "spiritual"? Consider the family, health care, education, or sexuality. Up to the late nineteenth century and early twentieth century, they were considered to be private, and were in effect controlled by religious norms. But the liberalizing and democratizing impulse of the modern welfare state has led to increased state regulation of these spheres.[15] As Kirstie McClure notes, modern conceptions of harm and inequality "operate to reconstitute as injurious, and hence political, 'facts' which were previously understood as civilly benign."[16] Ultimately, the secular democratic state is the final legitimate arbiter of the boundary between the public and the private.

States, not churches, have *Kompetenz-Kompetenz:* the authority to define their own spheres of competence, as well as those of other institutions. Beatrice Webb was once asked to explain how she and her husband Sidney managed to work together so effectively. She cited "a clear division of responsibility: Sidney takes all the important decisions, and I take all the unimportant decisions." Asked which of them decides whether any decision is important or unimportant, she said, "I do."[17] The state, I suggest, is exactly in the same position as Beatrice Webb: it is that which decides what is important and what is not. Here are a few examples of how state *Kompetenz-Kompetenz* is deployed in contemporary political and legal practice. Relying on the Lockean premise that inner belief cannot be coerced, but that external action can be regulated, states delimitate what constitute *forum internum* and *forum externum*, referring to a set of dualisms (mind and body, thought and action, belief and symbol) that are often alien to the religious individuals and groups whose activities are being regulated.[18] States define what constitutes *harmful* behavior—a key notion in the regulation of religion, as it sets out the boundary of permissible religious activities.[19] In freedom of speech law, they deploy secular notions of harm and offense, distinguishing between the (legitimate) critique of ideas and the (illegitimate) incitement of hatred against ethnicized religious groups.[20] States also assert the right to regulate what religious groups see as *intrinsically spiritual* activities: educating the young, providing health services, forming like-minded associations, delivering welfare, and so forth. In liberal egalitarian states, such activities are perceived as belonging to the "civil," secular sphere of education, health, employment, and welfare, and therefore to be subject to principles of fair access and equal opportunities. States even define what semiotic meanings to attach to religious symbols—secular courts have had to decide whether a crucifix, or a hijab, is an "active" or a "passive" symbol.[21]

Critical religion theorists have developed a rich and provocative analysis debunking this sovereign line-drawing prerogative. But—as I showed in Chapter 1—the implication of their critique is unclear. Is it their critique that states sometimes act unjustly or undemocratically in their determination of the boundary between the religious and the nonreligious (a critique that liberals make themselves)? Or is it that liberal democratic states have no *pro tanto* legitimacy in defining what counts as harm, as offense, as fair opportunity, and so forth? If the latter, critics owe us an alternative account of how political conflicts about religion are to be arbitrated fairly. Critics writing from Asadian, Foucauldian, or postcolonial perspectives presumably are not committed to the claim that religious groups' own understanding of what religion demands should be determinative of the rights of their members and of others.

Other critics, by contrast, have been less coy about their normative preferences. A group of thinkers, writing from perspectives more sympathetic to the claims of (notably Christian) churches against the seemingly secularist encroachments of Euro-Atlantic liberal states, have challenged state sovereignty in the name of what has been called the "New Religious Institutionalism." In what follows, I assess their criticism and show that state sovereignty cannot be wished away easily.

Contemporary legal constitutionalists such as Richard Garnett, Steven Smith, and Victor Muniz-Fraticelli advance the striking claim that there is no exclusive sovereignty of the state.[22] Here they take their cue from British pluralist critics of monism and modern constitutionalism who, in the early twentieth century, counterposed the independent authority of intermediate associations such as universities, churches, and trade unions against the sovereignty of the modern state.[23] Along similar lines, the main claim of today's religious institutionalists is that state sovereignty is *externally* limited by the authority of other associations, notably religious associations. The state, for example, does not have the legitimacy to force equality legislation (in particular, nondiscrimination norms) onto the church. Churches should be free to organize their own affairs, without interference from the secular state. This is because "the civil authority . . . lacks 'competence' to intervene in such questions, not so much because they lie beyond its technical or intellectual capacity, but because they lie beyond its jurisdiction."[24] On this view, the progressive state Secularia is illegitimate because, by denying any exemptions for churches from general laws of antidiscrimination, it violates a prior, pre-political principle of church autonomy. Churches should be seen to have jurisdictional autonomy: they must have the authority to determine the scope of their own competence. This means that they must share meta-jurisdictional sovereignty with the state.

What are we to make of this theory?[25] I shall suggest, first, that religious institutionalists misconstrue state sovereignty and, second, that their substantive proposals are not as radical as they imply, as they accept the core intuition behind the notion of state sovereignty. First, religious institutionalists wrongly assume that sovereignty in a liberal-democratic mode is essentially arbitrary, that the state acts *ultra vires* every time it trespasses on what churches take to be their jurisdictional domain.[26] But the fact that the state is sovereign does not mean it is a

Hobbesian or Schmittian state: it is a mistake to connect modern sovereignty to a purely voluntaristic account of unconstrained sovereignty, as Westphalian sovereignty evolved in a norm-bound, liberal-democratic direction.[27] On the view I defend, a sovereign state has liberal legitimacy only if it pursues a recognizably liberal conception of justice, and does so democratically. That is, sovereignty is *internally* limited by liberal democratic principles.

Consider a familiar implication in international law: a state may lose its claim to external sovereignty—its immunity from interference from other states—if it violates basic human rights. In cases of human rights violations, we can say that the state has acted *ultra vires*—that it has trespassed on a forbidden jurisdictional domain. Similarly, when a state persecutes dissidents, bans religious associations or forces them underground, directly appoints religious leaders, or dictates religious dogma, there is a sense in which it is acting *ultra vires*. It is trespassing on a core sphere of basic rights—a sphere over which individuals and groups have a jurisdictional claim of self-determination. The religious institutionalist critique, therefore, appeals to a plausible intuition: that the most egregious breaches of justice amount to *ultra vires* exercises of state power. It is correct that states have no legitimate claim to sovereignty in such cases.

But while basic rights violations are unacceptable injustices—and affect the legitimacy of the state—there is reasonable disagreement about the positive content of justice. This is because, I have insisted, liberal values are inconclusive and indeterminate about the scope and content of more specific liberal rights and liberties. In circumstances of reasonable disagreement, the state does not act *ultra vires* when it imposes and enforces a democratically arrived-at solution. On the contrary, it is the only institution with the legitimacy to do so, because it can reliably enforce a scheme of cooperation over time, and because it represents the interests of citizens as citizens. What religious institutionalists describe as illegitimate *(ultra vires)* exercises of power are not violations of basic rights. Instead, they concern disagreements about whether legitimate state power is exercised justly.

The focal point of their discussions concerns reasonable controversies about justice. Should the Catholic Church be exempt from antidiscrimination legislation? Can for-profit corporations owned by religious individuals be granted an exemption from compulsory contraception provision?[28] In such controversies, it is not clear that church autonomy acts as an external, jurisdictional limit on state sovereignty. Churches are not foreign states: their members are also citizens, and churches do not have unilateral authority to settle the normative claims of their members. Nor do churches have a preemptive right not to obey state laws—whether criminal laws against abuse and exploitation, or civil laws of tort, contract, and property. The jurisdictional view seems to imply that any interference is *pro tanto* suspect and illegitimate *(ultra vires);* whereas on my view, beyond violations of basic rights, there can be reasonable disagreement about the justice of state intervention. Most of the cases discussed by religious institutionalists concern justice in this sense, not legitimacy. Controversies arise at the margins, and the scope and limit of religious rights to autonomy are properly subject to democratic deliberations about justice, which are ultimately settled by the state.

Interestingly, no religious institutionalist in fact denies this. Talk of jurisdictional autonomy is used as a rhetorical device to emphasize the normative force of the rightful claims made on behalf of churches. Consider Steven Smith's thoughtful and nuanced defense of church jurisdictional autonomy. Smith argues that state sovereignty is not absolute; that the terms of state interference with religious life must be discussed and negotiated; that claims to jurisdiction can be rephrased in the liberal language of rights; and that, ultimately, state courts have "jurisdiction over jurisdiction": only the state can settle the content and limits of the rights of other associations. In asking whether state courts should defer to the special competence and authority of religious associations, the "live question," Smith writes, is not "who defers" but "whether to defer."[29] This is exactly right—there is no genuine controversy about where *Kompetenz-Kompetenz* lies.

Consider also Muniz-Fraticelli's robust defense of pluralism as an alternative to sovereignty. Muniz-Fraticelli rightly focuses on the intractability of conflicts of competence between state and church. Yet despite insisting in several places that church autonomy is an "external" limit to state sovereignty, Muniz-Fraticelli suggests that the state must "*internalise the external limit* imposed by the existence of a competing authority."[30] This, he adds, does not determine the conclusion of any particular conflict, because "the state need not defer to the reasons of persons *qua* members of association over their reasons *qua* citizens."[31] Again, this is exactly right: churches' claims have strong normative weight, and they must be taken into account ("internalised") by the state. But ultimately the state decides how much weight to give to them: that is the sense in which it is sovereign. Religious institutionalists confuse the source of sovereignty with the considerations that make its exercise just.

On my theory, the proper nature and scope of the authority of associations can only be determined democratically, in reference to broadly liberal principles, and finally settled by the state. Only the state can adjudicate the "rightful bounds of religious liberty," as exercise of this liberty must be compatible with the exercise of other liberties, as well as the pursuit of other important interests such as equality and nondiscrimination. Freedom of association in the minimal secular state is compatible with the granting to religious associations of a range of liberties, claim rights, and immunities, but it does not justify stronger claims of jurisdiction.[32] Religious associations do not have *Kompetenz-Kompetenz*: if they were able to unilaterally determine the rights and duties of their members and of other citizens, they would act out of a theocratic, not a democratic, principle of legitimacy.[33] Table 4 sets out the implications of sovereignty for jurisdictional prerogative.

Respect for freedom of association and freedom of religion, then, are liberal constraints on legitimate state authority. In the next section, and in Chapter 6, I defend a substantive theory of the justice of exemptions from general laws, derived both from freedom of association (the collective dimension of religious freedom) and individual integrity (the

Table 4 Sovereignty and Jurisdictional Prerogative

Liberal State	Liberal Value	Feature of Religion	Nonreligious Analogues	Neutrality toward the Good?
Sovereign	Democratic citizenship	Theocratic	Nondemocratic political ideologies	No: State has meta-jurisdictional prerogative

individual dimension of religious freedom). I articulate my preferred conception of the justice of both types of exemptions. This can be reasonably contested, because there are other reasonable conceptions of liberal justice, as I have insisted throughout. But the controversy over jurisdiction is a nonstarter. What theorists reasonably disagree about is the scope of the substantive rights that the sovereign state should grant, in justice, to religious groups.

Freedom of Association: Two Interests

In recent years the U.S. Supreme Court has ruled that religious groups can be exempted from various laws of general application, such as laws against disability discrimination or laws requiring all employers to provide contraception insurance.[34] Many liberal egalitarians have worried that this entrenched an exorbitant right of collective religious autonomy, which directly conflicts with individual freedom and rights against discrimination.[35] In this section I do not discuss the details of any particular controversy but instead apply my theory of disaggregation to the general puzzle of collective religious exemptions. In the previous section, I argued against the view that religious groups have jurisdictional autonomy. Here I argue—in line with a liberal egalitarian theory of justice—that whatever rights they should have, these are derived from liberal freedom of association. I then ask whether, and when, religious associations should be exempted from the application of laws against discrimination on the grounds of gender, sexuality, or race.

A preliminary point. Are churches merely "associations"? Critical religion theorists have questioned this individualistic construal of religion. Religious institutionalists, for their part, go further and argue that churches are real, singular entities with an independent ontological reality, not simply an aggregation of the individuals who compose it. They draw on the British pluralists who insisted that groups are no fiction of law but real persons animated by lives and will of their own.[36] More contemporary accounts of group agency point out that group decisions complexly transform individual decisions into corporate decisions, such that it makes sense to treat groups as agents capable of making their own decisions.[37] If groups can have agency, they can have moral personality; and if they are moral persons, they can have legal rights.

This is a rough sketch of what Richard Schragger and Micah Schwartzman call the "standard argument" for group rights. The problem, as they point out, is that one does not need to have a theory of a group's ontological nature in order to consider it as a right-and-duty-bearing unit. As H. L. A. Hart and John Dewey both argued, the ontological or metaphysical nature of groups is irrelevant to, or indeterminate about, the justification and scope of their rights.[38] For example, even if, with J. N. Figgis and other pluralists, we take intermediary groups to be corporate persons, the question of their rights vis-à-vis the state remains open, as the state is also a corporate person—and indeed has often been seen as the supreme and culminating person, or *primus inter pares,* notably in early twentieth-century corporatist theories of the state.[39]

Conceptions of personhood distract attention from the underlying facts and interests that ought to guide our legal and moral assessment of the rights and duties of different groups. They often offer rhetorical tools to advance preferred policy positions, but do not engage the interest that grounds particular right claims, nor do they provide a sense of how those interests are implicated within groups.[40] For some purposes—such as corporate liability—the law might well treat a group *as if* it were a person; but this says nothing about whether it is a real, preexisting person. Instead of engaging in the semantics of group ontology—"What is a group?"—we should be asking a different, interpretive question: "How would giving this group specific legal rights and duties affect our social relations?"[41]

Further, on my disaggregative theory, a "religious group" does not appear as a unified politico-legal category entitled to a specific bundle of rights and entitlements. For some purposes, religious groups can be treated as loose communities; for other purposes, by contrast, they need to be construed as formal legal corporations. Let me illustrate. When states seek to give political representation to ethno-religious diversity, to institutionalize interfaith dialogue (as in bioethics committees), or to protect members of vulnerable groups from certain forms of discrimination, the conception of "group" that does the work here is a loose notion of community, an ascriptive, transgenerational group with porous boundaries and a low level of institutional organization. By contrast, if religious groups seek to own and sell property, they must be treated like legal corporations with formal structures of authority, conditions of liability, and so forth.

For which specific purposes, then, should we treat religious groups as *voluntary associations?* The purpose is not, to reiterate, to postulate that religious groups are (ontologically) voluntary associations. The specific question we ask here is which particular interests, values, and relationships are promoted by religious groups, such that they can be granted *special* rights of exemption from antidiscrimination laws. It matters that groups are construed in a particular way if they are granted such rights, for two reasons. The first is that collective exemption rights are power *over* others. By contrast to other collective rights, they affect the normative status—the rights and entitlements—of the group's members (or employees). The second is that—on the progressive theory of egalitarian justice I endorse—protection against discrimination on morally arbitrary grounds (such as gender, race, or sexuality) is an essential way to respect citizens as free and equal. Groups, far more than natural persons, have the capacity to dominate individuals, exercising power over their choices and undermining their autonomy. So if they are to be allowed to discriminate among their members or employees on otherwise impermissible grounds, they have to be particular kinds of group. In what follows, I suggest that only groups that are voluntary and identificatory have *pro tanto* rights to discriminate. They must be voluntary, in the sense that members must be able to leave the group at no excessive cost (so that we can presume they consent to its formal authority structures, even if it is not democratic). And the groups must be identificatory, in the sense that they are groups that individuals join to pursue a conception of the good that is central to their identity and integrity. When this is the case, groups have an interest in maintaining their own collective integrity, including by enforcing their own norms of membership and leadership and by enjoying some immunity from the reach of antidiscriminatory legislation.

I shall say more about the value of integrity for individuals in Chapter 6. Here I simply postulate it is an important value, and I further assume that the protection of collective integrity is valuable insofar as it allows its members to live with integrity. Individuals join religious associations to be able to live by their deep commitments and beliefs, and religious associations provide the structure within which this is possible.[42] As Peter Jones has noted, what marks out a group as the kind of group that might bear rights is the integrity manifested by a group: a group must surmount a threshold of unity and identity if it is to be potentially capable of bearing rights.[43] In what follows, I show that collective integrity is an internally complex idea and that, if we disaggregate the values it protects, we can justify some of the collective rights claimed by religious groups. As will become clear, religious groups are not uniquely special here. While religious groups do not have any uniquely special feature, some of their activities exhibit an array of normatively relevant features that, put together, justify special treatment. Religious activities and practices can benefit from special exemptions, but this is not because religion, or freedom of religion, is special. Rather, it is because (and when) they meet the two criteria that independently justify exemptions: what I call their *coherence* interests and their *competence* interests. Table 5 sets out the two interests underlying freedom of association.

Table 5 Freedom of Association, Two Interests and the Specificity of Religion

Liberal State	Liberal Value	Feature of Religion	Nonreligious Analogues
Sovereign	Freedom of association	Associational interest in	(1) Identificatory associations
		(1) coherence (2) competence	(2) Expert-based associations, e.g., universities

Two Interests Outlined

I begin by offering a summary sketch of these two integrity-related interests. *Coherence* interests refer to associations' ability to live by their own standards, purposes, and commitments. *Competence* interests refer to associations' ability to interpret their own standards, purposes, and commitments. I argue that while many associations can appeal to coherence interests to defeat the application of some general laws, only some can, in addition, appeal to competence interests. Disaggregating associational interests into coherence interests and competence interests allows us to explain why religious associations are special, but not uniquely so.

In brief, here is the argument I shall develop in the rest of this chapter. Coherence interests can justify full exemptions from laws of general application. The Catholic Church's prerogative to exclude women from its clergy is a coherence interest, no different from the prerogative of other associations to enforce and live by their professed standards and principles. Courts—I shall argue—cannot hear suits of otherwise impermissible discrimination when such discrimination is part of the message of the association. Coherence interests justify *narrow but deep* associational rights—for example, formal statutory exemptions.

Competence interests are different. They become salient when only the association has the requisite competence to assess how to interpret and apply its doctrine and message. Religious associations are not uniquely special here: other associations similarly operate according to their own standards of competence and excellence. Universities, for example, are also expert-based associations. They use specialized criteria of scholarly evaluation in the selection and promotion of academic faculty. Likewise, churches employ ministers, officials, and teachers according to their specialized criteria of spiritual fitness, calling, and vocation. Courts—I shall argue—can hear suits of otherwise impermissible discrimination but, in adjudicating such disputes, they must substantively defer to the association's competence. Competence interests justify *broad but shallow* associational rights—typically, entitlements to minimum judicial deference.

The distinction between coherence and competence interests has been ignored in the literature on the rights of religious associations. Yet, I hope to demonstrate, it is an appealing alternative to the approach dominant in the United States, which postulates that religious groups enjoy a special right of "ministerial exception." As we saw in Chapter 2, the ministerial exception provides religious associations with full immunity from legal scrutiny in the employment of their ministers. In *McClure v. Salvation Army* (1972) the Fifth Circuit dismissed Mrs. Billie McClure's equal pay lawsuit against the Salvation Army, arguing that "the relationship between an organized church and its ministers is its lifeblood. The minister is the chief instrument by which the church seeks to fulfill its purpose. Matters touching this relationship must necessarily be recognized as of prime ecclesiastical concern."[44] Subsequently, courts have held that ministerial employment, because it lies at the core of church autonomy, should be exempt from any kind of judicial inquiry.[45] Since then, federal and state courts have broadened the exception to reject lawsuits by an ever-expanding category of "ministers" (school teachers, choir directors, and so on) from alleged violations of an ever-expanding category of labor laws (such as the Disabilities Act, Pregnancy Discrimination Act, and Fair Labor Standard Acts). In the unanimous *Hosanna-Tabor* decision, the Supreme Court constitutionalized the ministerial exception for the first time, applying it globally to "the church," shielding the church from liability under the Americans with Disabilities Act for a retaliatory dismissal of an employee, Cheryl Perich, who taught mainly secular subjects in a religious school.[46] At stake, the Court held, was no mere employment decision but the freedom of "internal governance of the Church." As many commentators have noticed, this creates a new, extended right of corporate religious freedom.

Yet despite the strikingly novel (in a U.S. context) corporate language and the potentially extensive scope of the exception suggested by *Hosanna-Tabor,* most U.S. legal commentators have accepted the principle of the ministerial exception, mostly because of their understandable reluctance to envisage state interference with the well-established Catholic tradition of all-male clergy.[47] Appeal to the idea of ministerial exception, however, is a mistake. As I shall argue, there is no need to appeal to such an exorbitant right to defend the right of churches to follow their doctrine.[48] I have already surveyed and criticized two influential theories justifying the ministerial exception. The first, the *jurisdictional autonomy* theory, is incompatible with the theory of state sovereignty and wrongly appeals to the idea that the state and churches somehow share sovereignty. The second, the *close association* theory, is more in line with liberal egalitarianism. It analogizes religious groups with other close groups, such as families and small-scale associations, under a general theory of freedom of association. In Chapter 2, however, I showed that the analogy is problematic and unable to support a ministerial exception for large-scale, hierarchical associations, such as precisely those churches that are committed to an all-male clergy.

Instead of identifying one single feature (church autonomy, close association) that justifies an exorbitant right of ministerial exception, I outline two features that explain why religious groups have special (but not uniquely special) rights. The approach I defend breaks with the ministerial exception developed by U.S. courts and comes closer to the balancing approach favored by the European Court of Human Rights.[49] The Court of Human Rights has declined to take a position on matters of religious significance, orthodoxy, and teaching, but has not shied away from weighing church autonomy against the rights of employees. Its approach, however, remains unsystematic and ad hoc. The distinction that I offer, between coherence interests and competence interests, outlines a more principled and structured account of both the normative force of religious association and the scope of the privileges it justifies.

Coherence Interests

Coherence interests refer to associations' ability to live by their expressed standards, purposes, and commitments. Individuals form associations to pursue the conceptions of the good they find valuable, and associations provide the structure within which this is possible. Coherence interests are interests that associations have in sustaining their integrity, that is, their ability to maintain a structure through which their members can pursue the purpose for which they have associated.[50] To have minimum associational integrity, groups must achieve some coherence between their purpose, structure, and ethos. Such a coherentist "fit" is central to the notion of collective integrity.[51]

In what follows, I set out the implications of coherence interests for the scope of freedom of association. I argue, first, that coherence interests justify associational prerogative to refuse or rescind association, but only if the prerogative is in furtherance of the association's doctrine or purpose. Second, I explain which types of associations have the relevant coherence interests. Third, I show that requiring associations to articulate a discriminatory doctrine, if they want to discriminate, is a legitimate restriction on their freedom of speech and expressive autonomy. Discrimination should not come cheap in liberal societies, and if it takes place at all, it should be open rather than insidious. Let me take these three points in turn.

First, it is easy to see how coherence interests include interests in refusing or rescinding association. Consider familiar cases: a support group for female rape victims should not be forced to accept a male manager; the Labour Party should not be forced to appoint a Conservative general secretary. The misalignment in such cases is such that the group that is compelled in that way would be unable to continue to be the group that it is: its integrity would be fatally undermined. Likewise, associations are entitled to enforce their ethos and standards on their members. My university will rightly discipline me if I plagiarize academic work; my political party will expel me if they find out I am an ideological opponent and have only joined cynically to influence the selection of its next leader. These are normal powers of associations, powers that directly flow from their coherence interests.

Religious associations, just like other associations, are entitled to enforce their standards on their members, and to refuse association with nonadherents. It would be a category mistake to complain that religious associations discriminate on religious grounds—a mistake not reflected in current law, which provides religious organizations with an exemption from prohibition of religious discrimination.[52] Associational coherence interests ground religious associations' right to prohibit apostasy and blasphemy for their members, to excommunicate heretics and dissidents, and to refuse entry to nonbelievers. A religious association that is unable to insist on adherence to its own religious tenets as a condition of membership is unable to be a religious association.[53] If extramarital sex is a sinful offense within a church, that church can rightfully terminate employment of its clergy, leaders, and teachers on this ground.[54]

Can a group rightfully invoke coherence interests to discriminate on otherwise impermissible grounds, such as race, gender, and sexuality? Not unless the professed doctrine of the group itself demands such differentiated treatment. To be able to discriminate, a religious group must show the religious nature or basis of the practice. Let me illustrate. In a U.S. case involving unequal pay in a religious publishing house, Seventh-Day Adventists were found guilty of discrimination against a female employee. The court ruled that "preventing discrimination can have no significant impact upon the exercise of Adventist beliefs *because the church proclaims that it does not believe in discrimination against women.*"[55] One implication of this line of thinking is that churches cannot discriminate on insidious grounds (that is, on grounds that it is not publicly committed to). Courts have held, for example, that prohibitions on extramarital *pregnancy,* by contrast to prohibitions on extramarital *sex,* cannot be applied equally to men and women, and therefore constitute insidious gender discrimination (assuming the church does not hold that extramarital sex is more sinful when committed by women).[56]

By contrast, if a church's tenets include some theologically justified exclusion, it can invoke coherence interests to exempt itself from antidiscrimination legislation. For governments to prevent groups from enforcing their own declared criteria of membership would be to strike at the core of associational freedom. So the Nation of Islam ("Black Muslims") cannot be forced to admit whites, just as white supremacist churches cannot be forced to admit blacks.[57] More controversially perhaps, the Jews' Free School cannot be forced to admit students that the school does not consider (ethnically) Jewish.[58] By analogy, the government cannot force the Roman Catholic Church to ordain female clergy—as long as the established doctrine of the church is that only men can be priests. Church authorities appeal to all-male priesthood as its established doctrine, grounded in scripture, the experience of Jesus and the Apostles, and its two-millennia-old tradition. They further claim that only men can represent Jesus, because of the "natural resemblance" between Christ and his ministers.[59] When discrimination is grounded in this way in religious doctrine—however objectionable the doctrine is—courts should treat it as a case of permissible religious discrimination. Such a commitment is, of course, subject to controversy within the Catholic Church itself, and there are powerful movements for reform.[60] But it is not for courts to force the church to change its doctrine: courts should respect the existing structures of authority within the church. Freedom of association would not be robust enough if it did not include this minimum associational integrity.[61]

Second, which associations have coherence interests? As intimated, associations have coherence interests only if (1) they are formally constituted as voluntary associations and (2) the primary mode of association is identificatory. Let me explain these two points in turn. First, only religious groups that are formally organized as associations (such as "organized religions" in UK law) are candidates for exemption from general laws. The key feature of associations is that they are voluntary (they can be entered and left without excessive costs), they have reasonably formal structures of authority, and they are formed around a specific doctrine or purpose. The implication is that diffuse, loose religious communities—such as "the Hindu community" or "the Muslim community"—cannot *qua* communities be candidates for exemptions from general laws for differential treatment of individuals according to caste, gender, or sexuality.[62] If forms of legal pluralism and regimes of personal law are allowed, they should be subjected to the common associational regime and to the ultimate sovereignty of civil law. The important point is to preserve individual freedom to enter and exit associations. This requirement is not easily met, but it is crucial for addressing the serious worry that exemption rights aggravate the vulnerability of "minorities within minorities"—sexual and gender minorities as well as children.[63] If a religious group seeks to discriminate on impermissible grounds, it must constitute itself as a voluntary association, guarantee freedom of exit for its members, and have an open doctrine that justifies (to its members) the differential treatment it takes to be central to its doctrine.

Does this, as critical religion theorists claim, amount to a Protestantization of religion, such that only religious groups that are voluntary count as properly religious? It does not. Recall that my approach is interpretive, rather than focused on the semantic or ontological question of what groups "really" are. To say that only religious groups that are constituted as voluntary associations can claim discrimination from general laws is not to postulate that only they are properly religious. Hindus, Jews, Catholics, and others rightly see themselves as belonging to religious nonvoluntary communities of fate. This is a perfectly legitimate, commonsense use of the term "religion," and one that, in addition, is relevant

for distinctive purposes such as interfaith dialogue, inclusive representation, and antidiscrimination. But the question that concerns us here
is a specific normative question, that of the justification of some legal
privileges. The question is not: What is a religious group? It is instead:
If a group *(any group)* wants to discriminate on impermissible grounds,
what kind of group must it be, for the purposes of the law? The normative
point is that, for some groups to be granted exorbitant powers to der-
ogate from general rules of justice, they must fulfill strict conditions
of voluntariness.

Second, only those voluntary groups where the primary mode of association is identificatory have the relevant coherence interests. Religious
associations have strong rights of "incorporated conscience" (what I call
coherence interests), but they have these rights only in virtue of being
identificatory associations, where individuals identify with the projects
and commitments that are at the core of the association's integrity.[64] Identificatory associations are those that allow members to integrate core aspects of their personal beliefs and commitments with associational goals
and values. Intuitively, it is easy to see that a church—a nonprofit, soli-
daristic, identificatory association—should enjoy robust associational discretion, while it is less clear that a profit-based commercial organization
can rightfully enforce the religious precepts of its owners on its nonad-
herent employees, as the U.S. Supreme Court allowed in the recent
Burwell v. Hobby Lobby decision (2014). There the Court held that a
closely held business association run by a religious family could be exempt
from the contraception mandate imposed under authority of the 2010
Affordable Care Act. Because Hobby Lobby had a religious basis for its
objection to providing insurance coverage for contraception, it was protected by the federal Religious Freedom Restoration Act (RFRA).

Much ink has recently been spilled on the question of whether
for-profit corporations can make freedom of religion claims. Critics of
Hobby Lobby, however, have not provided sufficient explanation of why
for-profit corporations do not have relevant standing in the law.[65] Two
arguments have been put forward: a *legal* argument about the fact of

incorporation, and a *functional* argument about the nature of market relations. But, I argue, neither is fully convincing. The legal argument runs as follows. Legal incorporation implies that the corporation is a separate legal person, not simply an *alter ego* of its founders or owners. The corporate veil protects shareholders from personal liability; in turn, they should be prevented from infusing the corporation with their personal beliefs and values. The problem with this is that, as a general fact about corporations, it is doubtful. The corporate form is not incompatible with the advancement of religion as the main purpose of a corporate entity. Indeed, many churches, synagogues, and mosques are corporate entities, so legal incorporation does not in itself rule out collective freedom of religion claims.[66]

The functional argument points more specifically to the nature of market relations, and draws on a well-established distinction between constitutive or expressive associations, on the one hand, and commercial associations, on the other. The thought is that once individuals (as individuals or acting via a corporation) operate in the market economy, their primary purpose is the maximization of profit, and they are subjected to the state's compelling interests of fair access to material resources and opportunities.[67] For *this* reason, they are not relevantly "religious" anymore: commerce and religion do not mix, so to say. But this is a radically reductive argument, both about the marketplace and about religion. People engage in the market economy for a variety of purposes— including the pursuit of values (ethical investments, corporate social responsibility), trading in religious goods (kosher or halal butchers, Bible sellers), and the provision of faith-based services such as health care. Many religious associations do not seek simply to engage in standardly religious activities such as praying, preaching, teaching, or otherwise participating in the rituals of the faith. They also aspire to foster a religiously integrated life for their members, and to bear witness to the faith in the public sphere and civil society: to deliver services, set up hospitals, run religiously inspired commercial enterprises. It would be arbitrary to claim that a kosher butcher or a Bible seller cannot make a religious freedom claim (in my preferred terminology: that it does not have the relevant coherence interest) just because it is engaged in a commercial activity. In such cases, as a U.S. court stated, because "the beliefs of a closely held corporation and its owner are inseparable, the corporation should be deemed the alter ego of its owners for religious purposes."[68]

Existing explanations for why for-profit corporations do not have relevant standing, then, are insufficient. We must look for a different interpretive criterion. Taking James Nelson's lead, I locate this criterion not in a legal or functional argument, but in a normative argument about the mode of association itself.[69] What I propose to call identificatory associations exhibit coherence or alignment among their purpose, structure, membership, and public.[70] Only associations that exhibit tight coherence in this sense have a claim for exemption from general laws—regardless of whether they are incorporated or whether they are mostly commercial in nature. This is because the natural persons that are involved in the workings of the collective entity—be they leaders, members, employees, or customers—are in the right (identificatory) relationship with the association. Therefore, the association is entitled to claim coherence as a key interest. In practice, most for-profit corporations do not exhibit the right kind of coherence—but some do, as long as they meet the test. So how can we test identificatory coherence? Clearly, the sincerity of the owner or shareholders is not sufficient: judges must look at the objectively ascertainable purpose, structure, and activities of the association.

First, there must be a fit between the main purpose of the association and the main purpose of its members in associating. Identificatory associations implicate the identity of their members; they allow them effectively to pursue a valued conception of the good, the ideal, or purpose. This is by contrast to mere organizations, where the dominant mode of relationship is detached—distant, instrumental, and impersonal.[71] Nonprofit churches and other religious associations are paradigmatically identificatory groups, whereas large-scale for-profit corporations are paradigmatic organizations. Generally, environmental conditions in modern corporate life encourage shareholders, officers, and directors to detach from their organizational roles.[72] However, personal or family businesses (with only a few employees) sometimes exhibit the right kind of identificatory coherence, even when they are incorporated and commercial. By contrast, Hobby Lobby, despite the religious ethos of its owners, is not an identificatory association. It is a large arts-and-craft chain with over 500 stores whose 13,000 employees cannot be assumed to share the owners' personal investment and moral commitments.

Second, there must be a fit between the association's purpose and the public it intends to serve or the customers it caters for. Ethical investment companies, kosher supermarkets, and Bible sellers exhibit relevant coherence interests insofar as their customer base is mostly self-selecting and identificatory. By contrast, what U.S. law calls "public accommodations"—businesses and other providers that are open to the public at large—do not have relevant standing. They have no relevant coherence interest that would allow them to refuse to serve all members regardless of race, gender, or sexuality.[73] This is not simply because their *pro tanto* coherence interests are trumped by compelling interests in equality of access. My claim is stronger: as soon as an organization claims to serve the public, it is not "religious" in the sense that matters to standing in exemptions from discrimination claims. If faith-based hospitals or charities are to serve the public, they must do so on a nonexclusive basis, on a par with secular organizations.[74]

Third, there must be a fit between the association's main purpose and the specific activity or function for which it claims an exemption from nondiscrimination laws. Even identificatory associations cannot claim coherence interests on behalf of all the activities they undertake. It is essential to distinguish between core and peripheral religious activities and assess the nexus between a group's activities and its purpose.[75] Religious groups, for example, cannot subject all their employees— regardless of their duties—to the tenets of their doctrine. A different view is proposed by Christopher Lund. Discussing the landmark case of *Corporation of the Presiding Bishop v. Amos* (1987), Lund appeals to what he calls "relational interests" to justify the dismissal by the Mormon Church of the janitor of a church-owned gymnasium, on the grounds that he was not a member in good standing of the church. Lund's relational interests are broader than what I call coherence interests, because they apply to all the activities engaged in by the association (in this case, employment in a sports facility).[76] The relational dimension of associations, in Lund's theory, gives them a prerogative to choose *all their members* (not only their leaders) on religious grounds, including those members employed in nondirectly religious activities.

This, in my view, is far too permissive. On the stricter construal that I favor, coherence interests apply only to the association's core purpose, and only to the activities and functions that are closely related to such purposes. The closer the association's discriminatory policy is to the core of its internal spiritual practices, the stronger its claim to exemptions based on its distinctively religious associational purposes becomes. As a practice becomes more distant from the core religious practices and activities of the association, it also becomes less relevant to associational coherence.[77] Religious employers cannot discriminate on religious grounds—or on any other impermissible ground—in relation to employees not doing religious work. When a church engages in educational or economic activities—activities where the state rightly claims jurisdiction—its claims to discriminate on coherence grounds weaken considerably.[78] The state has compelling interests in ensuring equal access to key opportunities such as housing, education, and employment; in protecting the liberty and the equality interests of both employees and nonmembers; and in respecting the freedom of conscience of nonadherents employees. When it comes to the marketplace, it has a compelling interest in eradicating discrimination on grounds of race, gender, and sexuality. Given the importance of these interests, religious associations should only have narrow latitude to discriminate on religious grounds, beyond core religious functions. The activities of a priest or a teacher of religion are relevantly religious, but the activities of a janitor in a gymnasium are not—there is obviously a wide range of intermediate functions and activities, and associational "latitude for discrimination" should vary accordingly.[79]

Only associations with coherence interests of this kind have a *pro tanto* claim to exemption. Some religious associations will qualify, and some will not; some of the activities that associations engage in will qualify, and others will not. The point is, it is not necessary, on my theory, to define what a "religious institution" is.[80] It is not the presumptively religious nature of the association, but rather the mode of association that it actually exhibits, that is relevant to its standing.

Let me now turn to my third and final point. Does my restrictive interpretation of coherence interests violate the freedom of *speech* of associations? In U.S. constitutional and political theory, a common way of defending what I call coherence interests has been to appeal to the *expressive* interests of associations. Because freedom of association is not explicitly mentioned in the U.S. Constitution, it has been derived from other constitutional rights, most influentially, rights of freedom of speech.[81] The First Amendment protects the expression of messages that are unpopular, objectionable, or even repugnant. When the primary purpose of an association is expression of a point of view, its freedom to select (and discipline) its members consistently with its expressive purpose is essential to its members' exercise of free speech through the association. A government that regulates the membership of a church or a political club or a social advocacy group in a way that defies its expressive purposes is also regulating its members' speech, unjustifiably and unconstitutionally so, no matter how morally misguided or factually mistaken the government may rightly believe the association's message to be.[82] As Justice O'Connor influentially wrote in the landmark case of *Roberts vs. U.S. Jaycees* (1984), "the formation of an expressive association is the creation of a voice, and the selection of members is the definition of that voice."[83] The expressive theory of freedom of association can be seen as a version of the coherence-based approach, which, arguably, follows from any plausible construal of freedom of association.

A crucial question, however, arises. How explicit must the association's expressive message be? Must associational coherence apply only to the association's declared purpose and mission? Controversy arose, in the United States, in the context of the much-discussed Supreme Court decision in *Boy Scouts v. Dale.*[84] At issue there was the question of whether the Boy Scouts had to demonstrate that homosexuality was incompatible with the ethos of scoutism to be allowed to let go of a gay scoutmaster called Dale. Influential critics, such as Seana Shiffrin, have argued that proper understanding of the expressive interests of associations requires respecting their right not to have to articulate a clear public message. Compelled association is a form of compelled speech, which dangerously interferes with the internal life of the association. Associations do not simply broadcast and amplify the ideas and commitments individually and *a priori* held by their members: they are also sites for the development of ideas, discussions, and disputes between them. Shiffrin's worry is that if associations have explicitly to justify a claim for exemption, their process of self-definition might be inhibited: fear of potential liability is likely to have a chilling effect on associational life. Moreover, forcing associations to articulate a message if they are to receive legal protection rewards the most discriminatory groups and discourages dissent, experimentation, and critical reexamination within them. On Shiffrin's view, the right to exclude should be "fairly absolute," lest courts interfere with the process of thought production and idea affirmation central to the formative and deliberative role of associations.[85]

In a spirited critique of the *Dale* decision, Andrew Koppelman has made compelling points in response to this line of argument. He argues that what critics such as Shiffrin describe as perverse effects of the message-based approach are, in fact, desirable. The point of the law is to eradicate insidious discrimination—discrimination undertaken for pretextual reasons that have nothing to do with the association's commitments. By forcing associations to articulate their discriminatory messages publicly, the message-based approach raises the cost of discrimination. Discrimination should not come cheap in a liberal society committed to eradicating prejudice. If associations seek to exclude women or LGBTQ, they must "come out" as sexist or heterosexist institutions; they should not be allowed insidiously to perpetuate patterns of prejudice. They must pay the cost of discrimination: they might lose members, scare away customers, and disqualify themselves from public funding. An additional point can be made. It is not clear that the message-based approach necessarily has a chilling effect on associations. It is, if anything, as likely to provoke intense internal debate and dissent, as members must decide whether they wish to be publicly associated with the relevant message. It is true that the message-based approach has the effect of offering exemptions only to the most obviously prejudiced speakers. But this too is appropriate: it does put pressure on the culture to become less discriminatory, but it does so in a way that is respectful of freedom of association and speech of dissenters.[86]

Koppelman's message-based approach parallels the coherence approach that I defend. However, because Koppelman thinks that religion should be subjected to a uniquely special regime, he would not apply the message-based approach to churches, endorsing instead the judicial doctrine of ministerial exception.[87] For my part, I see no reason to treat the coherence interests of churches any differently. Religious associations should be allowed to discriminate on otherwise impermissible grounds such as gender only if they can show that discriminatory messages are essential to their doctrine and mission. And they must live with the consequences, including be criticized as patriarchal or heterosexist institutions. They should not be allowed to discriminate insidiously: they should not use an exorbitant privilege of so-called ministerial exception to be shielded from scrutiny in all their employment decisions. The implication is clear. A woman cannot complain of gender discrimination when she is excluded from the clergy by the Catholic Church, because the commitment to an all-male clergy is (currently, and for better or worse) central to Catholic doctrine. But a woman could bring a discrimination suit against a liberal protestant church (or an Adventist publishing house) that is committed to gender equality.[88]

So far, so good. But there is something troubling here. Is it really the case that "churches are just like the Boy Scouts?"[89] Compare the following scenarios:

1. The Boy Scouts expel one of their scoutmasters, Martin. He is criticized for failing to fulfill his responsibilities adequately. Martin sues for insidious discrimination on grounds of his sexuality.
2. A Christian church expels one of its priests, Mark. He is criticized for failing to fulfill his responsibilities adequately. Mark sues for insidious discrimination on grounds of his sexuality.

On the theory I have proposed, neither association should receive a blanket exemption from discrimination suits, unless they are able publicly to articulate and justify their discriminatory position toward homosexuals. Assuming that neither does, no associational coherence interest is infringed, and both Mark and Martin can get a hearing in court. However, matters cannot rest here. There is an intuitively obvious sense in which Martin will get a more sympathetic—or at least more attentive—hearing than Mark. Plainly, secular courts are able to evaluate what the duties and responsibilities of a scoutmaster are, while they cannot assess what makes a good priest without inquiring into arcane and (to them) esoteric or inaccessible matters of theological doctrine or spiritual practice. If this is plausible, we need to account for the difference. In what follows, I draw attention to other interests that religious associations—among others—have, which I call competence interests. Such interests, I argue, do not justify blanket exemptions, but they demand judicial deference.

Competence Interests

While coherence interests refer to associations' ability to live by their professed standards, purposes, and commitments, competence interests

FREEDOM OF ASSOCIATION

refer to associations' special expertise in the interpretation and application of those standards, purposes, and commitments. Legal commentators and political theorists have generally eschewed reference to this epistemic dimension of freedom of association. They have either subsumed it under a broad, all-encompassing theory of jurisdictional autonomy, such as the ministerial exception, or they have explicitly denied that competence interests—such as the theological expertise of churches—ground any special right for associations. Yet it is important to identify, and to delimit, the nature and scope of competence interests, because they are crucial in accounting for the special rights that religious associations—among others—should have in the liberal state. Competence interests are at the intersection of free exercise and nonestablishment. They articulate a crucial sense in which the state must avoid "entanglement" with religion—which closely mirrors the sense in which some religious reasons are inappropriate justificatory reasons for public policy. If some reasons, doctrines, and ideas are inaccessible in public reason in the way that I describe in Chapter 4, then, *ceteris paribus,* they are also inaccessible as a basis for judicial interference in the internal life of associations.[90]

The basic intuition behind a theory of competence interests is drawn from another segment of U.S. common and constitutional law, which concerns property disputes within churches. It is there that the "hands-off" approach to religious associations has been developed.[91] When courts were faced with competing factions laying claims to church property, they would decide which faction had least departed from the basic doctrines of the church. Such inquiries, of course, are common in property law and in the law of contracts and trusts. However, they posed a particular problem in the case of churches, because they led courts into theological inquiries for which they are distinctively ill-suited. Judicial resolution of theological or ecclesiastical disputes, even when necessary to resolve litigation, would impermissibly entangle the government in the affairs of religion. Over the last thirty years or so, the Supreme Court has decided that such enquiries are barred by the religion clauses.

It has referred back to a precedent under federal common law (*Watson v. Jones*, 1871)[92] and asserted in *Jones v. Wolf* (1979) that courts must adopt a hands-off approach in matters of religious doctrine. This means that, in cases of property disputes, courts must either defer to the decisional structure of the religious organization, or they must apply so-called neutral principles of law. What they must *not* do is to take sides on disputed matters of doctrine.[93]

A logical extension of this is that courts should not take a position on the theological rationale of religious employment decisions—in particular, they should not adjudicate disputes concerning the selection and dismissal of clergy.[94] As one court put it, "it is axiomatic that the guidance of the state cannot substitute for that of the Holy Spirit and that a courtroom is not the place to review a church's determination of 'God's appointed.' "[95] If—to come back to my hypothetical example—a church dismisses Mark because he has failed to show the requisite spiritual qualities or he has preached an inaccurate interpretation of the Gospels, it would be difficult for courts to engage in the fact-finding inquiries that would allow them to qualify circumstances and justifications as merely pretexts for heterosexist prejudice. Even the best-intentioned courts are susceptible to error because they lack the competence properly to evaluate the "gifts and graces" of a minister. Only religious associations have the competence to interpret such qualities, and courts must accept the *prima facie* validity of the religious justifications proffered by the church. This is in contrast to the objective core tenets of religious associations, which, as we saw, underpin their coherence interests, and justify exemption from some antidiscriminatory legislation. The difference is crucial. If a religious association asserts in its defense that a minister violated a tenet against adultery, this is an objectively testable religious justification. But if a religious association asserts that a minister lacked the requisite spirituality, this is not within the competence of the court to assess. The meaning of adultery is accessible (to a secular court) in the way that the meaning of spirituality is not.

This does not mean that courts should altogether refuse to hear such cases. My argument is that they should exercise deference, but not grant immunity. Some authors have argued that a church's competence interests ground a full right of jurisdictional autonomy. This, as Lund and others have suggested, should be seen as the underlying rationale for the U.S. theory of ministerial exception.[96] Advocates of the ministerial exception argue that only a prophylactic hands-off approach, offering complete jurisdictional immunity to churches in *all* their employment decisions, would adequately address the risk of impermissible entanglement of church and state. The implication is that "government interference with clergy decisions is barred, *independent of the presence of theological questions.*"[97]

This, in my view, is again too permissive. It is only theological questions that courts, on my theory, do not have competence to resolve. But one need not grant full jurisdictional immunity to ensure that competence interests are respected. When courts inquire into whether a religious reason is used as a pretext for an employment decision, they are not automatically becoming entangled in theological questions over which they do not have competence. In discrimination cases, the question is not whether the asserted reason is true, but whether the defendant believed it to be true when he took the challenged action: it is an inquiry into sincerity, of the kind that is common in cases of individual freedom of religion.[98] Cases where religious reasons are produced only subsequently (or not at all), and where there is substantial evidence pointing to sexist, heterosexist, or racist prejudice, should be litigated, not subjected to a blanket jurisdictional exception. As Caroline Corbin has pointed out, "there is nothing inherently entangling about asking whether a religious reason was in fact the sole reason motivating a decision."[99]

Current legal practice supports this interpretation of competence interests. Even in the United States, where the ministerial exception is seen as barring most inquiries into employment disputes, some courts have declined to apply it when the employer's behavior is "wholly nonreligious in character." For example, in a case where a priest asserted that he had been discriminated against on racial grounds, and claimed that religious reasons were merely a pretext, the Second Circuit signaled that it would consider the case, provided it could avoid "intrusion into sensitive religious matters."[100] The European Court of Human Rights, for its part, has taken an even more robust position. While recognizing the rights of religious associations to rely on their own teachings, practices, and interests in making employment decisions, it has also held that religious associations must also consider the right to privacy, family life, and employment prospects of employees. Only if a proper weighing process has taken place, the European Court grants national courts (and churches) a fairly wide margin of appreciation.[101] Deference to associational competence, then, does not bar some *substantive* scrutiny. Nor should decisions made by religious associations be immune from *procedural* scrutiny. The European Court of Human Rights, for example, found fair hearing and free expression rights breached in the termination of a professor employed at a Catholic university (*Lombardi Vallauri v. Italy,* 2009).[102] In sum, many suits need not involve any religious dispute at all; in others, the sincerity—albeit not the validity or adequacy—of appeal to a religious reason is ascertainable by secular courts; and in yet others, the rights of the employees must be (minimally) weighed against the religious interests of the association. Advocates of the ministerial exception are right to point out the limits of state competence in matters of "purely ecclesiastical cognizance"—but they are wrong to deny state authority altogether.

Religious associations, then, have competence interests that justify courts in showing judicial deference in their adjudication of ministerial employment disputes. But are they the only associations that have such interests, and the employment discretion that they justify? They are not. Courts routinely defer to employers' judgments about subjective professional qualifications in highly specialized fields—such as academic scholarship for a professorship or analytical ability for a law firm partnership. Courts do not presume to know what qualities are necessary for professor or partner, nor do they second-guess subjective judgments about whether a plaintiff possesses those qualities. Consider, for example, academic tenure cases. Courts have declined to sit as "super-tenure review committees," whose work would involve "inquiry into aspects of arcane scholarship beyond the competence of individual judges." Courts have refused to second-guess academic tenure board decisions. For example, in *Weinstock v. Columbia,* the Second Circuit found that the provost's denial of tenure to a Barnard assistant chemistry professor because "her scholarship was not up to snuff" did not constitute wrongful gender discrimination, despite circumstantial evidence to the contrary.[103]

It is true that courts must rule whether competence-based reasons are merely pretexts, and such inquiries will be resisted: no association likes courts poking their noses into its internal affairs. But while a law firm or university or church may have expertise in knowing who is best suited for a job, courts have expertise in evaluating circumstantial evidence to ferret out discrimination. As with tenure cases, they will likely be overly cautious in interpreting the evidence they have been provided with. And the inquiry will be more sensitive in the case of churches than in the case of universities. But this is a difference of degree, not of nature. Religious associations have strong competence interests, which justify a high degree of judicial deference but not full jurisdictional immunity. Ira C. Lupu and Robert W. Tuttle have compellingly argued in their analysis of U.S. jurisprudence: "The Establishment Clause does generate respect for religious communities, by deferring to their answers to ecclesiastical questions. This deference, however, is limited by the government's retained power to decide which questions are ecclesiastical and which religious bodies have the authority to resolve them."[104]

Another way of putting the point is this. Religious associations, among others, have weighty competence interests. But they do not have

Kompetenz-Kompetenz: they do not have the prerogative to determine their own sphere of autonomy. They cannot appeal to competence interests to identify their own area of competence. In particular, they cannot claim that only they are competent to settle the rights and duties of their members and employees. Religious groups have interests both in coherence and in competence, but they do not have a right of jurisdictional self-definition.

6

⸏⸏⸏

Disaggregating Religion
in Freedom of Religion

Individual Exemptions
and Liberal Justice

I n this final chapter, I address the ethical salience issue head-on and
defend a theory of the justice of individual exemptions on religious,
as well as other ethically salient, grounds. I build on the pioneering work
of Dworkin, Taylor, Maclure, Eisgruber, Sager, and other liberal egalitarian authors, but I suggest that they have offered only a partial account
both of ethical salience and of the justice of exemptions. In part, I argue,
this is because they failed to see that religion has different relevantly normative dimensions, and that different principles of justice apply to these
different dimensions.

Ethical Salience and Integrity-Protecting Commitments

In this first section, I summarize my critique of the standard liberal egalitarian objection to exemptions, and then I show that exemptions apply

to an ethically salient category of integrity-protecting commitments (IPCs). The standard liberal egalitarian objection to exemptions goes roughly as follows:[1]

1. State neutrality prohibits judgments of ethical salience.
2. Religious exemptions assume the special ethical salience of religion.

Therefore

3. State neutrality prohibits religious exemptions.

Summarizing arguments I have presented in previous chapters, I show that premises 1 and 2 are both false. It follows that the standard egalitarian objection to exemptions is false.[2] I examine both premises in turn.

Premise 1 articulates a plausible thought about state neutrality, but unduly generalizes it beyond its core cases of application. The plausible thought is that the state should not draw on, or side with, comprehensive conceptions of the good, lest it infringe on personal liberty and on equal status. In this case, the injunction of neutrality applies to the justification of the law, regardless of the particular interest the law burdens. To illustrate: The state should not restrict some religious practice out of prejudice, distaste, or otherwise impermissible partiality toward the good. This is *not* because religion is a salient interest. Rather, it is because the *reasons* for restricting it are impermissible. The state's treatment of religion here is only an application of a broader principle of justificatory neutrality.

Chris Eisgruber puts the point eloquently: "Suppose there are two interests, X and Y, of any weight, and the government treats X worse than Y because X depends on a religious perspective that the government dislikes. That is a failure of equal regard—and it is a failure regardless of whether X and Y are profound or middling sorts of interests."[3] So it is, and there is no doubt that justificatory neutrality has normative force and central cases of application. Consider legal decisions such as the City of Hialeah ordinance against Santeria animal sacrifice, the French and Belgian ban on Muslim veils, or the Swiss ban on minarets.[4] Insofar as those decisions are motivated by (or can be justified only by) hostility toward Santerians or Muslims, they are straightforwardly in breach of liberal neutrality. And when liberal neutrality is breached in this way, it does not matter whether what is restricted is religious or not—whether it is ethically salient in any particular way.

To illustrate, consider another example drawn from international asylum law. When governments persecute religious minorities, they are wrong to do so, regardless of whether members of those minorities actually practice the targeted religion, or even whether membership of that group is a salient identity for them. The fact of persecution—the fact that the state restricts their rights out of hostility and prejudice—is sufficient for them to be candidates for asylum on grounds of religious persecution.[5] In such cases, the shift to justificatory neutrality—to an assessment of the reasons that the state can permissibly appeal to—displaces the need to assess the ethical salience of particular practices and identities. Not surprisingly, then, neutrality of justification is invoked by many authors as the key principle of liberal treatment of religion.[6] They appeal to the intuitively persuasive idea that governments should not draw on contested or comprehensive conceptions of the good to justify interfering with people's preferences and commitments, whatever they are.

Although this is an important principle, it is more limited than many liberal egalitarians assume. As I have argued, governments often appeal to good neutral reasons—public order, animal rights, gender equality—to ban or regulate certain practices, including Santerian ritual sacrifice and Muslim veiling. So neutrality of justification is not sufficient. If we are to protect Santerian ritual sacrifice or Muslim veiling, we need to say more about the nature of the interest that such practices protect, such that it cannot simply be trumped by any appeal to the general welfare, public order, and so forth. Workplace uniform regulations that accommodate Muslim veils but not clown hats implicitly judge Muslim veils to have greater ethical salience than clown hats. Are they *ipso facto* in breach of liberal neutrality?

They are not, because liberal political philosophy has more structure than a flat neutralism about values would suggest: it is rooted in what John Rawls called a thin theory of the good. It is compatible with judgments of ethical salience—judgments that rank certain freedoms and rights as essential to the exercise of basic human capacities. Freedom of religion or conscience is standardly recognized as a special kind of freedom by liberals. It is one of the "conclusively justified" commitments of liberalism, according to one of its foremost interpreters, Gerald Gaus.[7] In Rawls's contractarian liberalism, the basic liberties (which include conscience, speech, and association) have priority over other freedoms, because they are closely connected to two salient moral powers.[8] Charles Taylor, in a memorable comparison of Great Britain with communist Albania, showed that freedom of religion is more valuable than freedom to drive unimpeded by traffic lights, and argued that "strong evaluations"—evaluations of the ethical salience of particular liberties—are unavoidable.[9] Andrew Koppelman has concurred that there is no way for liberalism to avoid judgments of ethical salience in order to decide what rights are important.[10] Alan Patten has suggested that liberal neutrality (*qua* equal treatment) should be particularly "robust" in relation to certain important religious and cultural commitments.[11] Even a philosopher committed to strict justificatory neutrality such as Dworkin conceded that a law should not ride roughshod over the "sacred duties" Native Americans are burdened by.[12] And generally, Dworkin's commitment to justificatory neutrality did not dissolve the need for him to discriminate, at the level of justification, between religious matters of personal ethics and more impersonal matters such as environmental protection.[13]

So liberals are committed to the view that the state is not neutral toward higher-order interests or moral powers: it grants special protection to a class of ethically salient interests—as we saw in our explication of the connection between state neutrality and personal liberty in

Chapter 4. A law that burdens a central Muslim practice, even if it is justified by appeal to sound neutral reasons, might not be all-things-considered justified if it gravely infringes a salient interest. To see this, we can appeal to Rawls's notion of "strains of commitment": because parties in the original position seek to avoid excessive strains of commitment, it is plausible, given what they generally know about the importance of certain commitments to them, that they would want laws to avoid disproportionately burdening them. As Jonathan Quong has argued, the parties would arguably not commit themselves to a strict consequence-blind pursuit of justificatory neutrality. They would not want to put themselves in a position where the law would place on them intolerable strains—typically, burdens on their conscience.[14] On this view, religious persecution is wrong, not only because persecutors appeal to the wrong kind of reason (when they do), but because it gravely infringes on a salient interest of individuals. So premise 1 is false: liberal neutrality does not prohibit judgment of ethical salience, at the relevant level of abstraction.

Now consider premise 2: Religious exemptions assume the special ethical salience of religion. As my critique of premise 1 has established, the objection here cannot simply be that any judgment of ethical salience in itself breaches liberal neutrality. Rather, the objection must be that religious exemptions single out an inadequate category of ethical salience. This is because—the argument is often made—religion is not special. More precisely, religious beliefs and practices are not more ethically salient than nonreligious commitments and conceptions. Whatever feature of religion is highlighted as ethically salient (its connection to the sacred, its categorical nature, its centrality to personal identity, its relation to ultimate matters, its comprehensive nature) will also be found in many nonreligious commitments.[15]

The point is well taken, and has been one of the starting points of this book. However, as I have shown throughout, the fact that religion is not uniquely salient does not entail that religion does not belong to a broader category of commitments and practices that are themselves salient. We can say that religion should be protected, not in virtue of some feature it essentially and exclusively possesses, but in virtue of features it contingently possesses, along with other salient beliefs, conceptions, and identities. This is the upshot of the interpretive approach to freedom of religion that I have developed.

Next, to make some progress on the question of the justice of religious exemptions, we need to identify the class of beliefs and practices that are candidate claims for exemptions. A preliminary clarification. I have said that some practices are *candidate* claims for exemptions: the implication is that not all those claims will be granted, only that they have a *pro tanto* claim to be heard. In other words, I deploy a two-pronged test to exemptions: (1) Does the practice exhibit the correct interpretive values? (2) Should it be accommodated? My substantive theory of the fairness of accommodations will be the subject of the next section. For now, let us focus on the first prong of my test. What is it about religious claims that justifies the special concern exhibited in exemptions from general law? Recall that on my interpretive approach, it is not sufficient simply to say "religion is X and Y." What is required is to identify the specific normative values that the law has reason to protect—values that make X or Y legally salient.

The semantic and the interpretive step are distinct and should not be conflated. Consider, for example, the argument presented by a thoughtful and influential theorist of religion and the state, Robert Audi. Audi offers an answer to the critical religion challenge according to which, because religion cannot be reliably defined, the domain of freedom of religion is unclear. Audi retorts, sensibly enough, that providing a broad, multi-criterial conception of religion is not as difficult as critics imply. He lists nonexclusive features such as "beliefs in one or more supernatural beings," "a moral code believed to be sanctioned by the god(s)," "ritual acts focused on [sacred] objects," and so forth.[16] But here is the rub: Whatever conception of religion we opt for, we must explain in virtue of what it is worthy of special politico-legal concern. Why exactly do the features picked out by Audi merit special solicitude by the state?

A few pages later, Audi explains why religious freedom is (in his view) special. But, interestingly, he appeals, not to the intrinsic value of these features, but instead to their instrumental importance to individuals' well-being. The relevant interpretive principle is *how individuals relate to these features*. It generates what Audi calls "the principle of protection of identity" according to which "the deeper a set of commitments is in a person, and the closer it comes to determining that person's sense of identity, the stronger the case for protecting the expression of those commitments."[17] The interpretive move, here, is to say that religious beliefs and practices are typically central to the identity of individuals. But, of course, religion is not the only mode of identity; nor is religion only about identity. The gap between the semantic and the interpretive dimension of religion, then, opens the possibility that *not all* religion, and *not only* religion, meets the relevant interpretive value.[18]

In what follows, I present my theory of the interpretive value of freedom of religion as it relates to the question of the justice of exemptions from general laws.[19] In Chapter 4, I suggested that the ethically salient liberties that the state should generally refrain from infringing are *integrity-related liberties*. In what follows, I explicate this notion of integrity more fully. Integrity is an ideal of congruence between one's ethical commitments and one's actions. It expresses an ideal of "fidelity to those projects and principles that are constitutive of one's identity."[20] Integrity, then, is primarily a formal relation one has to oneself, or between parts or aspects of one's self; and it has an ethical content, in the broad sense that it relates to normative evaluations of the good, bad, just, and unjust. Integrity is a coherentist principle: it focuses on the fit between what individuals are committed to and what they do, with minimal external assessment of the validity, orthodoxy, or objective importance of their commitments.

The class of ethically salient commitments, for exemption purposes, is that of *integrity-protecting commitments* (IPCs). An integrity-protecting commitment is a commitment, manifested in a practice, ritual, or action (or refusal to act), that allows an individual to live in accordance with how she thinks she ought to live. Following Bernard Williams, we can define integrity in relation to the commitments that people identify with most deeply, constituting what they consider their life is fundamentally about. Integrity requires that persons act out of their own convictions, that is, out of commitments with which they deeply identify.[21] Ultimately the value of integrity is grounded in the values of identity, autonomy, moral agency, and self-respect.[22] Importantly, individuals acting in accordance with the demands of their conscience possess integrity even if they are mistaken about what moral duties they have. The value of integrity explains why important ethical and moral commitments, but not mere preferences, are *pro tanto* candidates for exemptions. These commitments cannot be sacrificed without feelings of remorse, shame, or guilt, by contrast to preferences, which can.[23] *Contra* critics of exemptions, then, integrity provides us with a plausible criterion for identifying ethically salient claims and commitments.[24]

The notion of integrity is grounded in widely shared values that are not sectarian, and it can be valued as a good both by religious and nonreligious citizens.[25] This is because the content of integrity—the particular commitments and actions that it commands—cannot be drawn from any objective, person-independent conception of the good: it can only be defined by the individual whose integrity is at stake. As Paul Bou-Habib rightly notes, "the integrity argument gives nonreligious persons a way of understanding 'what is so special about religion'—or, at least, 'what's so special about a religious person's being able to practice his religion'—namely, that this enables him to instantiate in his life something they themselves value as moral agents: their integrity."[26] It follows that integrity underwrites what Taylor and Maclure call a subjective theory of freedom of religion.[27] Not surprisingly, many liberal egalitarians have been drawn to justify religious exemptions by reference to something like integrity. Martha Nussbaum's conception of freedom of conscience, for example, protects the deep ethical convictions that define the practical identity of persons. It is through those convictions, she argues, that a person tries to "identify the value and point of human life and the relationships, achievements and experiences that would realize that value in her own life."[28]

Furthermore, integrity connects the individual's own standards of the good life to specific *actions and practices*. As a result, the notion of integrity is particularly apt to interpret exemption claims, which are typically claims to act (or not to act) in particular ways. Therefore, the integrity view is not vulnerable to the critical religion charge, discussed in Chapter 1, according to which the liberal construal of religion is biased toward individualistic notions of autonomy or Protestant modes of belief. The integrity view is not thus biased, because it does not put any premium on individualistic, chosen, or antecedently existing beliefs. Integrity-protecting commitments may or may not be based on beliefs in the Protestant sense; practices may or may not be communal; and there is no assumption that beliefs somehow precede and supervene on practices. Practices are not necessarily mandated by beliefs; rituals often give shape to, and embody, the religious life itself—consider, for example, the bodily discipline of Jewish or Muslim praying rituals. The integrity view, then, nicely accommodates the practice-centered, embodied conception of religion described by Winnifred Sullivan, Saba Mahmood, and others.[29]

Integrity-protecting commitments, then, are *pro tanto* candidates for exemptions. But which test should judges use to assess integrity? I set out two tests, which I call *thick sincerity* and *thin acceptability*.

The first test, in line with the subjective conception of religious freedom, is a test of individual sincerity. In exemption cases, individuals themselves are best placed to explain why some of their commitments and practices are central to *their* integrity. My approach, therefore, departs from objective conceptions of the demands of religion (or culture).[30] Individuals might be mistaken about what is demanded of them; they might come up with wildly eccentric or idiosyncratic beliefs and practices; they might press highly heterodox interpretations of their religion, and so forth. But as integrity is understood as an individual, subjective value, it follows that only the individual is competent to determine what her own integrity demands. The alternative—judging individual practices in relation to some religious orthodoxy—is unacceptable to liberal egalitarians.[31] As the Supreme Court of Canada suggested in its noted *Amselem* decision, claimants "need not show some sort of objective religious obligation, requirement or precept to invoke freedom of religion."[32]

This approach has not gone unchallenged. In her book *Reasons of Identity*, Avigail Eisenberg forcefully argues that the "sincerity approach"— as she calls it—is deficient and should be complemented with an objective conception of identity claims. She presents two arguments. The first is that appeal to well-established spiritual practices and communal traditions provides "accessible and compelling" evidence of the authenticity of claims (such as a peyote exemption for Native Americans). The second is that individualized claims might damagingly distort the authenticity of these communal traditions. Both arguments, however, are problematic. They wrongly assume that the moral force of exemption claims resides in their compatibility with communal traditions, and that individual exemptions should not undermine communal authenticity. But, I have argued, the moral force of individual exemption claims lies, instead, in their importance to individual integrity, not in their advancement of objective or collective goods such as "religion" or "tradition." This obviously does not entail that communal membership has no value, but it does entail that communal membership has the value that the individual herself gives it.[33]

Now, why do we need *thick* sincerity? It is because individuals should properly honor the values that integrity expresses. Recall that integrity captures the salient value involved in doing what you think is good or right, as opposed to what you would prefer to do. Integrity involves what Charles Taylor called a strong evaluation: an evaluation about better or worse, important or trivial conceptions of the good life, views that are not reducible to mere preferences, desires, and inclinations, but are instead the standards by which desires, preferences, and inclinations can be judged.[34] Individuals must show that the practice for which they claim an exemption is *nontrivial:* that it touches on something that is connected to their sense of self, to their moral or ethical identity, not simply to a whim, preference, or unreflected prejudice. And they must show that it is *important:* that it actually occupies a pivotal place in their life as they want to live it, and is not simply a peripheral, incidental, or occasional commitment.[35] The standard of thick sincerity, then, requires that individuals show that a particular IPC is actually important to their life and to the standards by which they attempt to live it. Sincerity tests are commonly used by judges in all areas of the law. Of course, judges cannot and should not pry into individual consciences, but should simply check minimum coherence between what is said and what is done by the claimant. Judges have, in practice, not found it difficult to identify clear cases of religious fraud.[36] Hard cases might be cases where claimants successfully mimic religion in order to get access to benefits and exemptions,[37] or cases where claimants sincerely argue that a *prima facie* preference—such as their devotion to a football team—plays such a role in their lives that it becomes an integrity-protecting commitment. We have to live with such cases, and the fact that we are unsure about whether this or that practice is really an IPC does not entail that the category of IPC is meaningless.

Thick sincerity is a standard internal to integrity, in the sense that it remains normatively bounded by the individual's own subjective ethical standards.[38] There is, however, an additional, nonsubjective standard, which I call *thin acceptability.* It is nonsubjective in the sense that, although individuals sincerely believe, and can show, that a particular practice is central to their lives and implicates their ethical identity, their claim nonetheless is not *pro tanto* permissible. This concerns a category of claims that I shall call morally abhorrent claims—claims that are flatly incompatible with the basic rights of others. At the end of Chapter 2, I suggested that liberal egalitarians such as Taylor and Dworkin have made it too easy for themselves, by only considering largely inoffensive, self-regarding practices, such as the ingestion of peyote or the wearing of religious signs. What can we say about the harder cases of other-regarding, potentially harmful, practices?

Take, for example, a person who believes she has a sacred duty to perform infant sacrifice. Evidently, that person should not receive an exemption from laws criminalizing murder. But this conclusion can be justified in different ways. One could suggest, first, that morally abhorrent claims are flatly incompatible with the pursuit of integrity. People of integrity cannot do abhorrent things, even if they are acting sincerely and in accordance with their core commitments. On this view, far-right Nazi murderers or religiously motivated terrorists cannot be said to act with integrity.[39] The performance of infant sacrifice is so abhorrent that it cannot be pursued with integrity. There is no IPC, and so the claim does not go through *at the first stage*. Or on a second view, one may allow the claim to perform infant sacrifice to go through at the first stage, as a sincerely held, integrity-protecting commitment. But it is then turned down at the second stage, when it is weighed against the basic right to life of the infant. These are two plausible positions, but both—I shall argue—have limitations.

The first position relies on a moralized view of integrity, which runs against my subjective theory of freedom of religion. The position wrongly suggests that individuals who are sincerely committed to the pursuit of a wicked cause cannot be said to act with integrity. Instead we should say that they act with integrity, but that integrity is not the paramount or overriding value. Bernard Williams held the view that a Nazi can be a man of integrity, although it would be better if he did not have integrity. It is not correct to say, as some have, that just because individuals possessing personal integrity may be wicked, integrity is without value.[40] There is value in people pursuing the subjectively held projects and commitments that are central to their life and worldview—but the pursuit of integrity cannot justify the performance of morally abhorrent actions. The second position avoids the moralization of integrity by shifting all the burden of justification to the second stage. All integrity-protecting claims qualify as *pro tanto* worthy of protection, and it is at the second stage that morally abhorrent claims (as well as other claims that conflict with the public conception of justice) are turned down. This comes at a cost, however. The strategy problematically homogenizes all first-stage claims: a claim to perform infant sacrifice is treated in exactly the same way as a claim to inflict mild corporal punishment on a child. Both go through as IPC and both, on the public liberal theory of justice, can be turned down at the second stage. The fact that infant sacrifice is abhorrent, whereas mild corporal punishment is not, is lost from sight.

In response, let me sketch a third, alternative position, which avoids the pitfalls of the other two. On my view, the claim to perform infant sacrifice should not go through at the first stage, but this is not because it does not adequately express the value of integrity. It is an IPC, but it does not qualify as a *pro tanto* claim, because it is morally abhorrent. There are two advantages to this account. First, it is more in line with considered judgments about the structure of liberal rights. To qualify for protection under any basic right—of association, of enterprise, of speech—practices must meet a threshold of moral acceptability. A claim by a mafia to associate purely for criminal purposes, for example, does not even *pro tanto* qualify as a freedom of association claim—regardless of whether the association has integrity-based value for its members. Second, and crucially for my theory, this account allows us to take seriously reasonable disagreement about liberal justice. Let me explain. While morally *abhorrent* claims are rejected at the first stage, morally *ambivalent* claims go through. Liberal justice is not compatible with violation of basic rights and of minimal standards prohibiting cruelty, murder, rape, and so forth. Morally abhorrent claims are claims, such as that of the Nazi or the fundamentalist terrorist, that are incompatible with any reasonable conception of morality and justice. Morally abhorrent demands—perform infant sacrifice, stone "dishonorable" women, attack physicians performing abortions—even if they are sincere and located into a worldview that is central to a person's sense of self, should be ruled out at the first stage.

But recall that in Chapter 4 I allowed that there can be reasonable disagreements about liberal justice. Morally ambivalent claims, I suggest, are claims that can be fitted into one or other recognizably liberal conception of justice. They are claims that might be defeated at the second stage (when judges enforce the particular conception of justice that has been publicly endorsed) but that go through at the first stage (because they would go through under an alternative conception of liberal justice). On this view, a claim to perform infant sacrifice is rejected, whereas a claim to inflict mild corporal punishment on one's children goes through at the first stage: it is heard, because it is compatible with one reasonable conception of parental authority and children's rights, even though it can be rejected at the second stage.[41]

At this point, an obvious objection arises. Are there such things as morally ambivalent claims? Why should not all claims that are incompatible with the public liberal conception of justice be ruled out at the *first* stage (as per the first strategy adduced above)? If infant sacrifice is an unacceptable IPC, why not corporal punishment of children? And why should practices that breach liberal norms of equality and nondiscrimination (those treating women or LGBTQ citizens differentially, for example) be candidates for exemption at all? There is—the objection continues—no intermediate category between the morally abhorrent and the illiberal, as both are unreasonable. Illiberal citizens should have rights of free speech and freedom of association (as long as they do not infringe other people's rights), but they should not have *pro tanto* rights to claim exemptions on the basis of their illiberal beliefs.[42]

In response, let me clarify what I mean by morally ambivalent claims, and explain why it is important to grant such claims first-stage recognition. Morally ambivalent claims arise out of reasonable disagreement about liberal justice. People think seriously and conscientiously about justice and what it implies—about what it means to treat people as free and equal—and they naturally disagree about many things, including, for example, the scope of adults' rights to discipline children. Morally ambivalent claims typically emerge at the intersection of different liberal principles, when people disagree about the relative weight and importance of attendant rights of privacy, free speech, free expression, or free association. Let me give a few examples.

Strict parent. A parent sincerely believes that strict discipline—including justly administered mild corporal punishment—serves the moral edification of her child, and that this decision pertains to her discretionary authority. This claim, insofar as it concerns the scope of parental rights, is morally ambivalent.

Muslim puritan. A Muslim pupil in a Swiss school refuses to shake a teacher's hand. Swiss authorities have ruled that religious belief is no excuse to opt out of a common practice of civility that is universally respected in that country. But refusing to shake someone's hand (if this refusal is extended to men as well as to women) is not in itself morally abhorrent: norms of civility and social mores should not be confused with matters of basic justice.[43]

Message on a cake. A bakery owner in Northern Ireland does not mind serving a gay customer but objects to writing a pro-same-sex marriage slogan on the cake that the customer wishes to purchase. This is an ambivalent claim. The shop owner might be wrong that his freedom of speech is properly implicated; but to think so is not a morally abhorrent failure of judgment.[44]

Polyamorous lovers. Three individuals have lived in a loving relationship all their adult lives. One of them is terminally ill, and they object to a provision permitting only one partner to be present at the patient's bedside in a palliative care unit. Because there is reasonable disagreement about which unions the state should extend legal recognition to, this is a morally ambivalent claim. (Perhaps polyamorous unions prefigure what liberals will think is just in the future, just as LGBTQ couples have transformed mainstream understandings of marriage.)[45]

On my theory, because these morally ambivalent claims are claims that can be inserted into one or other conception of liberal justice, they should be allowed at the first stage (even if they are turned down at the second stage). If we accept that there is not one but several conceptions of liberal justice, we must accept, as *pro tanto* IPCs, commitments that are compatible with one or another of such conceptions of justice—even if it is not the conception that we (as political theorists) personally favor, nor the one that has been endorsed through fair democratic procedures. Citizens ought to get a hearing for those claims that conflict with the publicly endorsed conception of liberal justice, insofar as their claims are not morally abhorrent. This also allows and facilitates continuing democratic deliberation about the content of justice: liberal standards about the permissibility of corporal punishment of children, norms of civility and social mores, the nature of legally recognizable amorous unions, and the reach of antidiscrimination norms, change over time. First-stage admissibility is one way in which liberal democratic polities, while committed to enforcing a determinate conception of justice, leave open the possibility that their principles and standards evolve over time.

First-stage admissibility, then, follows from the admission of reasonable disagreement about liberal justice; and it helps affirm the equal status of citizens as participants in democratic debate about justice. This provides an answer to Richard Arneson's vigorous argument that we have no reason to defer to conscience if a person is mistaken about what moral duties she has.[46] *Contra* Arneson, I have argued that we have two compelling reasons to grant first-stage admissibility (though, as I argue in the next section, not necessarily to defer). The first is that it validates the claim in question as an integrity-protecting commitment—one rooted in deeper values of moral agency or self-respect, instead of a mere preference that can be dismissed without compelling reason. The second is that the claim might be protected under an alternative conception of liberal justice, and therefore first-stage admissibility recognizes the legitimacy of certain disagreements about justice and the right. Generally, liberal rights include rights to do wrong—the right to do and say hateful and objectionable things, within the boundaries set by the basic rights of others—out of respect for reasonable pluralism.[47]

How different is this from a more standard Rawlsian account? Rawls argued that political liberalism has to respond to the plurality of *reasonable comprehensive doctrines*. By contrast, what I call morally ambivalent claims are acceptable, not because they are derived from a reasonable comprehensive doctrine, but because they can be *detached* from such a doctrine and inserted into a liberal conception of justice. This difference is crucial. Rawls's approach invites us to assess the reasonableness of claims by reference to their standing within comprehensive doctrines that are themselves politically reasonable (that is, that accept the public conception of justice). On that view, a socially conservative, patriarchal demand is reasonable *because* it is inscribed within a well-established Christian or Muslim religious worldview (provided that worldview does not deny the basic moral equality of men and women). But this amounts to saying that claims are respectable because they are embedded within well-established religious traditions: religious misogyny is more acceptable, so to say, than nonreligious misogyny, just because it is religious.

Rawls's concern was in one sense understandable: his political liberalism was motivated by the need for citizens to converge, via an overlapping consensus, on principles of justice from the perspective of different comprehensive doctrines. This might be a plausible theory of liberal legitimacy.[48] But this account, with its focus on the reasonableness of doctrines instead of the reasonableness of citizens, is ill-suited to justifying the *pro tanto* permissibility of exemption claims. Recall that such claims are rooted in individual integrity, and their permissibility does not depend on their conformity to some established tradition or orthodoxy. I prefer to detach exemption claims from the particular conceptions of the good they are inscribed in (it suffices that individuals relate to them in the right way, according to the thick sincerity test). Such claims are then evaluated by reference to their compatibility with a recognizably liberal conception of justice. The upshot is this: demands of exemption from antidiscriminatory legislation on integrity grounds are morally

ambivalent, not because they have respectable standing within traditional religions, but because they can be supported by (a reasonable
interpretation of) liberal rights of free speech, free association, privacy,
and so forth.

The advantage of disaggregating religious comprehensive doctrines
into single, detachable IPCs for purposes of exemptions is that this is
more consistent with the liberal egalitarianism that inspired Rawls and
Rawlsians. In exemption cases, I have argued, what does the normative
work is not respect for religion as such, not even for "reasonable" religion—but, rather, respect for individuals and their particular ethical
claims. This means that individuals with nonreligious IPCs are treated
on a par with individuals with religious IPCs. It also means that individuals who are members of non-Western, non-monotheistic, unfamiliar,
or unusual religions are treated on a par with members of well-known
religions—there is no assumption that, because one's ethical claim
belongs to a familiar comprehensive religious doctrine, it is deserving
of more *pro tanto* respect. As should be clear by now, the implication of
this thoroughgoing egalitarian disaggregation is a permissive first stage
of qualification. This is because the set of morally ambivalent IPCs
(religious, secular, idiosyncratic) is potentially very large. Is this a problem?
One commonly voiced concern is the risk of exemption proliferation.
My theory, however, is not vulnerable to that worry because it does not
assume that just because something is an IPC, it will be granted an exemption. Rather, claims get scrutinized at the second stage by reference
to the public conception of liberal justice. My two-pronged theory (Is
this an IPC? Should it be granted an exemption?) allows us to distinguish clearly between the *metric* and the *principles* of justice.

Before I move on to clarify my preferred liberal conception of the
justice of exemptions, I need to say something more about the content
of IPCs. The paradigmatic case of an IPC, for many liberals, is that of
conscientious objection to war. This is a case of a strict obligation (in
this case, not to perform a certain act). Yet while obligation has an undeniable normative pull, it does not encompass all the value of integ-

rity. On the Williams-inspired view of integrity I sketched above, I act with integrity when I live by my ideal of the kind of person I should be—when I follow a valued way of life, when I realize my ideals of ethical excellence, and so forth.[49] As Alan Patten has noted, "attachments to a culture can be of crucial importance to individuals in ways that track, if at some distance, the importance of religious convictions—violating a cultural attachment may not produce a feeling of having sinned, but it may lead to a sense of having betrayed or compromised a relationship of community that is of central importance in an individual's life."[50]

Patten's point that cultural attachments track "at some distance" the importance of religious convictions suggests that we should draw a distinction between two kinds of IPCs, with different ethical salience. I call them obligation-IPCs and identity-IPCs.[51] Let me briefly explain the difference between the two, as it will be relevant to the theory of the justice of exemptions I develop in the next section. Obligation-IPCs have great salience because they express the intuition that coercing people to act against what they feel they are *obligated* to do is a severe threat to their integrity. This was the intuition behind Taylor and Maclure's defense of freedom of conscience. And as they rightly argued, obligation-IPCs need not be traditionally religious in content. Secular conscientious objectors can feel obligated by their deepest normative principles and ideals. My notion of obligation-IPC is closely related to Taylor and Maclure's, but improves on theirs in two ways.

First, obligation-IPCs need not be tied to too narrow a view of conscientious duty. Cultural and communal practices can have comparable salience as conscientious duties—if they are experienced as obligatory by the claimant. This successfully rebuts the charge, which we discussed in Chapter 1, that liberal accounts of religion are biased toward Protestant construals of religion as conscience. They need not be. We can acknowledge the strong normative pull of obligation, but obligation need not be rooted in conscience, nor is it exclusive to Protestant religion. Second, not all religious claims are obligation-IPCs, because not all religion is about obligation. As Andrew Koppelman has argued, "the emphasis on conscience focuses excessively on duty. Many and perhaps most people engage in religious practice out of habit, adherence to custom, or happy religious enthusiasm, rather than a sense of obligation or fear of divine punishment."[52] This is correct. But while Koppelman concludes that religion as such must therefore benefit from special categorical protection, I draw a different conclusion. Insofar as "habit, adherence to custom or happy religious enthusiasm" are not integrity-protecting commitments, they do not fall under the salient, exemption-worthy category. We should bite this bullet: If a person's integrity is not compromised, it is not clear that the person suffers any ethically salient burden.[53]

Yet it is true (as Koppelman perhaps meant to imply) that the non-obligatory dimensions of religion can also be central to one's integrity. This is the case, I argue, when they take the form of identity-IPCs: non-obligation-imposing commitments and practices that comprehensively regulate the lives of the claimant. Recall Saba Mahmood's description of the religious life as consisting of embodied practices of piety, exhibiting the virtues of fidelity, devotion, care of the self and others, and so on. Most of the practices associated with such a religious way of life are ethically salient, even though they are not duties of conscience, or even obligations. Yet, taken together, they form a complex web of social and ethical meanings. Here religion looks a lot like culture—particularly the all-encompassing notion of culture referred to by theorists of multiculturalism.[54] Non-Western or non-monotheistic religions, such as African religions or Native American religions, "look like" culture more than they look like (Western) religion, insofar as they lack the attributes of divine command, strict separation between the profane and the sacred, a sacred text, and religious authorities.[55] Yet they also contain integrity-protecting commitments in my sense: the notion of identity-IPCs, in this way, provides a compelling response to the Protestant critique explicated in Chapter 1.

The argument that, for purposes of exemptions, religion should be interpreted not only as conscientious duty but also as one form of meaning-giving, integrity-protecting cultural commitment has often been resisted by political theorists. Yet this suspicion is rooted in the mistaken assumption that religion is essentially different from culture. Of course, one can provide theological, sociological, anthropological, political, and phenomenological accounts of this difference. The question that preoccupies us, though, is a narrower, interpretive question.

When we think of the object of exemptions, the question we ask is as follows: What kinds of commitment are so important to people that their integrity would be threatened, were they prevented from acting on them? The onus is on critics to explain why certain kinds of cultural commitments are not as central to people's integrity as traditionally understood religious commitments. I am prepared to grant, however, that identity-IPCs are less salient than obligation-IPCs, because the violation of integrity caused by restriction on culture is weaker and more indirect than that caused by coercing individuals not to act on their sense of obligation.[56] A law that burdens a non-obligatory practice infringes integrity only indirectly. As I argue later, the severity of a burden is relevant to how we think about the justice of exemptions.

In the next section, I shall outline my preferred theory of the justice of exemptions—one, it turns out, that is quite restrictive about granting exemptions that infringe on important interests of others. My preferred theory of justice is distinctively progressive rather than conservative, in the sense that it sets the individual rights of children, women, and sexual minorities as limits to the pursuit by others of their integrity-protecting commitments. But I am prepared to allow that there are other permissible liberal conceptions of the justice of exemptions—both more restrictive and more permissive than mine.[57]

Just Exemptions: Two Principles

In this section I set out my preferred substantive theory of the justice of exemptions. I defend two principles—*disproportionate burden* and *majority bias*—and show how they relate to the two kinds of IPCs:

obligation-IPCs and identity-IPCs. On an egalitarian theory of justice, the mere fact that an individual has an IPC does not entail that she should benefit from an exemption from the law. There are two main reasons for this. First, there is no presumption that, just because an IPC is burdened by a law, that burden is thereby unfair. Egalitarian theorists rightly reject liberty-based accounts of religious freedom, which posit a baseline of maximal freedom, against which each law must be justified in relation to some compelling state interest.[58] Egalitarian theorists argue that legal and political arrangements unavoidably limit the untrammeled pursuit of people's life projects, because they provide a fair framework for the sharing of the burdens and benefits of common life. Of course, as we saw above, governments should not repress some religious practice out of prejudice or animus, nor selectively accommodate some religious practice over others. But many general laws burden IPCs incidentally, without being thereby unfair. Consider a law making safety motorcycle helmets compulsory. It does burden Sikh motorcyclists who wear a turban, but it is not obvious that it is thereby unfair. Sikhs are not persecuted or discriminated against on grounds of their IPC. The law does not prevent them from wearing a Sikh turban, it merely prevents them from riding a motorcycle without a helmet.[59] The law sets out a general health-and-safety requirement, and the fact that it (incidentally) burdens those with reasons not to comply with it is not sufficient to make it unjust.

The second skeptical thought about exemptions resides in the value of the rule of law. The notion is intrinsically connected to egalitarian ideals because it emerged in reaction to the hierarchical order where different social groups had different laws, and the rich and privileged could exempt themselves from the burdens of common life. From this point of view, exemptions begin to look not so much like fair accommodation as like unfair privilege. It is easy to see the intuitive appeal of the notion that if there is a law, it should be the same for all. Intuitions, however, can lead us astray. Regimes of exemptions, if they can be designed and administered transparently, are a feature of modern legal regimes and do not in themselves undermine the rule of law.[60] This is particularly the case when the law is able to identify categories of citizens for whom differential treatment would not defeat the purpose of the legal regulation in question. Accommodation of citizens with disabilities, pregnancy and maternity workplace arrangements, special provisions for the elderly, and so forth, fall under that category. On reflection, then, there must be something troubling about IPC exemptions that does not also apply to these less controversial exemptions.

What is troubling about them, it seems, is that they are connected to people's life projects and conceptions of the good, and that the only reason for the exemption is that people object to the fact that the law frustrates their realization. Yet a just state cannot guarantee the success of all (or any) life projects; it is only there to provide a fair framework for the compossible pursuit of different and conflicting life plans. In Rawls's terms, there should be a social division of responsibility between the state—which provides a fair framework of justice—and individuals, who have to take responsibility for adjusting their life projects to the common framework.[61] Talk of responsibility, I hasten to add, does not entail the problematic view that people should be compensated for unchosen circumstances and bad luck but should take personal responsibility for the choices they make. Such a "luck egalitarian" framework is wholly inappropriate to the understanding of the ethical status of IPCs in a theory of justice.[62] IPCs are not worthy of respect because they are somehow "chosen"—here the critics of the liberal language of choice and religious freedom have a point. Rather, they are worthy of respect because they are connected to people's integrity—to the projects, beliefs, and commitments that people happen to identify with. It makes a moral difference that people (by and large) positively endorse and embrace IPCs whereas they (by and large) prefer not to suffer from a disability. One may object here that people may also embrace, and identify with, their state of pregnancy, age, or disability. This is correct, but it misses the point: there are separate reasons for accommodating such states of being or cycles of life. IPC exemptions, by contrast, arise principally out of a conflict between the law and a given belief or project. An incidental burden on an IPC should be construed not as a disadvantage worthy of compensation but instead as one of the costs of (well-ordered) freedom. To use Peter Jones's pithy expression, people must, generally, "bear the consequences of their beliefs."[63]

But—as Jones himself eloquently argued—people should take responsibility for their beliefs *only if background circumstances are fair.* A liberal state should not equalize people's success at maintaining integrity, but it should provide a fair framework for them to pursue their IPCs. So we need to identify more precisely what counts as an unfair background. Let me set out two distinct types of background unfairness that bear on justice toward IPCs.

> *Disproportionate burden.* Pursuit of some state regulatory interest makes it impossible for some citizens to fulfill an obligatory requirement of their faith or culture, yet makes it possible to relieve them of the burden without excessive cost. Disproportionate burden scenarios invite a *strict balancing test,* which weighs up the interests pursued by the law, the severity of the IPC burden, and the costs incurred in alleviating it. To illustrate: It would be unfair to compel Orthodox Jews to endure an invasive postmortem autopsy in case of nonsuspicious death, if they consider this a desecration of the body.[64] There seems to be a *disproportion* between the aims pursued by the law and the burden it inflicts on the claimants.
>
> *Majority bias.* Minority citizens are unable to combine the pursuit of a core societal opportunity with an IPC, whereas the equivalent opportunity set is institutionally available to the majority. Majority bias scenarios invite a *contextual evaluation* test, which compares burdens between similarly situated groups in relation to core opportunities whose exercise is facilitated by a background of institutional majority precedence. To illustrate: It would be unfair to deny Muslims some time off on Fridays, as Christians can both go to church on Sundays and hold a regular job.

As we shall see later, both types of unfairness can be present in any case of exemption—but each of them is sufficient to trigger a demand of justice. Let me say a bit more about the rationale, scope, and limits of both justifications for exemption.[65]

Disproportionate Burden

In this section, I argue that obligation-IPCs should be protected against disproportionate burden. Recall Rawls's argument for the priority of freedom of conscience. Given what they know about the weight and ethical salience of obligations of conscience, Rawls argued, parties in the original position would not want to gamble with them, and, to avoid suffering "strains of commitment," they would opt for laws that guarantee equal freedom of conscience. The argument can be generalized to apply to exemptions. Given what we know about obligation-IPCs, we should not want laws simply to have a sound public justification, nor to guarantee formally equal treatment: we should want laws to avoid disproportionately burdening certain kinds of commitments.[66]

But what is a disproportionate burden? Four criteria are relevant to the overall balance of considerations:

1. How direct is the burden?
2. How severe is the burden?
3. How proportionate is it to the aim pursued by the law?
4. Can it be alleviated without excessive cost-shifting?

Let me explain these four criteria in turn.

1. DIRECTNESS

The directness of a burden is measured in relation to the costs incurred by individuals in avoiding subjection to the law or regulation in the first place. Typically, laws of universal application—for example, laws mandating compulsory military service—are directly burdensome, because they apply to all citizens, though here in a given age (and often gender) group. Directly burdensome regulations are also paradigmatically found in closed, authoritarian institutions such as prisons or boarding schools, where inmates and students are mandatorily subjected to a system of compulsory rules. Regulations concerning specific professions and activities, by contrast, are less direct, because—on principle—people enjoy the market freedoms that allow them to avoid being subject to them. For example, a law compelling nursing homes to provide 24/7 care is only indirectly burdensome, because care workers who observe a regular day of rest can opt to work in environments where their commitments can be more easily accommodated. In such cases, something like the "specific situation rule," articulated by the European Court of Human Rights, applies.[67]

The higher the costs of not taking up a particular social opportunity or position are for an individual, the more the burden is a direct one, and the more scope there is for *(pro tanto)* accommodation. Such costs can be measured objectively, in relation to alternative social opportunity sets available to individuals. To illustrate, consider again a Sikh turban example, but this time in relation to a law compelling the wearing of safety helmets for all workers on construction sites. Assume—as is the case in the UK—that in many areas Sikh men are employed in the construction industry, and that there are high costs for them in retraining or relocating. In cases such as these, an exemption is permissible. The relevant difference between the motorcycling and the construction site health-and-safety regulations is that the latter, but not the former, are a direct burden on a Sikh IPC. The costs of losing one's job in the construction industry (when this is the chief employment opportunity available) is higher than the cost of having to forgo riding a motorcycle (which is not a vital human interest or core societal opportunity).[68]

2. SEVERITY

While the directness of the burden is law-dependent, the severity of the burden is IPC-dependent. Intuitively, obligation-IPCs are more severe than identity-IPCs. Earlier, I argued that IPCs are particularly ethically salient when they are *experienced as obligatory*. They are connected to individual subjective *experience:* they do not need to be validated by any objective religious authority or text. But they are experienced as *obligations:* something that the individual feels she must do, if she is to act with integrity, faithful to her conscientious, theological, or communal commitments. Classically, if one's conscience (religious or secular) dictates that one must not kill other human beings, then this works as a categorical imperative whose moral force cannot be overridden by any contextual or consequentialist consideration. But many religious rituals, as well as cultural practices, although not strictly speaking mandatory, are also experienced as having the force of obligations by those who engage in them. If they are central to an individual's life, such that her sense of self and integrity is bound up with them, they can have comparable weight as categorical obligations.[69]

However, not all IPCs have this obligatory force. Some religious practices are relatively flexible: although they are important to religious life, no particular exercise of them need be experienced as being obligatory. One may value going to pray in a mosque, synagogue, or church without feeling it is mandatory to do so. One may feel religiously motivated, though not obligated, to wear a cultural or religious symbol. Consider Sunali Pullay, who wore a nose stud to Durban Girls High School as an expression of her Hindu cultural and religious heritage.[70] Or consider the reasoning of the claimant in *SAS v. France,* who claimed that she sometimes wore a full-face veil, "depending on her mood."[71] In such cases, the burden of uniform laws is less severe than in the case of perceived obligations. Undoubtedly, in most cases Muslim veiling is *experienced* as an obligation. On the subjective interpretation of freedom of religion that I favor, it is irrelevant whether veiling is objectively one of the five pillars (compulsory practices) of Islam. If it is the case that it is experienced by women as a practice that engages their integrity in ways that a uniform restriction on the practice makes it a particularly severe cost, then it is an obligation-IPC.

This interpretation of veiling is, in my view, more plausible than the two alternative accounts that judges of the Court of Justice of the European Union recently wrestled with in their opinion about religious expression at work (July 2016).[72] The dilemma they posed was stark and misleading. Should religious expression be seen as a mere "belief" or "opinion"—not deserving of any special protection? Or should it be construed as an "identity," akin to race or gender, and therefore a candidate for strong antidiscrimination protections? To be sure, these are two plausible dimensions of religion, and on my disaggregative strategy, they have salience in specific legal and political contexts. Consider, for example, freedom of speech. In most cases, religious convictions should be analogized to ideas and opinions open to public critique. But when the target of the speech is not the beliefs themselves but some prejudiced, libelous, or offensive characteristic attributed *to the group* itself, we can talk of hate speech via the racialization of religion, and the second dimension of religion comes to the fore.[73] In cases of exemptions, however, I have suggested that the salient dimension of religion is neither "belief" nor "race." It is, rather, what I have called integrity-protecting commitments. They are weightier than mere belief (which may or may not be connected to integrity). And they are not an externally assigned, racelike identity: they are commitments that individuals positively identify with, which should not be construed as a disability or disadvantage.

Even if religious practices are not rooted in obligatory duties, they can still express the ethically salient value of integrity. Individuals act with integrity when they are faithful to relationships of community—be they cultural, linguistic, or religious—that are of central importance to their lives. As we saw, legal burdens on non-obligatory practices are less severe than burdens on obligatory practices. This does not mean, however, that non-obligatory practices can never be accommodated. They can, but under a slightly different rationale. There are cases when a minority religious practice should be exempted, not because it is a weighty obligation, but because it is unfairly accommodated in relation to some comparable majority practice that is itself given privileged status by the state. Such a worry is central to the literature on multicultural equality.[74] In my view, this is quite a distinct rationale for exemptions, which I call majority bias, and which I set out and elucidate below. In cases that concern us here (disproportionate burden), by contrast, the (noncomparative) severity of the burden is the crucial criterion to factor into the proportionality test.

The more an IPC is perceived as an obligation, the more severe the burden is. This does not imply that it must never, in justice, be borne. Conscientious objectors sometimes must bear the consequences of their beliefs and face the legal consequences of their action; and sometimes they can be required to shoulder their share of the burdens of social cooperation in other ways.[75] All-things-considered judgments about justice do not consider the severity of the burden as the only criterion relevant to decisions about exemptions. But it remains the case that the severity of the burden is a key dimension to be considered under *disproportionate burden*.

3. AIM OF THE LAW

The third criterion draws attention to the importance and centrality of a particular law in promoting egalitarian justice. The more tightly a law promotes a goal of egalitarian justice, and the more it requires universal and uniform compliance for its effectiveness, the less it will tolerate exemptions.

Consider three cases.

A. A law is demanded by justice, and requires universal and uniform compliance. In such cases, no exemption is permissible, even if burdens are direct and severe. Consider, for example, a law forcing parents to provide their children with appropriate medical care, including lifesaving blood transfusions if necessary. Such a law directly and severely burdens Jehovah's Witness families, but it should be enforced even against them.[76] Similar reasoning applies regarding the array of laws against rape, abuse, and exploitation; as well as laws setting out universal civic obligations such as the payment of taxes and compulsory education.

B. A law is demanded by justice, but its objectives can be achieved in different ways. Consider a law guaranteeing the right of all women to have adequate access to abortion and contraception. The aim of the law is not necessarily defeated if a small number of practitioners refuse on conscientious grounds to offer the service, as long as the service is adequately provided, on a universal basis, by someone. Such reasoning has served to justify the right of Catholic surgeons, in many countries, not to be forced into performing abortions. What matters is that the rights of the individuals that the law is designed to protect are actually protected, even if exemptions are granted.[77]

C. A law is not demanded (but is permitted) by justice. For example, it protects welfarist or regulatory interests. It is in relation to such laws and regulations that the case for exemptions is strongest. Consider regulations about dress and uniform in workplaces. There are good reasons to have such regulations (corporate visibility, esprit de corps, professional reputation); and in addition to their intrinsic benefits, they are presumptively not incompatible with basic rights of justice (such as freedom, privacy, or freedom of expression). But nor do they directly promote any basic right of justice. So if a given dress or uniform regulation clashes with an individual's IPC, there is scope for accommodation—the specific situation rule should not be applied harshly.[78] Another example of eligible regulation is that requiring postmortem autopsies. Assuming that the point of the regulation—the swift identification of the causes of death—can be met through less invasive procedures such as body scans (at least in the cases of nonsuspicious deaths), it makes sense to allow Orthodox Jews to require the latter procedures. This is because Jews regard invasive autopsies, defined by one Jewish leader as "cutting open a body and removing internal organs," as a desecration of the body—a severe and direct burden on a strict religious obligation.[79]

Arguably, most controversies about the justice of exemptions revolve around interpreting condition (3) regarding the aim of the law. On the interpretation I favor, justice requires robust protection of the rights of women, children, and sexual minorities. IPCs that involve denying those rights should, in my view, be defeated at the second stage, because of the paramount importance of these rights. But I am prepared to accept that this particular interpretation of liberal justice is not the only reasonable one. There can be reasonable disagreement, within liberal theories of justice, about how to interpret and weigh different rights, especially those that are rooted in what I earlier called morally ambivalent claims. Whether public officials infringe the dignitarian rights of LGBTQ couples when they refuse (unbeknownst to the latter) to officiate LGBTQ marriages; whether freedom of speech protects refusals to bake cakes celebrating same-sex marriages; whether refusals to shake hands in certain social situations infringe on basic rights or on more negotiable, conventional norms of civility; and whether different forms of religious education infringe on children's right to equal educational opportunities: all these questions, in my view, are matters for reasonable disagreement in liberal democratic societies. Liberals should accept that these cases are not on a par with morally abhorrent cases of sexist or heterosexist discrimination, or child abuse. My theory formalizes this intuition, by allowing such morally ambivalent claims to be considered as *pro tanto* claims for consideration, instead of being dismissed as illiberal at the first stage.

4. COST-SHIFTING

This last dimension is crucial to liberal egalitarian theories, for which the benefits and burdens of social cooperation must be shared fairly. Exemptions are sometimes said to be inherently unjust simply because they involve cost-shifting.[80] But this cannot be right. First, the permissibility of cost-shifting must be balanced against the other dimensions of severity, directness, and the interests pursued by the law. Second, many extra costs that are generated by exemptions are negligible or reasonable. This is the case, notably, of dress and uniform exemptions. Likewise, allowing coroners to require MRI scans instead of postmortem autopsies for Orthodox Jews does not involve excessive cost-shifting. Somewhat more complicated are exemptions from health-and-safety measures. Allowing Sikhs working on construction sites to wear turbans shifts the costs of suffering head injuries onto them, but also onto collective health systems, so these costs must be factored into the proportionality test. Even more tricky are workplace exemptions concerning timetable and work schedules: they can be costly for employers and co-employees, and it is right that the jurisprudence on reasonable accommodation, in Canada and Europe, for example, has consistently suggested that accommodations are not reasonable if they entail "undue hardship" for the organization.[81]

I suggest, therefore, that exemptions are compatible with justice if the balance of these four reasons renders the burden disproportionate. One implication of this balancing exercise is that severe burdens are not automatically alleviated, as in the case of the Jehovah Witnesses' rejection of blood transfusions on their children. Conversely, burdens that are not that severe can sometimes be alleviated: in the case of workplace uniform regulations, where no principle of justice is at stake and costs are low, claimants do not need to show that wearing religious signs or dress is a strict obligation for them. In between these two cases, however, the severity of the burden will make a difference in the overall weighing process.

Now, is disproportionate burden an egalitarian principle? In a broad sense, it is. All individuals should have a *fair* opportunity not to have their IPCs disproportionately burdened. The principle is an implication of the liberal commitment to equal freedom of religion and conscience.[82] But in a narrower sense, disproportionate burden is not a comparative principle. To grant an exemption to X, we do not need to identify a Y that is already advantaged. This, as I demonstrated in Chapter 2, is one of the limits of Eisgruber and Sager's analysis. They argue that religious exemptions should be granted out of a principle of equality, such that religious needs and interests should not be discriminated against in relation to already protected or otherwise advantaged nonreligious interests. They would grant an exemption to the Newark police officers on the ground that officers with disabilities are already accommodated.[83] On my approach, by contrast, it is sufficient to say that the Muslim police officers have suffered a disproportionate burden, regardless of whether other officers are accommodated on grounds of disability.[84] This also avoids us having to draw unsatisfactory analogies between religious commitments and disabilities (which are not IPCs). It also avoids us having to search for hypothetical, presumptively advantaged non-religious comparator groups, in relation to which religious groups are discriminated against.

In the next section, I turn to the second principle and identify the cases of unfair background where equality concerns do come to the fore. They are cases of majority bias—where the relevant majority is the historically dominant religious majority.

Majority Bias

Exemptions on grounds of majority bias are justified because laws and regulations are enacted against a baseline of precedence of a historically dominant religion. An egalitarian demand is generated because, in many societies, the politico-legal baseline is itself one that has accommodation for the religious majority built into it.[85] As Eisgruber and Sager have shown, the point of many religious exemptions is to rectify the status of religious minorities in societies historically dominated and shaped by the majority religion (Protestant Christianity, in the United States). Recall their reading of the Sabbatarian case *Sherbert:* On their view, denying Sherbert unemployment benefits was unfair against a background of institutionalized advantage of mainstream Christians. Justice, here, is a demand of reciprocity: it ensures that minorities do not suffer undue disadvantage in relation to the majority.[86]

The idea that exemptions can be supported by specifically egalitarian considerations is, of course, a key starting point of the liberal political philosophy of multiculturalism.[87] But in what sense, exactly, does multicultural diversity generate unjust inequalities? After all, in culturally and religiously diverse societies, individuals will not be equally successful in living by the demands of their religion or culture, nor should they expect that their religion or culture be kept alive, supported, and recognized by the state. Majorities will naturally be more successful than minorities in the cultural marketplace. Following Alan Patten, I reject both the view that the erosion of minority societal cultures is bad *per se,* regardless of the justice of institutions; and the view that states have an all-embracing purpose of recognizing ethical and cultural identities.

Instead, Patten rightly locates unfair background in the "formatting" of public institutions: the endowing of those institutions with particular characteristics in ways that unequally disadvantage certain citizens on the basis of their beliefs and identities. Patten focuses on holidays, language, jurisdictions, and boundaries.[88] In Chapter 4, I showed that symbolic endorsement by the state of one culture or religion sometimes unfairly excludes minority members from the imaginary community of citizens. In this section, I turn to cases where majority bias unfairly limits the material (not merely symbolic) rights and opportunities of minority citizens. Majority bias is not necessarily illegitimate: as we saw in Chapter 4, it does not in and by itself breach norms of nonestablishment (the inclusive state) or religious freedom (personal liberty). However, here I argue that when it involves denial of certain core opportunities to minorities due to the institutional recognition of the religious culture of the majority, it demands rectificatory accommodations. As Jonathan Quong has suggested, minority citizens should not be unduly disadvantaged, because of the cultural formatting of public institutions, in their access to a specific opportunity set: the possibility of combining a core societal opportunity with the pursuit of their cultural and religious commitments (IPCs in my preferred terminology).[89] Two points need to be further clarified in order to elucidate the specific logic of majority bias: the nature of the opportunities, and the content of the IPC.

First, what kind of inequality of opportunity should we be concerned about? Core societal opportunities paradigmatically relate to access to primary goods, work, and education. Consider the UK case of *Ahmad v. Inner London Education Authority* (1976). By being prevented from attending a mosque on Friday afternoons, Ahmad was being denied the opportunity to be a teacher in a state school as a Muslim—a significant infringement of equality in societies where members of the majority can both join others in prayer and be full participants in the workplace, especially in such crucial positions as state school teachers.[90] Accommodating his Friday schedule is a way of equalizing his opportunity set in relation to the advantaged Christian majority.[91]

In majority bias scenarios, then, the reasoning is straightforwardly egalitarian. Majority bias does not give us reason to accommodate; it gives us reason only to accommodate, or not accommodate, in even-handed fashion. So it is dependent on a prior account of whether the existing majority accommodation is itself permissible. To rectify majority bias, equality can take two forms: upward and downward equality. If the majority privilege is not defensible in the first place, justice requires, not that the privilege be extended to minorities, but instead that it be abolished altogether. This, I have argued elsewhere, is the main flaw of proposals (in a UK context) in favor of "multifaith establishment"—the extension of privileges historically granted to the Christian majority (such as the right of bishops to sit in the House of Lords) to religious minorities. In that case, one first needs to ascertain whether religious representation in the Lords is compatible with democratic justice. If the majority privilege is not defensible, the right thing to do is to "equalize downward," not to "equalize upward."[92]

Assume, however, that the majority privilege is not unjust, because it serves ends that are not incompatible with the pursuit of justice. This is the case, for example, with regulations imposing a shared weekly day of rest—in post-Christian societies: Sunday. There are good reasons for having a shared day of rest, and the choice of Sundays does not infringe on the liberty of nonreligious citizens.[93] However, because it favors (mainstream) Christians, it unfairly disadvantages members of religious minorities. So justice demands that, when possible, members of minorities' request to absent themselves from work to attend a mosque, synagogue, or temple should be the object of reasonable accommodations. In such cases, it is acceptable to ask the employer (or society at large, if the costs amount to undue hardship for the employer) to pick up (some of) the costs of belief, in order roughly to equalize the opportunity sets of majority and minorities. Majority bias scenarios, then, invite comparative contextual assessment of how minorities fare, in their access to core societal opportunities, in a given society. The costs incurred in compensating them for majority bias are costs that must be borne, in justice, by society at large.

Second, which IPCs should be accommodated? Both obligation-IPCs and identity-IPCs can be accommodated, but the majority bias principle, as a broadly egalitarian principle, is particularly well suited to rectifying identity-related inequalities. Evidently, obligation-IPCs can be accommodated under majority bias as well as under disproportionate burden. If the cultural formatting of institutions allows the majority to comply with obligation-IPCs and pursue core opportunities, while blocking access to the same set for members of religious minorities, then minority obligation-IPCs have a claim to be accommodated. What we have here is an inequality of treatment between (1) a minority claim that is particular weighty in its own right and (2) a majority claim with comparable weight. Minority members are seriously burdened, while majorities are advantaged, by religiously biased institutions. For example, a society where all or most schools are broadly Christian, with no accommodation for the dietary or ritual obligations of religious minorities, would fall foul of the majority bias principle. It is worse for minority obligation-IPCs to be relatively burdened, in relation to majority obligation-IPCs, by laws and institutions that are biased toward the latter. Of course, the obligation-IPCs of religious minorities can also be burdened incidentally—for example, by a secular (religiously neutral) system of schooling. Then they qualify under disproportionate burden. But it is clear that majority bias in the case of obligation-IPCs is a particularly egregious injustice because it combines an absolute with a comparative wrong.

That said, majority bias scenarios are particularly well designed to accommodate identity-IPCs. They allow us to capture discrete forms of comparative inequality, which relate to the broadly cultural dimensions of religion. In particular, they allow us to recognize the distinctive social and intersubjective salience of identity-IPCs. Recall that these do not need to map onto obligations. Instead, they pick up broader dimensions of the religious experience—the dimensions where (ordinary descriptions of) "religion" and "culture" meet. Religion appears here as a way of life, an embodied habitus, a set of practices, none of them essential or central but which, put together, create a thick web of ethical and social meanings. It is in relation to majority bias that what I call identity-IPCs become particularly relevant. Such IPCs are morally salient, not simply because they are important to one's moral, ethical, or cultural identity, but also because they have intersubjective recognitional salience.[94] They are imbricated in socially specific patterns of institutional and social recognition. Under majority bias, it does not matter whether an IPC is an obligation—a duty of conscience, a compulsory tenet of a faith, or a central practice. Generally speaking, the burden does not need to be as severe as in the disproportionate burden scenario.

What matters is that minorities and majorities find that their roughly comparable IPCs are burdened unequally. It is irrelevant whether attendance at a church or mosque or synagogue is experienced as obligatory or not; or whether the ingestion of peyote or the consumption of communion wine is central to devout practice. What matters is that similar IPCs are not accommodated on the same basis in a given society because of the majoritarian formatting of public institutions. On this view, Muslims do not need to show that going to the mosque on Fridays is a religious obligation to have a valid claim for reasonable accommodation. (On a textual reading, it is *not* one of the five compulsory pillars of Islam, whereas prayer [*salat*] five times a day is). Nor do individual claimants have to show that they themselves experience it as an obligation (although, on my subjective theory, it is of course open to them to do so). What matters is that, in a society where joining together in weekly prayer has acquired social salience and institutional recognition, members of minorities can pursue IPCs comparable to those of the majority—when the latter is still advantaged by existing institutions.

Now this raises difficult questions. The Ahmad example is relatively straightforward. Here, the relevant IPC is [*attend a place of prayer once a week*]. Insofar as the Christian, Muslim, and Jewish religions include, as one of their important (if not necessarily compulsory) rituals, weekly attendance of a place of prayer, it is easy to equalize majority and minority religion. This simplified model assumes, however, that different religions are isomorphic: that they have the same structure of demands and rituals. But what about the following IPCs: [*pray five times a day*], [*cremate bodies on an open pyre*], [*bleed animals to death before meat consumption*]? Such demands are difficult to accommodate on the majority bias account because there is no obvious majority equivalent, and therefore it is not clear what treating majorities and minorities equally might entail. They should instead be considered under disproportionate burden—and subjected to the somewhat more stringent test of success that applies there. This simply means that all religious believers must take some responsibility for the pursuit of their integrity-protecting practices, out of consideration for the fair pursuit of other citizens' projects and opportunities.

From the perspective of Muslims, the fact that majority bias egalitarian reasoning accommodates [*going to the mosque every week*] but not [*praying five times a day*] might seem arbitrary, insofar as both practices are key IPCs within Islam (and, as we saw, only praying is standardly considered compulsory). It is this thought that motivates the oft-voiced criticism, which we discussed in Chapter 1, that Western law reshapes non-Christian religion according to its own (Christian) standards: it homogenizes religious practice into a set of clearly identifiable obligations and duties on the Christian model. There is undoubtedly some force to this criticism. But the majority bias approach helps mitigate it. The point of exemptions, on this approach, is not to equalize opportunities to practice one's religion, regardless of the demands of that religion. It is, rather, to equalize opportunities to practice IPC opportunities equivalent to those of the already privileged majority, where the criterion of equivalence is a rough, culturally mediated approximation of already accommodated practices. What is at stake here is the equal status of minorities in societies that already accommodate the majority religion.

Interestingly, many exemptions for minority members can be justified under either the disproportionate burden or the majority bias principle, or both. Consider again the Ahmad case. We can say that Ahmad was unfairly treated against a majoritarian background where similarly situated workers do not have to choose between complying with their job's requirements and attending a place of prayer on their preferred day. Or we could say that dismissal from a teaching position is a disproportionate burden on a weighty obligation. The fact that some religious exemptions qualify under both scenarios should not come as a surprise. It denotes the multidimensionality of religious claims and practices: religion is both a historical mode of minority domination (as "culture") as well as a particularly stringent set of moral, ethical, or cultural obligations. Thus, [*going to the mosque*] can be interpreted either as a cultural minority practice isomorphic to an already accommodated majority practice (under majority bias) or as an especially stringent demand of the Islamic faith (under disproportionate burden). Minority religious IPCs—for example, the wearing of religious dress and symbols—will often qualify for exemptions under both approaches.

But what about majority religious IPCs, and nonreligious IPCs, such as secular obligations of conscience? For their holders, the burden of proof is higher because they rarely qualify under majority bias and must instead show a disproportionate burden. To see this, we need to say more about what counts as an unfair background. Consider a nonreligious person who objects to the religious bias of some rules and regulations: for example, she cannot leave work on Friday to attend her trade union meeting (whereas the Muslim can go to the mosque). Or consider a Christian who claims she is disadvantaged by the secular background of rules and regulations: for example, she cannot leave work on Good Thursday, because the calendar does not recognize all Christian religious festivals. Does either have an exemption claim under the majority bias approach? I think not, because neither background is unfair in the way that is picked out by the majority bias strategy. The moral force of demands for accommodation of religious minorities is rooted in recognition of the pervasive role played by the majority religion in shaping seemingly neutral institutions; and in the deleterious impact of this majoritarian baseline for the current equal standing of religious minorities.

The nonreligious person has no claim against residual religious privilege because such privilege is purely residual: whatever claim of equalization it generates, it does so out of compensatory recognition of the unequal historical standing of minority groups in particular societies. In a society where there is no official weekly day of rest, neither Christians, nor Muslims, nor trade unionists have a *pro tanto* right to leave work on grounds of fairness: whatever rights Muslims currently acquire are grounded in claims of reciprocity, rooted in an acknowledgment of the privileges historically enjoyed by members of the majority religion. Muslims and Jews can complain of indirect discrimination on grounds of their minority status. Under majority bias, they are owed redress, not because the law is secular, but because the law advantages Christians, that is, is not secular enough.[95] So what about the Christian who seeks a Good Thursday exemption? She has no *pro tanto* claim against nonreligious rules and regulations because there is nothing unfair, in and by itself, in rules and regulations being nonreligious. This, however, is not the end of the matter. Both the nonreligious and the majority-religion citizen can press a claim under the disproportionate burden approach. But here, I have suggested, the test is more stringent. Not only do they have to show that the burden is direct and disproportionate to the aim of the law, but they must also meet some criterion of severity and show that alleviating the burden would not shift excessive costs onto others.

In this chapter, I have covered a lot of ground. Much existing literature about exemptions takes the form of what we may call a simple *Sherbert v. Smith* dilemma: Do religious believers have a presumptive right to be exempted from general laws *(Sherbert)*? Or do general laws trump demands for special treatment of religion *(Smith)*? I have suggested, however, that this simple dilemma obscures a series of conceptual and normative puzzles. The first distinction I introduced is between the *metric* of accommodation and the *justice* of accommodation. Questions of metric invited analysis of the ethical salience of different beliefs and commitments; as well as a crucial distinction between morally abhorrent and morally ambivalent claims. I argued that ambivalent claims (for example, religiously conservative demands) can be accepted within one or another reasonable liberal conception of justice. I then presented my own preferred theory of justice—a theory substantively progressive rather than conservative, in the sense that religiously conservative demands should (on my view) be limited by the rightful claims of women, children, and sexual minorities. I also distinguished between two cases of just exemptions, with different normative implications: a noncomparative principle of disproportionate burden, and a comparative principle of majority bias.

How does my analysis help us think through the simple *Sherbert v. Smith* dilemma? *Smith* is wrong in its categorical rejection of exemptions, though correct to assert that religious believers have no presumptive right to be exempted from the burdens of general laws. I am more sympathetic to *Sherbert*-style reasoning, although the balancing test I propose is much stricter than the one used by U.S. courts, more discriminating in how it conceptualizes background unfairness, and less focused on religion as such. A less ethnocentric, more egalitarian regime of exemptions should move away from the category of religion altogether, and instead take as its focus integrity-protecting commitments—whether these are ethical, cultural, or traditionally religious.

Conclusion

Liberalism's religion—the conception of religion that liberal political theory relies upon—is internally complex. In this book I have explored the multidimensional features of religion and shown how they connect to different liberal values. Table 6 summarizes the results of my disaggregative analysis. The top half of the table captures the liberal values associated with the nonestablishment of religion and the neutrality of the state. It identifies what the liberal state has good reason to contain or separate itself from. The bottom half of the table analyses the liberal values associated with freedom of religion, both in its individual and in its collective dimension. It identifies what the liberal state has good reason to give special protection to. The upshot is that "religion" is not the same in nonestablishment and in freedom of religion. Further, the normatively relevant features of religion are themselves plural, depending on which more specific liberal values are invoked.

Disaggregating religion in this way has allowed me to respond to the critical religion challenge. Liberals need not construe religion as a belief-based, individually held, voluntarily chosen conception of the good. Liberal values can be defended by explicating how the state and the law relate to a variety of discrete features of religion—conscience, truth claims, culture, projects and preferences, modes of association, political ideology, community, ways of life—features that themselves can also be found in nonreligious conceptions. So it is not the case that my liberalism privileges a narrow, Christian, Protestant-inflected account of true religion. If liberal values are contestable, they need to be challenged on their own ground (say, as rooted in the liberal axiom of moral individualism), not on the ground that they rely on an ethnocentric view of religion. There is one claim of critical religion theorists, however, that hits its mark: the claim that liberalism relies on a presumption of state sovereignty. It is the state, in liberal democratic thought, that has the jurisdiction to define the religious and the nonreligious, the public and the private, the political and the personal—as and when this line drawing is relevant to specific decisions about deference, regulation, accommodation, and recognition. Liberals must come to terms with and justify democratic state sovereignty, if they are to take seriously reasonable disagreement about liberal justice, as I argued they should.

Disaggregating religion has also allowed me to reconstruct liberal theory itself by rearranging and reassembling its building blocks.[1] Moving away from vague notions of state neutrality toward the good, I have shown that the liberal state need only be committed to restricted neutrality. The state need not be separate from religion when religion does not threaten the foundations of liberal legitimacy. And the state need not be agnostic about the ethical salience of religion and other integrity-protecting commitments, as they are closely related to the thin liberal theory of the good and key moral individual powers.

The arguments of *Liberalism's Religion* have not only been analytical and conceptual, however. I have also defended normative proposals about how best to secure the fair treatment of religion in the state. For it is

Table 6 Liberalism and Disaggregated Religion

Liberal Value	Dimension of Religion	Nonreligious Analogues
NONESTABLISHMENT		
Justifiable state	Nonaccessible	Personal experience
Inclusive state	Socially salient and divisive	Vulnerable and divisive identities
Limited state	Comprehensive	Comprehensive worldviews
Sovereign democratic state	Theocratic	Nondemocratic political ideologies
FREE EXERCISE		
Freedom of association	Group coherence	Identificatory associations
	Group competence	Expert-based associations
Negative freedom	Preference, commitments, and projects	Any kind of individual preference, commitment, and project
Special concern (1)	Integrity-protecting commitment: Obligation	Secular conscience
Special concern (2)	Integrity-protecting commitment: Identity	Cultural minorities

obvious that, even if my disaggregated account of religion is accepted, there will remain broad disagreement about which substantive rights religious and nonreligious citizens and groups should have in the liberal state. In an attempt to come to terms with the scope and depth of reasonable pluralism about liberal justice itself, I presented liberal theory as a dualist normative theory. I described fundamental questions about whether a state is liberal at all as questions of liberal *legitimacy*. A state is legitimate, I argued, if it meets a number of desiderata concerning the justification of its constitutional framework, the inclusiveness of its political arrangements, and its entrenchment of key liberal principles. But agreement on the basic foundations of this minimal secularism is compatible with large disagreements about justice, and minimal secularism can accommodate both a progressive liberal state (Secularia) and a conservative liberal state (Divinitia).

Moving next to more specific questions about the *justice* of specific laws—in particular, laws granting special exemptions to some individuals and groups—I have allowed for substantive yet reasonable disagreement. My preferred conception of liberal justice allows only a restricted scope for individual exemptions from general laws, in particular when these exemptions undermine the rights of others. Some collective exemptions are also compatible with my theory of justice, but only insofar as exempted groups are voluntary associations and have robust coherence and competence interests—two conditions that, put together, can justify group rights against their own members. But I am prepared to accept that this conception of justice is only one among a family of reasonable conceptions of liberal justice. There is more permissible variation in the justice of state-religion relations, it turns out, than most Western liberals have so far recognized. This, I hope, is another response to those who worry that liberalism, far from being a potentially universal framework for the democratic and fair resolution of conflicts about religion, is in fact the sectarian, comprehensive ideology of Western progressives—the religion of liberals.

NOTES

ACKNOWLEDGMENTS

INDEX

Notes

1. Liberal Egalitarianism and the Critique of Religion

1. Ronald Dworkin, *Religion without God* (Cambridge, MA: Harvard University Press, 2013); Christopher Eisgruber and Lawrence Sager, *Religious Freedom and the Constitution* (Cambridge, MA: Harvard University Press, 2007); Charles Taylor and Jocelyn Maclure, *Secularism and Freedom of Conscience* (Cambridge, MA: Harvard University Press, 2011); Micah Schwartzman, "What if Religion Is Not Special?," *University of Chicago Law Review* 79, no. 1351 (2012); Micah Schwartzman, "Religion, Equality, and Anarchy," in *Religion in Liberal Political Philosophy,* ed. Cécile Laborde and Aurélia Bardon (Oxford: Oxford University Press, 2017); Jonathan Quong, *Liberalism without Perfection* (Oxford: Oxford University Press, 2011).

2. John Locke, *A Letter concerning Toleration,* reprinted in *A Letter concerning Toleration in Focus,* ed. John Horton and Susan Mendus (London: Routledge, 1991), 17.

3. Amy Gutmann, *Identity in Democracy* (Princeton: Princeton University Press, 2003); Gutmann, "Religion and State in the United States: A Defense of Two-Way Protection," in *Obligations of Citizenship and the Demands of Faith*, ed. Nancy L. Rosenblum (Princeton: Princeton University Press, 2000), 127–164.

4. Talal Asad, *Genealogies of Religion: Discipline and Reasons of Power in Christianity and Islam* (Baltimore: Johns Hopkins University Press, 1993); Asad, "Thinking about Religious Belief and Politics," in *Cambridge Companion to Religious Studies*, ed. Robert Orsi (New York: Cambridge University Press, 2012); William T. Cavanaugh, *The Myth of Religious Violence: Secular Ideology and the Roots of Modern Conflict* (New York: Oxford University Press, 2009); Stanley Fish, "Mission Impossible: Setting the Just Bounds between Church and State," in *Law and Religion: A Critical Anthology*, ed. Stephen M. Feldman (New York: NYU Press, 2000), 383–410; Tim Fitzgerald, *The Ideology of Religious Studies* (Oxford: Oxford University Press, 2005); Saba Mahmood, "Religious Reason and Secular Affect," *Critical Inquiry* 35, no. 4 (Summer 2009): 836–862; Mahmood, *Politics of Piety: The Islamic Revival and the Feminist Subject* (Princeton: Princeton University Press, 2005); Elizabeth Shakman Hurd, *Beyond Religious Freedom: The New Global Politics of Religion* (Princeton: Princeton University Press, 2015); Stephen D. Smith, "Discourse in the Dusk: The Twilight of Religious Freedom," *Harvard Law Review* 122, no. 1869 (2009); Smith, *The Disenchantment of Secular Discourse* (Cambridge, MA: Harvard University Press, 2010); Winnifred Fallers Sullivan, *The Impossibility of Religious Freedom* (Princeton: Princeton University Press, 2005); Winnifred Fallers Sullivan, Elizabeth Shakman Hurd, Saba Mahmood, and Peter G. Danchin, eds., *The Politics of Religious Freedom* (Chicago: University of Chicago Press, 2015).

5. Fish, "Mission Impossible."

6. John Rawls, *Political Liberalism* (New York: Columbia University Press, 1996), xxiii–xxx, 148–149, 154, 159, 303–304.

7. Texts I have found useful include these: Jeffrey R. Collins, "Redeeming the Enlightenment: New Histories of Religious Toleration," *Journal of Modern History* 81 (September 2009): 607–636; Benjamin Kaplan, *Divided by Faith: Religious Conflict and the Practice of Toleration in Early Modern Europe* (Cambridge, MA: Harvard University Press, 2007); Ian Hunter, "Religious Freedom in Early Modern Germany: Theology, Philosophy and Legal Casuistry,"

South Atlantic Quarterly 113, nos. 37, 39 (2014); John Dunn, *The Political Thought of John Locke* (Cambridge: Cambridge University Press, 1969); Cavanaugh, *Myth of Religious Violence.*

8. Kaplan, *Divided by Faith,* 356.

9. From an abundant literature, see, e.g., Gil Anidjar, "Secularism," *Critical Inquiry* 33, no. 1 (Autumn 2006): 52–77; Joseph A. Massad, *Islam in Liberalism* (Chicago: Chicago University Press, 2015).

10. Mark Lilla, *The Stillborn God: Religion, Politics, and the Modern West* (New York: Vintage Books, 2008).

11. Saba Mahmood and Peter Danchin, "Immunity or Regulation? Antinomies of Religious Freedom," *South Atlantic Quarterly* 113, no. 1 (Winter 2014): 129–158. See also Nehal Bhuta, "Two Concepts of Religious Freedom in the European Court of Human Rights," *South Atlantic Quarterly* 113, no. 1 (2014): 9–35.

12. For a powerful recent study, see Saba Mahmood, *Religious Difference in a Secular Age* (Princeton: Princeton University Press, 2016).

13. In a discussion of whether it is acceptable for the London Jews Free School to use an ethnic criterion in its admission policy, for example, Peter Danchin writes that "as a matter of justice, neither position seems entirely satisfactory"—but it is unclear why his own appeal to justice is exempt from the *aporias* of liberalism that his article exposes so carefully. Peter G. Danchin, "Religious Freedom as a Technology of Modern Secular Governance," in *Institutionalizing Rights and Religion: Competing Supremacies,* ed. Leora Batnitzky and Hanoch Dagan (Cambridge: Cambridge University Press, 2017), 184–205. Another common example of smuggled normative criteria is when liberal politicians are criticized for disparaging Islam as radically incompatible with liberalism. In taking such a view, Elizabeth Shakman Hurd writes, liberalism "fails to acknowledge and engage alternative forms of religious accommodation, such as the clerical moderates in postrevolutionary Iran. Neglecting these forms of non-theocratic politics gives way to ideologues like Khomeini who seek to dissolve the boundary between public and private. . . . Yet this usurpation of public-private divide is historically foreign to Muslim-majority societies." In this kind of argument, what is doing the normative work is the rejection of theocracy, and the distinction between public and private—these are basic liberal criteria. Elizabeth Shakman Hurd, *The Politics of Secularism in International Relations* (Princeton: Princeton University Press, 2008), 72.

14. J. Judd Owen, "Church and State in Stanley Fish's Antiliberalism," *American Political Science Review* 93, no. 4 (December 1999): 911–924; Nancy Fraser, "Foucault on Modern Power: Empirical Insights and Normative Confusions," *Praxis International* 1, no. 3 (1981): 272–287. Saba Mahmood is one of the few critics to explicitly recognize the internal normative potential of liberal secularism. As she puts it, "Secularism is not something that can be done away with any more than modernity can be. . . . To critique a particular normative regime is not to reject or condemn it; rather, by analyzing its regulatory and productive dimensions, one only deprives it of innocence and neutrality so as to craft, perhaps, a different future. Insomuch as secularism is one of the enabling conditions of religious conflict today, it behooves us to understand its paradoxical operations so as to mitigate its discriminatory effects" (*Religious Difference in a Secular Age*, 21, 22). She later clarifies: "My own argument may be read . . . as an assessment that denies the possibility that religious minorities could be treated equally in secular liberal polities. This does not, however, capture the argumentative arc of this book. If majoritarian prejudice is one side of secular liberal law, then the other is its promise of civil and political equality for all citizens irrespective of their religious status. Minorities often contest the discriminatory practices of secular law through the same legal instruments that enshrine majoritarian privilege" (176).

15. For the ideas of this paragraph, I have drawn on Wilfred Cantwell Smith, *The Meaning and End of Religion* (Minneapolis: Fortress Press, 1991 [1962]); Jonathan Z. Smith, "Religion, Religions, Religious," in *Critical Terms in Religious Studies*, ed. Mark Taylor (Chicago: University of Chicago Press, 1998), 269–284; Brent Nongbri, *Before Religion* (New Haven: Yale University Press, 2013); Winnifred Fallers Sullivan, *Paying the Words Extra: Religious Discourse in the Supreme Court of the United States* (Cambridge, MA: Harvard University Press, 1994); Talal Asad, *Formations of the Secular: Christianity, Islam, Modernity* (Palo Alto, CA: Stanford University Press, 2003); Jonathan Z. Smith, *Relating Religion: Essays in the Study of Religions* (Chicago: University of Chicago Press, 2004); Fitzgerald, *Ideology of Religious Studies;* Fred Donner, *Muhammad and the Believers: At the Origins of Islam* (Cambridge, MA: Belknap Press of Harvard University Press, 2010).

16. Richard S. Dunn, *The Age of Religious Wars: 1559–1715* (New York: Norton, 1979); Cavanaugh, *Myth of Religious Violence.*

17. John Locke, *Letter on Toleration* (Oxford: Clarendon Press, 1968), 68.

18. S. N. Balagangadhara, *The Heathen in His Blindness: Asia, the West, and the Dynamic of Religion* (Leiden: Brill, 1994); Richard King, *Orientalism and Religion: Post-Colonial Theory, India and the "Mystic East"* (New York: Routledge, 1999); Arvind-Pal S. Mandair, *Religion and the Specter of the West: Sikhism, India, Postcoloniality, and the Politics of Translation* (New York: Columbia University Press, 2009); Tomoko Masuzawa, *The Invention of World Religions: Or, How European Universalism Was Preserved in the Language of Pluralism* (Chicago: University of Chicago Press, 2005).

19. Smith, *Meaning and End of Religion*.

20. Fitzgerald, *Ideology of Religious Studies*. For an example of a substantive approach to religion, see also Martin Riesebrodt, *The Promise of Salvation: A Theory of Religion* (Chicago: University of Chicago Press, 2010). For influential functional approaches, see Emile Durkheim, *The Elementary Forms of the Religious Life: A Study in Religious Psychology* (1915); Clifford Geertz, *The Interpretation of Cultures* (New York: Basic Books, 1973).

21. Hurd, *Beyond Religious Freedom*, 6.

22. Asad, *Genealogies of Religion*, 28.

23. Asad, "Religious Belief and Politics."

24. Kirstie McClure, "Difference, Diversity and the Limits of Toleration," *Political Theory* 18, no. 3 (August 1990): 361–391, at 367–368.

25. Asad, *Genealogies of Religion*, 47. See also his "Religious Belief and Politics."

26. Mahmood, "Religious Reason and Secular Affect."

27. James Boyd White, "Talking about Religion in the Language of the Law: Impossible but Necessary," *Marquette Law Review* 81, no. 2 (Winter 1998): 177–202, at 186. See also William P. Marshall, "Religion as Ideas; Religion as Identity," *Journal of Contemporary Legal Issues* 7 (1996): 385–406.

28. Sullivan, *Impossibility of Religious Freedom*, 8.

29. As Yvonne Sherwood has noted, there is something paradoxical about this Protestant construal of freedom of religion. Religious belief has to be sufficiently weighty to count as a stringent obligation instead of a mere preference or opinion; yet it cannot be so compelling as to make the individual unfree—unable to critically reflect on her beliefs. This is what Sherwood vividly calls "the unbearable lightness of belief." Yvonne Sherwood, "On the Freedom of the Concepts of Religion and Belief," in Sullivan et al., *Politics of Religious Freedom*, 29–44. For stimulating Foucauldian reflections about religion and

freedom, see Wendy Brown, "Religious Freedom's Oxymoronic Edge," in Sullivan et al., *Politics of Religious Freedom*, 324–334.

30. Charles Taylor, *The Secular Age* (Cambridge, MA: Belknap Press of Harvard University Press, 2007).

31. Michael Sandel, "Religious Liberty: Freedom of Choice or Freedom of Conscience?," in *Secularism and Its Critics,* ed. Rajeev Bhargava (Oxford: Oxford University Press, 1998).

32. Mahmood, *Politics of Piety.* See also her "Religious Reason and Secular Affect."

33. Webb Keane, "What Is Religious Freedom Supposed to Free?," in Sullivan et al., *Politics of Religious Freedom*, 57–64, at 61.

34. Frits Staal, *Rules without Meaning,* cited in Jeff Spinner-Halev, "Hinduism, Christianity and Liberal Religious Toleration," *Political Theory* 3, no. 1 (February 2005): 28–57, at 36. Spinner-Halev's article offers a penetrating and pioneering analysis of what I call here the Protestant critique of liberalism.

35. For a Catholic-influenced critique of the Protestant language of the law, see White, "Talking about Religion." White points out that for many people the religious life is not about individual assent to creedal propositions but, rather, about gathering together in community, through rituals and practices— it is often the religious practices that are least understood (funerary and wedding rites, carol singing, prayers) that are adhered to most stoutly.

36. Sullivan, *Impossibility of Religious Freedom*. In his ethnography of the French Conseil d'Etat, *The Making of Laws,* Bruno Latour describes the effect that law has on life as being analogous to faxing pizza—the law flattens life, remaking it for law's own purposes. This tragic dimension of law has been thoughtfully explored in Sullivan's important work. For another illustration of the mismatch between legal tools and the unruly lived experience of religion, see Benjamin L. Berger, *Law's Religion: Religious Difference and the Claims of Constitutionalism* (Toronto: Toronto University Press, 2015). For discussion on this theme, see Cécile Laborde and Winnifred Fallers Sullivan, "Dialogue on the Impossibility of Religious Freedom," *Quaderni di diritto e politica ecclesiastica* (Rome), no. 1 (April 2013): 5–17.

37. Winnifred Fallers Sullivan, "New Discourse and Practice in Law and Religion," in Feldman, *Law and Religion,* 35–53, at 39.

38. Sullivan, *Impossibility of Religious Freedom,* 10.

39. Asad, *Formations of the Secular.* Asad's target is secularism, but what he means by secularism—state neutrality toward religion and the protection

of individual freedom of belief—is what I call liberalism. In Chapter 4, I shall explore the relationship between liberalism and secularism in more detail.

40. Winnifred Fallers Sullivan, Robert Yelle, and Mateo Taussig-Rubbo, eds., *After Secular Law* (Palo Alto, CA: Stanford University Press, 2011).

41. Winnifred Sullivan, "Requiem for the Establishment Clause," *Constitutional Commentary* 25 (2008): 309, 315–316; Winnifred Fallers Sullivan and Lori G. Beaman, eds., *Varieties of Religious Establishment* (London: Ashgate, 2013).

42. Hurd, *Beyond Religious Freedom*.

43. Hussein Ali Agrama, *Questioning Secularism: Islam, Sovereignty, and the Rule of Law in Modern Egypt* (Chicago: Chicago University Press, 2012); Markus Dressler and Arvind-Pal S. Mandair, *Secularism and Religion-Making* (New York: Oxford University Press, 2011).

44. Paul F. Campos, "Secular Fundamentalism," *Columbia Law Review* 94, no. 6 (October 1994): 1814–1827; Fish, "Mission Impossible"; Steven Smith, "The Pluralist Predicament: Contemporary Theorizing in the Law of Religious Freedom," *University of San Diego School of Law, Public Law and Legal Theory Research Paper Series* (2004).

45. Carl Schmitt, *Political Theology: Four Chapters on the Concept of Sovereignty* (Chicago: University of Chicago Press, 2006). As William Cavanaugh has powerfully illustrated, the fact that Christianity is construed as a religion, whereas nationalism is not, ensures that the Christian's public and lethal loyalty belongs to the nation-state. Cavanaugh, *Myth of Religious Violence*.

46. In previous work I introduced the label "egalitarian theories of religious freedom." I am now inclined to use the broader term "liberal egalitarianism" because it addresses questions both of religious freedom (free exercise) and of the secularity or neutrality of the state (nonestablishment). The value of nonestablishment is not entirely derived from free exercise: the secular nature of the state protects a range of other values, as we shall see in Chapter 4.

47. In this sense, liberal egalitarianism is not a departure from traditional liberalism but instead a clarification of its claims to *equal* liberty. Liberal egalitarianism is in the same broad family of views as Rawls's political liberalism, but it focuses most specifically on the place of religion in the liberal state. It clarifies the crucial point that while religion has a special place in liberal theory, it is not a uniquely special place. I have benefited from discussions with Aurélia Bardon on this point.

48. Ronald Dworkin, "Liberalism," in *A Matter of Principle* (Oxford: Clarendon Press, 1985), 191.

49. For a magisterial historical survey, see Rainer Forst, *Toleration in Conflict: Past and Present* (Cambridge: Cambridge University Press, 2011).

50. John Rawls, *A Theory of Justice* (Cambridge, MA: Belknap Press of Harvard University Press, 1971), 205–206.

51. Jeremy Waldron, "Liberalism, Political and Comprehensive," in *Handbook of Political Theory,* ed. Gerald F. Gaus and Chandran Kukathas (London: Sage, 2004), 92.

52. David A. J. Richards, *Identity and the Case for Gay Rights: Race, Gender, Religion as Analogies* (Chicago: University of Chicago Press, 1999). See also his more general liberal egalitarian interpretation of the U.S. religion clauses in Richards, *Toleration and the Constitution* (New York: Oxford University Press, 1986).

53. Rawls, *A Theory of Justice,* 206.

54. Ronald Dworkin, *Justice for Hedgehogs* (Cambridge, MA: Harvard University Press, 2011), 376.

55. This shift is well documented in Noah Feldman, "From Liberty to Equality: The Transformation of the Establishment Clause," *California Law Review* 90, no. 673 (May 2002): 1–59; and Ira C. Lupu and Robert Tuttle, "The Distinctive Place of Religious Entities in Our Constitutional Order," *Villanova Law Review* 46, no. 5 (2001).

56. For an excellent elucidation of the logic of liberal egalitarianism and religion, in relation to alternative positions both in U.S. constitutional law and in liberal political theory, see Schwartzman, "What if Religion Is Not Special?"; and Schwartzman, "Religion, Equality, and Anarchy."

57. Note that commitment to the unique specialness of religion does not necessarily lead to the "two-way protection" view of separationism. Consider two other positions. One influential position is that of "accommodationists." Michael McConnell, for example, has argued that religious freedom is unique and distinctive; it is the "first freedom" in the liberal state. Religious freedom cannot be analogized with, or reduced to, other freedoms, as it serves to protect a uniquely special human good, an autonomous sphere of conscience, ritual, and community, from state interference and regulation. The Establishment Clause is derived from the Free Exercise Clause and does not have separate foundations. It does not forbid state recognition, endorsement, and promotion

of religion, as long as there is no coercion on religious grounds. Michael W. McConnell, "Accommodation of Religion," *Supreme Court Review* (1985): 1–59. At the other end of the spectrum, we find "secularists." Some argue that religion is too valuable for the state to be allowed to meddle with it. See Andrew Koppelman, "Corruption of Religion and the Establishment Clause," *William and Mary Law Review* 50, no. 1831 (2009). Others, such as some French commentators on *laïcité,* focus on the "dark side of religion" and seek to protect the state from religious interference and influence. Cécile Laborde, *Critical Republicanism: The Hijab Controversy and Political Philosophy* (Oxford: Oxford University Press, 2008). For a useful taxonomy of different theories, see Schwartzman, "Religion, Equality, and Anarchy."

58. Eisgruber and Sager, *Religious Freedom.*

59. Ludwig Wittgenstein, *Philosophical Investigations,* 2nd ed. (Oxford: Basil Blackwell, 1958), 31–32, paras. 66–67. For a good general discussion, see Victoria S. Harrison, "The Pragmatics of Defining Religion in a Multi-Cultural World," *International Journal of Philosophy of Religion* 59 (2006): 133–152.

60. Kent Greenawalt, "Religion as a Concept in Constitutional Law," *California Law Review* 72, no. 5 (September 1984): 753–816. See also George C. Freeman, "The Misguided Search for the Constitutional Definition of 'Religion,'" *Georgetown Law Journal* 71 (1982–1983): 1519–1565; and Eduardo Peñaver, "The Concept of Religion," *Yale Law Journal* 107, no. 3 (December 1997): 791–822.

61. Andrew Koppelman, "Religion's Specialized Specialness," *University of Chicago Law Review Dialogue* 79 (2013): 71–83, at 78; Koppelman, "Neutrality and the Religion Analogy," paper presented to the APSA Annual Meeting, Washington, DC, August 28–September 1, 2014 (available at http://papers.ssrn.com/sol3/papers.cfm?abstract_id=2454399). See also Andrew Koppelman, *Defending American Religious Neutrality* (Cambridge, MA: Harvard University Press, 2013).

62. Ronald Dworkin, *Freedom's Law: The Moral Reading of the American Constitution* (Oxford: Oxford University Press, 1996), 78. "The key issue in applying these abstract principles to particular political controversies is not one of reference but one of interpretation, which is very different."

63. George Letsas, "Accommodating What Needn't Be Special," *Law and Ethics of Human Rights* 10, no. 2 (2016): 319–340.

64. Ira Lupu and W. Tuttle also draw an illuminating analogy between the treatment of the family and of religion as legal terms: "Just as the definition of 'family' may depend on whether the rule in question is designed to protect settled patterns of cohabitation (in housing law) or the public purse (in welfare benefits law), the legal meaning of 'religion' also depends on the term's function within the relevant legal norm." C. Lupu and Robert W. Tuttle, *Secular Government, Religious People* (Grand Rapids, MI: Eerdmans, 2014), 21–22.

65. Dworkin, *Freedom's Law*, 107. Other interpretive theories of religion in the law include Timothy Macklem, "Faith as a Secular Value," *McGill Law Journal* 45, no. 1 (2000): 1–64; Dworkin, *Religion without God;* Koppelman, "Religion's Specialized Specialness." For a thoughtful piece on U.S. First Amendment jurisprudence, which also introduces both an interpretive (non-semantic) and a polyvalent approach to controversies about religion and the law, see Nelson Tebbe, "Non-Believers," *Virginia Law Review* 97, no. 1111 (2011).

66. Dworkin "Liberalism," in *A Matter of Principle*, 191.

67. I leave aside the question whether the law should avoid religion as a *semantic* category altogether. James Nickel, in an important and pioneering article, "Who Needs Freedom of Religion," *University of Colorado Law Review* 76 (2005): 941–964, has argued that all the values of freedom of religion could be adequately protected under other liberal rights. For some discussion, see my "Religion in the Law: The Disaggregation Approach," *Law and Philosophy* 34, no. 6 (November 2015): 581–600, at 581, and further below in Chapter 6.

68. In Chapter 6, I shall develop this "two-pronged" approach further.

69. Bhuta, "Two Concepts"; Peter Danchin, "Islam in the Secular Nomos of the European Court of Human Rights," *Michigan Journal of International Law* 32, no. 663 (2011); Mahmood and Danchin, "Immunity or Regulation?"; Samuel Moyn, "Religious Freedom and the Fate of Secularism," in *Secularism and Constitutional Democracy,* ed. Jean L. Cohen and Cécile Laborde (New York: Columbia University Press, 2016), 27–46; Christian Joppke, "Pluralism vs. Pluralism: Islam and Christianity in the European Court of Human Rights," in Cohen and Laborde, *Secularism and Constitutional Democracy,* 89–111. Critics see this bias as the unavoidable by-product of Western, statist and Christian technologies of governance: on their view, Article 9 is "poisoned at the root" and structurally unable to accommodate non-Christian minorities. For a nuanced critique of this genealogical determinism, see Jason A. Springs, "Tentacles of the Leviathan? Nationalism, Islamophobia, and the Insufficiency-yet-Indispensability of Human Rights for Religious Freedom

in Contemporary Europe," *Journal of the American Academy of Religion* 84, no. 4 (2016): 1–34. Thanks to Christoph Baumgartner for pointing me to this reference, and for stimulating discussion.

70. Michael Sandel, *Liberalism and the Limits of Justice* (Cambridge: Cambridge University Press, 1982).

71. Sandel, "Religious Liberty."

72. Ronald Dworkin, *Sovereign Virtue* (Cambridge, MA: Harvard University Press, 2000), 81–82.

73. Martin Luther, *Works,* ed. Jaroslav Pelikan (St. Louis: Concordia Publishing House, 1958), 32:112.

74. Compare McClure, "Difference, Diversity," 378: "It is precisely the civil criterion of worldly injury that operates to circumscribe the scope and limits of what might be advanced as an appropriate expression of religious belief and practice in the first place."

75. For critical discussions of French *laïcité* and veiling bans, see Joan Scott, *The Politics of the Veil* (Princeton: Princeton University Press, 2007); John R. Bowen, *Why the French Don't Like Headscarves: Islam, the State, and Public Space* (Princeton: Princeton University Press, 2008); Laborde, *Critical Republicanism;* Catherine Audard, "Pluralisme religieux et égalité: Une critique de la laïcité," in *Etant Donné le Pluralisme,* ed. Marc-Antoine Dilhac and Sophie Guérard de Latour (Paris: Publications de la Sorbonne, 2013), 104–135; Mayanthi Fernando, *The Republic Unsettled: Muslim French and the Contradictions of Secularism* (Durham, NC: Duke University Press, 2014). French *laïcité* works with a rigid conception of the separation between public and private, of the importance of voluntary choice in religion, and thickly cultural notions of citizenship. Liberal approaches, by contrast, are suspicious of the permissibility of direct bans on religious practices. As I shall show in Chapter 6, the hard case for liberals concerns laws of general application that only *indirectly and non-intentionally* burden practice. I shall argue that, in these cases, liberals need a thicker account of the value of religious practice if they are to justify exemptions.

76. For another liberal response to what I call the Protestant critique advanced by Mahmood and others, see Andrew March, "Speech and the Sacred: Does the Defense of Free Speech Rest on a Mistake about Religion?," *Political Theory* 40, no. 3 (June 2012): 318–345.

77. Talal Asad, "Trying to Understand French Secularism," in *Political Theologies: Public Religions in a Postsecular World,* ed. Hent de Vries and

Lawrence Sullivan (New York: Fordham University Press, 2006), 494–526; Agrama, *Questioning Secularism*.

78. Christopher L. Eisgruber and Lawrence G. Sager, "Does It Matter What Religion Is?," *Notre Dame Law Review* 84, no. 2 (2009): 807.

79. Fraser, "Foucault on Modern Power."

80. Danchin, "Religious Freedom as a Technology," 185.

81. Eisgruber and Sager, *Religious Freedom*.

82. For the argument that political liberalism is indeterminate between separation and establishment, see also Cécile Laborde, "Political Liberalism and Religion: On Separation and Establishment," *Journal of Political Philosophy* 21, no. 2 (March 2013): 67–86.

83. Stanley Fish, *The Trouble with Principle* (Cambridge, MA: Harvard University Press, 1999), 157. Kent Greenawalt forcefully makes the general point: "A court orders a state to desegregate its schools, the country goes to war, educational funds are made available equally to men and women. The government has implicitly rejected religious notions that (1) God wishes rigid racial separation, (2) all killing in war violates God's commandments, (3) all women should occupy themselves with domestic tasks. A vast array of laws and policies similarly imply the incorrectness of particular religious views." Kent Greenawalt, "Five Questions about Religion Judges Are Afraid to Ask," in Rosenblum, *Obligations of Citizenship*, 196–244, at 199.

84. Fish, "Mission Impossible," 392.

85. Stephen Lukes, *Liberals and Cannibals: The Implication of Diversity* (New York: Verso Books, 2003), 67.

86. On the religious aspects of Rawls's liberalism, see Paul Weithman, "Does Justice as Fairness Have a Religious Aspect?," in *A Companion to Rawls*, ed. Jon Mandle and David A. Reidy (Oxford: Wiley Blackwell, 2014).

87. Laborde, *Critical Republicanism*.

2. Liberal Egalitarianism and the Exemptions Puzzle

1. Accommodationists such as Michael McConnell argue that religious freedom is basic and distinctive; it is the "first freedom" in the liberal state. Religious freedom cannot be analogized with or reduced to other freedoms, as it serves to protect a uniquely special human good—an autonomous sphere of conscience, ritual, and community—from state interference and regulation.

Michael W. McConnell, "Accommodation of Religion," *Supreme Court Review* (1985): 1–59; McConnell, "The Problem of Singling Out Religion," *DePaul Law Review* 50 (2000): 9–12. For a good critique, see François Boucher, "Exemptions to the Law, Freedom of Religion and Freedom of Conscience in Postsecular Societies," *Philosophy and Public Issues* 3, no. 2 (2013): 159–200. Other accommodationist approaches are found in Douglas Laycock, "Religious Liberty as Liberty," *Journal of Contemporary Legal Issues* 7, no. 313 (1996); Michael Paulsen, "The Priority of God (A Theory of Religious Liberty)," *Pepperdine Law Review* 39, no. 5 (2013); Thomas Berg, "Can Religious Liberty Be Protected as Equality?," *Texas Law Review* 85 (2007); Andrew Koppelman, "Is It Fair to Give Religion Special Treatment?," *University of Illinois Law Review* 571 (2006); Steven D. Smith, "Non-Establishment under God? The Nonsectarian Principle" (University of San Diego Public Law Research Paper No. 04-08, 2004). More generally, and in a European context, see Rex Adhar and Ian Leigh, *Religious Freedom in the Liberal State* (Oxford: Oxford University Press, 2005).

2. See the Introduction.

3. Ronald Dworkin, *Religion without God* (Cambridge, MA: Harvard University Press, 2013), 132–133.

4. This is a distinction Dworkin had introduced in *Justice for Hedgehogs* (Cambridge, MA: Harvard University Press, 2011), 152–157. The terms "general rights" and "special rights" are confusing as they are the same ones used by H. L. A. Hart (and generally accepted) to distinguish rights everyone has, and those one has by virtue of a special relationship (citizen, family, etc.).

5. Dworkin, *Religion without God*, 131.

6. Also in support, see Koppelman, "Is It Fair?," on Dworkin on equality of resources and expensive tastes.

7. Dworkin, *Religion without God*, 132.

8. Ibid., 117.

9. Ibid.

10. Ibid., 125–126.

11. Ibid., 137.

12. Brian Barry, *Culture and Equality: An Egalitarian Critique of Multiculturalism* (Cambridge: Polity Press, 2001); Cécile Laborde, *Critical Republicanism* (Oxford: Oxford University Press, 2008).

13. A justification is "directly" non-neutral if government invokes a particular view of the good to justify some regulation, and it is "indirectly" non-neutral

if government relies on the fact that a majority endorses that particular view of the good (Ronald Dworkin, "Religion without God," unpublished manuscript, December 14, 2011, on file with author). Dworkin presented the original text of *Religion without God* at the Bern Einstein Lectures; see Ronald Dworkin, Einstein Lectures (December 12–14, 2011), archived at http://perma.cc/G9SF -3JDR. He presented a draft to the NYU Colloquium in Legal, Political and Social Philosophy; see Dworkin, "Religion without God," NYU Colloquium in Legal, Political, and Social Philosophy, Working Paper, 2011, archived at http://perma.cc/Y3EB-2T4H. This distinction was removed from the final text, but Dworkin has maintained the reference to "covert" non-neutrality. Ethical independence outlaws "any constraints neutral on its face but whose design covertly assumes some direct or indirect subordination." Dworkin, *Religion without God,* 134. A better expression than "covert," however, might be "inadvertent," as the kind of cases of discrimination that Dworkin has in mind are clearly unintentional. I am grateful to Daniel Sabbagh for this point.

14. Ibid., 136. My emphasis.

15. Ibid., 138–139.

16. On the internal tension between two theories of rights in Dworkin, see Richard Pildes, "Dworkin's Two Conceptions of Rights," *Journal of Legal Studies* 24 (January 2000): 309–315. The "reason-constraining" view denies the state the power to appeal to certain impermissible reasons, typically prejudicial or paternalistic reasons, whereas the "immunities view" demarcates fundamental interests, spheres of belief, and conduct insulated from majoritarian preferences. On this topic, I have benefited from discussions with Matthew Clayton and Guy Aitchison-Cornish.

17. Ronald Dworkin, *Life's Dominion: An Argument about Abortion, Euthanasia and Individual Freedom* (New York: Vintage Books, 1993).

18. Two recent articles have expanded on, and responded to, this criticism of Dworkin (which I first developed in Cécile Laborde, "Dworkin on Freedom of Religion without Religion," *University of Boston Law Review* 94 [2014]: 1255–1271). Paul Bou-Habib, in "Reconstructing Religion without God" (unpublished manuscript, on file with author), makes the case that neutrality of justification is not sufficient and that Dworkin should be independently committed to negative freedom (in matters touching on individual integrity or authenticity). Matthew Clayton, in "Is Ethical Independence Sufficient?," in *Religion in Liberal Political Philosophy,* ed. Cécile Laborde and Aurélia Bardon (Oxford:

Oxford University Press, 2017), argues that Dworkin's views should be situated within his broader account of political morality, and his theory of religious freedom should be integrated with his other principles of political morality such as distributive justice, political legitimacy, or the value of community.

19. Christopher L. Eisgruber and Lawrence G. Sager, *Religious Freedom and the Constitution* (Cambridge, MA: Harvard University Press, 2007).

20. Ibid., 6.

21. Ibid., 202–203.

22. See, for example, Barry, *Culture and Equality;* William Marshall, "The Case against the Constitutionally Compelled Free Exercise Exemption," *Journal of Law and Religion* 7, no. 2 (1989): 363–414.

23. Eisgruber and Sager, *Religious Freedom,* 202–203.

24. Ibid., 90.

25. McConnell, "Singling Out Religion."

26. *Fraternal Order of Police Newark Lodge v. City of Newark,* 170 F.3d 359 (3d Cir. 1999).

27. Eisgruber and Sager, *Religious Freedom,* 89.

28. Ibid., 14–15.

29. Ibid., 92.

30. Ibid., 52.

31. Ibid., 59.

32. Peter Westen, "The Empty Idea of Equality," *Harvard Law Review* 95, no. 3 (1982): 537–596; Joseph Raz, *The Morality of Freedom* (Oxford: Clarendon Press, 1986), 240; Kent Greenawalt, "How Empty Is the Idea of Equality?," *Columbia Law Review* 83 (June 1983): 1167.

33. Adhar and Leigh, *Religious Freedom,* 116.

34. McConnell, "Singling Out Religion."

35. For different positions, see Véronique Munoz-Dardé, "Is the Family to Be Abolished Then?," *Proceedings of the Aristotelian Society* 99 (1999); Elizabeth Brake, "Minimal Marriage: What Political Liberalism Implies for Marriage Law," *Ethics* 120 (2010): 302–337; Stephen Macedo, *Just Married: Same-Sex Couples, Monogamy, and the Future of Marriage* (Princeton: Princeton University Press, 2015); Clare Chambers, "The Marriage-Free State," *Proceedings of the Aristotelian Society* 113, no. 2 (2013): 123–143; Greg Walker, "Rawls, Political Liberalism, and the Family: A Reply to Matthew B. O'Brien," *British Journal of*

American Legal Studies 3 (2014): 37–70; Walker, "Public Reason Liberalism and Sex-Neutral Marriage: A Response to Francis J. Beckwith," *Ratio Juris* 28 (2015): 486–503.

36. In a separate paper, "Equal Liberty, Non-Establishment and Religious Freedom," *Journal of Legal Theory* 20, no. 1 (2014), I show that Eisgruber and Sager take it for granted that religious interests should be protected, before they look for a relevant comparator in existing law. This approach, however, remains too wedded to U.S. doctrine: the reasoning is *ad hoc* and does not reflect on the justness of existing arrangements, i.e., the baseline problem. So it does not get to the heart of the normative questions I raise here. For other commentary on the theory of equal liberty, see Berg, "Can Religious Liberty Be Protected"; Abner S. Greene, "Three Theories of Religious Equality . . . And of Exemptions," *Texas Law Review* 87, no. 5 (2009): 963–1007; Kent Greenawalt, *Religion and the Constitution*, vol. 1, *Free Exercise and Fairness* (Princeton: Princeton University Press, 2006); Greenawalt, "How Does 'Equal Liberty' Fare in Relation to Other Approaches to the Religion Clauses?," *Texas Law Review* 85, no. 5 (2007): 1217–1246; Koppelman, "Is It Fair?"; Andrew Koppelman, "Conscience, Volitional Necessity, and Religious Exemptions," *Legal Theory* 15, no. 3 (2009): 215–244; Ira C. Lupu and Robert W. Tuttle, "The Limits of Equal Liberty as a Theory of Religious Freedom," *Texas Law Review* 85, no. 5 (2007): 1247–1272; McConnell, "Singling Out Religion"; Stuart White, "Religious Exemptions: An Egalitarian Demand?," *Law and Ethics of Human Rights* 6, no. 1 (2012): 97–118; Jeremy Webber, "Understanding the Religion in Freedom of Religion," in *Law and Religion in Theoretical and Historical Context*, ed. Peter Cane, Carolyn Evans, and Zöe Robinson (Cambridge: Cambridge University Press, 2008), 26–43; Lisa Schultz Bressman, "Accommodation and Equal Liberty," *William and Mary Law Review* 42, no. 3 (2001): 1007–1051; Alan Patten, "The Normative Logic of Religious Liberty," *Journal of Political Philosophy*, early view, December 1, 2016.

37. Following Kasper Lippert-Rasmussen, I define discrimination as differential treatment of individuals based on their membership in socially salient groups that potentially determines the allocation of scarce goods among them. Kasper Lippert-Rasmussen, *Born Free and Equal? A Philosophical Enquiry into the Nature of Discrimination* (Oxford: Oxford University Press, 2014), 30. Discrimination is not necessarily wrongful, as I shall suggest in the rest of this book. For example, some discrimination on religious grounds by

religious associations is permissible (Chapter 5); as is merely indirect discrimination that incidentally burdens religious believers (Chapter 6). On this topic, I have benefited from helpful discussions with Daniel Sabbagh.

38. Unless it can be shown that peyote is more dangerous than alcohol. Eisgruber and Sager, *Religious Freedom*, 92–94.

39. Christopher L. Eisgruber and Lawrence G. Sager, "The Vulnerability of Conscience: The Constitutional Basis for Protecting Religious Conduct," *University of Chicago Law Review* 61, no. 4 (1994): 1245–1313, at 1266.

40. Eisgruber and Sager, *Religious Freedom*, 101.

41. Koppelman, "Is It Fair?" For Taylor's notion of strong evaluation, see Charles Taylor, "What's Wrong with Negative Liberty?," in *Philosophy and the Human Sciences: Philosophical Papers* (Cambridge: Cambridge University Press, 1985), 211–229.

42. Eisgruber and Sager, *Religious Freedom*, 113–114. See *United States v. Seeger* (2rd Cir. 1964) and *Welsh v. United States* (1970). In *Welsh*, the Court noted that what is necessary is "that one's opposition to war stemmed from one moral, ethical, or religious beliefs about what is right and wrong and that these beliefs be held with the strength of traditional religious convictions."

43. Eisgruber and Sager, *Religious Freedom*, 91.

44. Ibid., 101, 104.

45. See, for example, the essays in Paul Kelly, ed., *Multiculturalism Reconsidered: "Culture and Equality" and Its Critics* (Cambridge: Polity, 2002); and, for a critique of "luck multiculturalism," Jonathan Quong, "Cultural Exemptions, Expensive Tastes and Equal Opportunities," *Journal of Applied Philosophy* 23, no. 1 (2006): 53–71.

46. Andrew Shorten, "Are There Rights to Institutional Exemptions?," *Journal of Social Philosophy* 46, no. 2 (2015): 242–263.

47. Barry, *Culture and Equality*, 36–37; Ronald Dworkin, *Sovereign Virtue: The Theory and Practice of Equality* (Cambridge, MA: Harvard University Press, 2000), 297. For alternative views, see Jonathan Wolff, "Disability among Equals," in Kimberly Brownlee and Adam Cureton, eds., *Disability and Disadvantage* (Oxford: Oxford University Press, 2011); Miklos Zala, *The Devout and the Disabled: Religious and Disability Accommodation as Human Variation*, unpublished manuscript, on file with author.

48. Peter Jones, "Religious Exemptions and Distributive Justice," in Laborde and Bardon, *Religion in Liberal Political Philosophy*. In the version of

the paper presented at the RAPT conference in London (June 15, 2015), Peter Jones forcefully argued that the Sherbert case illustrates the possibility of a double wrong: the nondistributive wrong being denied the religious freedom one is constitutionally entitled to and the distributive wrong of having been accorded less religious freedom than others.

49. Christopher Eisgruber and Lawrence Sager, "Equal Regard," in *Law and Religion: A Critical Anthology*, ed. S. Feldman (New York: NYU Press, 2001). See also Eisgruber and Sager, "The Vulnerability of Conscience."

50. Lawrence Sager, "Why Churches (and, Possibly, the Tarpon Bay Women's Blue Water Fishing Club) Can Discriminate," in *The Rise of Corporate Religious Liberty*, ed. Micah Schwartzman, Chad Flanders, and Zoe Robinson (Oxford: Oxford University Press, 2016), 77–102.

51. Eisgruber and Sager, *Religious Freedom*, 64–65; *Boy Scouts of America v. Dale*, 530 U.S. 640 (2000).

52. Sager, "Why Churches . . . Can Discriminate," 86, 88.

53. Eisgruber and Sager also suggest that there might be a strategic rationale for carving more extensive protections for churches than would be allowed by the strict demands of equal liberty. It is that judges are prone to prejudicial determinations about the risk of unfair discrimination by religious groups, and undue interference with employment relationships that are essential to associational autonomy. Eisgruber and Sager, *Religious Freedom*, 249–252. I say more about this "hands-off" rationale in Chapter 5.

54. John Rawls, *A Theory of Justice* (Oxford: Oxford University Press, 1972), secs. 32–35; Martha Nussbaum, *Liberty of Conscience* (New York: Basic Books, 2008).

55. Paul Bou-Habib, "A Theory of Religious Accommodation," *Journal of Applied Philosophy* 23, no. 1 (2006): 109–126.

56. Gerald Gaus, *Justificatory Liberalism: An Essay on Epistemology and Political Theory* (Oxford: Oxford University Press, 1996), 175; Chandran Kukathas, *The Liberal Archipelago: A Theory of Freedom and Diversity* (Oxford: Oxford University Press, 2003), 55.

57. Quong, "Cultural Exemptions."

58. A good is lexically prior if no small sacrifice of it can be incurred for the (even great) gain of another good. Rawls argues that freedom of conscience can never be traded against a substantial improvement of socioeconomic resources. For discussion, see, e.g., Robert S. Taylor, "Rawls's Defense of the

Priority of Liberty: A Kantian Reconstruction," *Philosophy and Public Affairs* 31, no. 3 (Summer 2003): 246–271.

59. Bou-Habib, "Theory of Religious Accommodation." For a different reading of Rawls on freedom of religion, see Andrew Koppelman, "A Rawlsian Defense of Special Treatment for Religion," in Laborde and Bardon, *Religion in Liberal Political Philosophy.*

60. Jocelyn Maclure and Charles Taylor, *Secularism and Freedom of Conscience* (Cambridge, MA: Harvard University Press, 2011), 76.

61. Ibid., 94. For Rawls, "a moral conception is . . . comprehensive when it includes conceptions of what is of value in human life, and ideals of personal character, as well as ideals of friendship and of familial and associational relationships, and much else that is to inform our conduct, and in the limit to our life as a whole." John Rawls, *Political Liberalism* (New York: Columbia University Press, 1996), 13.

62. Maclure and Taylor, *Secularism,* 96.

63. Charles Taylor, *Sources of the Self* (Cambridge, MA: Harvard University Press, 1989).

64. They explicitly draw on Paul Bou-Habib's "A Theory of Religious Accommodation."

65. Martin Luther, *Works,* ed. Jaroslav Pelikan (St Louis: Concordia Publishing House, 1958), 32:112.

66. Ronald Dworkin, Einstein Lectures (December 12–14, 2011), archived at http://perma.cc/G9SF-3JDR.

67. Charles Taylor, "What's Wrong with Negative Liberty?," in *Philosophy and the Human Sciences: Philosophical Papers* (Cambridge: Cambridge University Press, 1985), 211–229.

68. Maclure and Taylor, *Secularism,* 81.

69. I originally developed this line of criticism in "Protecting Freedom of Religion in the Secular Age." Jocelyn Maclure has replied to this line of criticism in his paper "Conscience, Religion and Exemptions: An Egalitarian View" (unpublished paper, on file with author). I shall say more about duties, obligation, and piety in Chapter 6.

70. A version of this interpretive critique (of Taylor and Maclure, as well as of Laborde, "Protecting Freedom of Religion") can be found in George Letsas, "Accommodating What Needn't Be Special," *Law and Ethics of Human Rights* 10, no. 2 (2016): 319–340.

71. Charles Taylor, "The Politics of Recognition," in *Multiculturalism: Examining the Politics of Recognition*, ed. Amy Gutmann (Princeton: Princeton University Press, 1994 [1992]); Will Kymlicka, *Multicultural Citizenship: A Liberal Theory of Minority Rights* (Oxford: Oxford University Press, 1995); Joe Carens, *Culture, Citizenship, and Community: A Contextual Exploration of Justice as Evenhandedness* (Oxford: Oxford University Press, 2000); Alan Patten, *Equal Recognition: The Moral Foundations of Minority Rights* (Princeton: Princeton University Press, 2014).

3. Liberal Egalitarianism and the State Neutrality Puzzle

1. An important alternative view, which I do not discuss here, is found in Andrew Koppelman, *Defending American Religious Neutrality* (Cambridge, MA: Harvard University Press, 2013). Koppelman shows that commitment to neutrality is not incompatible with special treatment of religion. For some discussion, see Cécile Laborde, "Religion and the Law: The Disaggregation Approach," *Law and Philosophy* 34, no. 6 (2015): 581–600.

2. Ronald Dworkin, "Liberalism," in *A Matter of Principle* (Cambridge, MA: Harvard University Press, 1985), 191.

3. I borrow the notion of restricted state neutrality from Steven Wall, "Neutralism for Perfectionists: The Case of Restricted State Neutrality," *Ethics* 120 (January 2010): 232–256.

4. Ronald Dworkin, *Freedom's Law: The Moral Reading of the American Constitution* (Cambridge, MA: Harvard University Press, 2011).

5. Ronald Dworkin, *Religion without God* (Cambridge, MA: Harvard University Press, 2013), 108.

6. Ronald Dworkin, *Justice for Hedgehogs* (Cambridge, MA: Harvard University Press, 2011), 376.

7. Micah Schwartzman, "Religion, Equality, and Public Reason," *Boston University Law Review* 94, no. 1321 (2014); John Inazu, "The Limits of Integrity," *Law and Contemporary Problems* 75 (2012): 181–200, at 191–195.

8. Dworkin, *Religion without God*, 137–147.

9. Dworkin, *Justice for Hedgehogs*, 368. My emphasis.

10. For a good discussion of this ambivalence, see Paul Bou-Habib, "Reconstructing Religion without God," unpublished manuscript, on file with the author.

11. Dworkin, "Liberalism," in *A Matter of Principle*, 191.

12. He argued that both believers in God and atheists can share a religious attitude, namely, one of awe at the ineffable mystery and beauty of human life and of the universe. Dworkin, *Religion without God*, 103–104.

13. Ibid., 117–118.

14. Ibid., 123.

15. Ronald Dworkin, "Can a Liberal State Support Art?," in *A Matter of Principle*, 222.

16. John Rawls, *A Theory of Justice* (Oxford: Oxford University Press, 1972), 332.

17. Ronald Dworkin, *Life's Dominion: An Argument about Abortion, Euthanasia, and Individual Freedom* (New York: Alfred A. Knopf, 1993).

18. Ibid., 154.

19. Ibid., 157.

20. Dworkin's argument is that we owe it to future generations to leave them with a fair share of resources, and these resources include a set of cultural opportunities or a cultural "structure." Such resources are a generic constituent of the good life, though not a detailed conception of it. Dworkin stipulates that people are better off when the opportunities their culture provides are more "complex and diverse," and the state should act as a trustee for the future complexity of this culture (Dworkin, "Can a Liberal State Support Art?," 232). He also argues that a rich cultural structure presents options that are "innovative" and "diverse" and display "complexity and depth" (Dworkin, *A Matter of Principle*, 229). The difficulty with the argument is that it is not clear that Dworkin can avoid specifying the content of this cultural structure in ways that do not favor some, and disfavor other, ways of life, in breach of neutrality. As critics have pointed out, members of conventional religious groups, as well as disadvantaged citizens with presumptively simple, unsophisticated aesthetic tastes, may rightly object (for different reasons) to being compelled to sacrifice part of their income in order to subsidize opera or the purchase of Titian paintings for public museums. It is hard to see how any justification for cultural policy—even one that appeals to a generic interest in a "complex" cultural structure—can be compatible with neutrality about the good. For criticisms of Dworkin along these lines, see Samuel Black, "Revisionist Liberalism and the Decline of Culture," *Ethics* 102, no. 2 (January 1992): 244–267; Harry Brighouse, "Neutrality, Publicity, and State Funding for the Arts," *Philosophy & Public Affairs* 24, no. 1 (Winter 1995): 35–63; Colin Macleod, "Liberal Neutrality

or Liberal Tolerance?," *Law and Philosophy* 16, no. 5 (September 1997): 529–559; Richard C. Sinopoli, "Liberalism and Contested Conceptions of the Good: The Limits of Neutrality," *Journal of Politics* 55, no. 3 (August 1993): 644–663.

21. Dworkin, *Life's Dominion,* 154.

22. Ronald Dworkin, *Is Democracy Possible Here? Principles for a New Public Debate* (Princeton: Princeton University Press, 2008), 71.

23. Ibid., 72–73.

24. Matthew Clayton, "A Puzzle about Ethics, Justice and the Sacred," in *Dworkin and His Critics,* ed. Justine Burley (Oxford: Blackwell, 2004), 99–109, at 106. In his response to critics such as Clayton, Frances Kamm, and Eric Rakowski in that volume, Dworkin confirms the importance of "the distinction I draw between ethical convictions that are central to personality, like convictions about abortion, and other convictions, that I think are not" (358). He later clarifies: "Only certain intrinsic values are essentially religious: I define these to include all convictions about whether, how, and why human life is important, whether or not these convictions are drawn from assumptions about a supernatural god" (374).

25. See Colin Bird, "Does Religion Deserve Our Respect?," *Journal of Applied Philosophy* 30, no. 3 (August 2013): 268–282.

26. As an example, he refers to the argument that a pornography-free environment (a presumptively religious demand) is better for the education of children and more generally for the health of the public culture. This is, admittedly, not a compelling argument insofar as there are unconventionally religious arguments for restricting pornography too.

27. Dworkin, *Is Democracy Possible Here?,* 77.

28. Ibid., 75.

29. See Sinopoli, "Liberalism and Contested Conceptions." Sinopoli rightly notes: "If the principle asserted is that it is better to broaden the range of artistic experience, why should we not say the same thing about religious experience, on one extreme, and trivial enjoyments like games of marbles or pushpin on the other? If, for example, the southern Baptist faith was dying out, should the state act to preserve it so that this denomination would remain available to future generations? What if, on the other hand, the game of marbles found fewer adherents today than it used to have, as is the case? Should the state endorse marbles clinics to preserve this entertainment for others who might someday enjoy it? If it should do so in the case of arts as opposed to marbles, it must be because preserving an artistic heritage is more valuable.

And if this value judgment is a controversial conception of the good life, or an element in such a conception as Dworkin clearly believes, he is violating his own neutrality constraint by advocating state support for art" (648).

30. Dworkin, *Religion without God*, 138.

31. Ibid. and 134n16.

32. See my argument in Chapter 2.

33. See, in particular, *Life's Dominion*.

34. For persuasive criticisms of Dworkin's argument along those lines, see John Tomasi, "Liberalism, Sanctity, and the Prohibition of Abortion," *Journal of Philosophy* 94, no. 10 (October 1997): 493; Eric Rakowski, "Reverence for Life and the Limits of State Power," in Burley, *Dworkin and His Critics*, 241–263; Inazu, "The Limits of Integrity," 191–195.

35. This tallies with the idea that public reason is incomplete and indeterminate about key issues such as prenatal moral status. For a good discussion, see Jeremy Williams, "Public Reason and Prenatal Moral Status," *Journal of Ethics* 19, no. 1 (2015): 23–52.

36. In Chapter 2, I focused on their interpretation of the Free Exercise Clause.

37. Christopher L. Eisgruber and Lawrence G. Sager, *Religious Freedom and the Constitution* (Cambridge, MA: Harvard University Press, 2007), 70.

38. Ibid., 6–7.

39. Ibid., 17.

40. Ibid., 212–215. In the particular case of Cleveland, however, they note that the absence of good-quality public schools provided insufficient options for parents, and generated an unfair advantage to the religious schools.

41. Much more remains to be said, however, about what it means for a religious organization to provide a public service "on the same terms" as a nonreligious one. The issue of direct public funding for faith-based initiatives is complex and controversial, insufficiently examined by Eisgruber and Sager.

42. The voucher program in *Zelman* allowed indirect, not direct, funding for religious organizations: it allowed parental choice, not the direct subsidy of religious education.

43. Elizabeth S. Anderson and Richard H. Pildes, "Expressive Theories of Law: A General Restatement," *University of Pennsylvania Law Review* 148, no. 5 (2000): 1509, 1520.

44. See also Daniel Brudney, "On Non-Coercive Establishment," *Political Theory* 33, no. 6 (December 2005): 812–839; Cécile Laborde, "Political

Liberalism and Religion: On Separation and Establishment," *Journal of Political Philosophy* 21, no. 2 (March 2013): 67–86; Simon Căbulea May, "Democratic Legitimacy, Legal Expressivism, and Religious Establishment," *Critical Review of International Social and Political Philosophy* 15, no. 2 (2012): 219–238; Sune Laegaard, "What's the Problem with Symbolic Religious Establishment? The Alienation and Symbolic Equality Account," in *Religion in Liberal Political Philosophy*, ed. Cécile Laborde and Aurélia Bardon (Oxford: Oxford University Press, 2017).

45. Eisgruber and Sager, *Religious Freedom*, 19.

46. Kent Greenawalt, *Religion and the Constitution*, vol. 2, *Establishment and Fairness*, 2:182–191; Martha Nussbaum, *Liberty of Conscience* (New York: Basic Books, 2008), 229, 253, 265–266, 270.

47. Justice O'Connor, cited in Nussbaum, *Liberty of Conscience*, 247.

48. Eisgruber and Sager, *Religious Freedom*, 122–123.

49. Ibid., 124–136.

50. For a penetrating criticism of the non-endorsement test and the jurisprudence of symbolism and neutrality, see Steven D. Smith, "Symbols, Perceptions, and Doctrinal Illusions: Establishment Neutrality and the 'No Endorsement' Test," *Michigan Law Review* 86, no. 2 (November 1987): 266–332. I shall return to these questions in Chapter 4.

51. Eisgruber and Sager, *Religious Freedom*, 164.

52. The "three plastic animals rule" was another legacy of *Lynch*, the Pawtucket crèche display. Justice O'Connor had argued that by surrounding the crèche with a few Santas and flying reindeers, the town had distanced itself from its theological content. Eisgruber and Sager disagree: "The Santa and the reindeer neither secularize the crèche nor mark it as only one of several competing religious and philosophical symbols valued by citizens" (134). For stimulating reflections on the interplay of legal, social, and religious meanings in *Lynch*, see Winnifred Fallers Sullivan, *Paying the Words Extra: Religious Discourse in the Supreme Court of the United States* (Cambridge, MA: Harvard University Press, 1994).

53. Eisgruber and Sager, *Religious Freedom*, 138–139.

54. Ibid., 128.

55. Ibid., emphasis added.

56. Ibid., 126.

57. Michael W. McConnell, "The Problem of Singling Out Religion," *DePaul University Law Review* 50, no. 1 (2000): 1–47; Abner Greene, "The Political

Balance of the Religion Clauses," *Yale Law Journal* 102 (1992): 1611; Ira C. Lupu and Robert W. Tuttle, "The Limits of Equal Liberty as a Theory of Religious Freedom," *Texas Law Review* 85, no. 5 (2007): 1247–1272.

58. *West Virginia v. Barnette*, 319 U.S. 624 (1943), held that students should not be required to salute the flag.

59. See Christopher L. Eisgruber and Lawrence G. Sager, "Chips Off Our Block? A Reply to Berg, Greenawalt, Lupu and Tuttle," *Texas Law Review* 85, nos. 1273, 1274 (2007). They argue that a municipal sign such as "Finn a Town for Straight Folks" would be unconstitutional on this ground: "Race, sex and sexual orientation should all be constitutionally protected against disparagement."

60. Eisgruber and Sager, *Religious Freedom*, 170, 192.

61. Ibid., 169–170.

62. Ibid., 170.

63. Ibid.

64. For more general criticisms, see Lupu and Tuttle, "Limits of Equal Liberty"; Thomas Berg, "Can Religious Liberty Be Protected as Equality?," *Texas Law Review* 85, no. 5 (2007): 1185.

65. See *Mozert v. Hawkins* (1987), concerning Christian parents' objection to the curriculum in a Tennessee school. See Stephen Macedo, "Liberal Civic Education and Religious Fundamentalism: The Case of God v. John Rawls," *Ethics* 105, no. 3 (1995): 468; Nomi May Stolzenberg " 'He Drew a Circle That Shut Me Out': Assimilation, Indoctrination, and the Paradox of a Liberal Education," *Harvard Law Review* 106, no. 3 (1993): 581–667.

66. Eisgruber and Sager, *Religious Freedom*, 183.

67. Ibid., 190.

68. Ibid., 195.

69. Eisgruber and Sager reject the epistemic arguments of, e.g., Abner Greene (compare Abner Greene, "The Political Balance of the Religion Clauses," *Yale Law Journal* 102 [1992]) because, they argue, religious arguments are not more or less open to critical discussion than secular arguments. This is true. But I'll add two caveats. First, as I argue in Chapter 4, as public justifications for state coercion, arguments must be accessible to all, not simply intelligible. Second, although theories about the origin of life, such as creationism and intelligent design, are perfectly valid topics to introduce in ethics and religion classes, there are specifically epistemic reasons why they are not suitable for biology classes. For critical discussions, see Thomas Nagel, "Public

Education and Intelligent Design," *Philosophy & Public Affairs* 36, no. 2 (2008): 187–205; Alvin Plantinga, "Creation and Evolution: A Modest Proposal," in *Intelligent Design Creationism and Its Critics: Philosophical, Theological, and Scientific Perspectives,* ed. Robert T. Pennock (Cambridge, MA: MIT Press, 2001), 779–791; Francis J. Beckwith, "Rawls's Dangerous Idea: Liberalism, Evolution and the Legal Requirement of Religious Neutrality in Public Schools," *Journal of Law and Religion* 20, no. 2 (2004–2005): 423–458; Cristobal Bellolio, *Political Liberalism and the Scientific Claims of Religion,* unpublished PhD thesis, University College London, 2017.

70. Eisgruber and Sager, *Religious Freedom,* 196.

71. John Rawls, *Political Liberalism* (New York: Columbia University Press, 1996), xxv, paperback edition.

72. Public reason liberalism is the dominant brand of liberal theory today, and is associated with John Rawls, Jürgen Habermas, Charles Larmore, Thomas Scanlon, Brian Barry, Gerald Gaus, Thomas Nagel, and Jonathan Quong, among others.

73. Christopher Eberle, *Religious Convictions in Liberal Politics* (Cambridge: Cambridge University Press, 2002), 14.

74. Jonathan Quong, *Liberalism without Perfection* (Oxford: Oxford University Press, 2011).

75. Ibid., 12–15.

76. Ibid., chap. 7, "Disagreement and Asymmetry." Quong's theory importantly differs from theories, such as Brian Barry's, that ground liberal neutrality in epistemological and moral skepticism. Quong is not committed to such skepticism: he does not assert that conceptions of the good are less epistemically secure than conceptions of the right. Rather, religious conceptions are excluded because the disagreements or controversies over religious and other comprehensive doctrines are deeper or more foundational, and lack the normative common ground that characterizes reasonable disagreements over matters of justice and individual rights (192–220). So the view I attribute to Quong is not that religious conceptions of the good are less epistemically secure than conceptions of justice. It is, instead, the claim that disagreement about the good goes to foundations that are not shared or mutually accessible. This is an epistemic argument, which draws, and expands, on Rawls's own epistemic theory of the burdens of judgment. An earlier, influential statement can be found in Thomas Nagel, "Moral Conflict and Political Legitimacy,"

Philosophy & Public Affairs 16, no. 3 (Summer 1987): 215–240. I am grateful to Jon Quong for his comments on this section.

77. Rawls, *Political Liberalism*, 55–57.

78. For various formulations of the asymmetry objection, see Simon Caney, "Anti-Perfectionism and Rawlsian Liberalism," *Political Studies* 42 (1995): 248–264; Caney, "Liberal Legitimacy, Reasonable Disagreement, and Justice," in *Pluralism and Liberal Neutrality,* ed. Richard Bellamy and Martin Hollis (London: Frank Cass, 1999), 19–36; Jeremy Waldron, *Law and Disagreement* (Oxford: Oxford University Press, 1999); Joseph Chan, "Legitimacy, Unanimity, and Perfectionism," *Philosophy & Public Affairs* 29 (2000): 5–42; Simon Clarke, "Contractarianism, Liberal Neutrality, and Epistemology," *Political Studies* 47 (1999): 637–641.

79. Stephen Lecce, *Against Perfectionism: Defending Liberal Neutrality* (Toronto: Toronto University Press, 2008).

80. Quong, *Liberalism without Perfection*, 201.

81. Lecce, *Against Perfectionism*, 230.

82. Quong, *Liberalism without Perfection*, 196–198. Compare Rawls: "In addition to conflicting comprehensive doctrines, political liberalism does recognize that in an actual political society a number of differing liberal political conceptions of justice compete with one another in society's political debate . . . this leads to another aim of political liberalism: saying how a well-ordered liberal society is to be formulated given not only reasonable pluralism [of comprehensive conceptions] but a family of reasonable liberal conceptions of justice" (Rawls, *Political Liberalism*, xlvi).

83. Quong, *Liberalism without Perfection*, 204.

84. Ibid., 205.

85. Ibid., 204.

86. Ibid., chap. 5.

87. Ibid., 205–206.

88. Ibid., 197, 207. Quong here closely follows Rawls's reasoning in a much commented-upon footnote (Rawls, *Political Liberalism*, lv n. 31; 243n32) but refrains from concluding—with Rawls—that there is only one reasonable balance of values.

89. In previous sections we saw that the fact of disagreement about the good also played a role in other theories. In Dworkin's argument, it provided one of the premises that justified state neutrality toward personal ethical views

about abortion. In Eisgruber and Sager's theory, it was combined with the fact of historical conflict and discrimination to explain why certain social identities are particularly vulnerable to disparagement. The difference between their account and Quong's, however, is that they explicitly rejected the epistemic conception of disagreement. Dworkin took the view there is as much disagreement about justice and the good; and preferred to ground neutrality in substantive, if thin, liberal values, rather than in procedural rules of contractualist reasoning. Eisgruber and Sager, for their part, explicitly reject the "epistemic" argument against the teaching of religion in schools.

90. Quong, *Liberalism without Perfection,* 197.

91. Ibid., 150–151.

92. Eberle, *Religious Convictions,* 14–15.

93. Quong, *Liberalism without Perfection,* 206.

94. Joseph Chan, "Legitimacy, Unanimity, and Perfectionism," *Philosophy & Public Affairs* 29, no. 1 (2000): 5–42.

95. Quong, *Liberalism without Perfection,* 215.

96. Ibid., 197.

97. Ibid., 200.

98. For an interesting argument showing that the problem lies with how Quong construes the justificatory constituency of reasonable citizens, see Paul Billingham, "Liberal Perfectionism and Quong's Internal Conception of Political Liberalism," *Social Theory and Practice* 43, no. 1 (2016): 79–106. Billingham suggests that reasonable citizens could also be said to endorse some ideals about the good (such as the good of individual autonomy): it is only because Quong stipulates that reasonable citizens have foundational disagreements about the good that he is able to insist that perfectionist policies cannot be justified to them.

99. T. M. Scanlon, *What We Owe to Each Other* (Cambridge, MA: Harvard University Press, 1998).

100. In Chapter 5, Quong describes in this way the view he criticizes: "Different citizens may have different perfectionist reasons for disvaluing drug addiction, but so long as there is an overlapping consensus on its disvalue, then it can be the legitimate target of state sanctions." He then comments, "This is an illiberal outcome, and one that is inconsistent with the basic tenets of political liberalism." But this is not an adequate response. Liberal states restrict freedom all the time, and when they do so in the name of "the right," the out-

come is not illiberal. But as Quong seeks to *explain* why coercion in the name of "the good" is illiberal (by reference to the epistemic nature of disagreements about the good), he cannot merely stipulate that it is (Quong, *Liberalism without Perfection*, 150).

101. One option open to Quong at this point would be to retort that it would be impossible to have a proper public debate about (say) the policy implications of the badness of addiction without bringing in the deeper, comprehensive reasons that justify this belief. Those who think addiction is bad because, but only insofar as, it harms others will defend more liberal policies toward drug or alcohol use than those who think addiction is only a worse case of an intrinsically bad behavior. Public debate about thin values of the good will inevitably draw on deeper, thicker conceptions of the good. This is correct. But, I would argue, exactly the same is true of disagreements about the right. Quong discusses the case of abortion, and argues that it is sufficient that public reasons—respect for life, women's rights—be put forward. But such public reasons, because they point in different directions, do not generate a determinate conclusion: they cannot be weighed and ranked without appealing to substantive views about the moral status of the fetus. Quong attempts to specify the contours of what a "reasonable balance of values" in the abortion case would be, but his argument seems to me to be vulnerable to the penetrating criticism that Patrick Neal has made of Rawls's early formulation of the same argument. See Patrick Neal, "Rawls, Abortion and Public Reason," *Journal of Church and State* 56, no. 2 (2012): 323–346.

102. Quong, *Liberalism without Perfection*, 215.

103. Rawls, *Political Liberalism*, 178–180.

104. Quong, *Liberalism without Perfection*, 215.

105. Jonathan Quong, "Cultural Exemptions, Expensive Tastes and Equal Opportunities," *Journal of Applied Philosophy* 23, no. 1 (2006): 53–71.

106. Ibid., 66.

107. Quong, *Liberalism without Perfection*, 218.

108. Quong writes that "given the way reasonable persons are defined within political liberalism, perfectionists cannot claim that there are judgements about [the good] that all reasonable persons must accept" (ibid., 217). This is true, but it is only because neutrality about the good is built into the Rawlsian conception of reasonableness. Quong argues that the defense of the ideal of reasonableness—such as it is—is independent of the discussion of the asymmetry charge. But it

is difficult to see why this is the case, insofar as the notion of reasonableness itself presupposes that a relevant distinction has already been drawn between the good and the right.

109. Different formulations appear in ibid. at 38, 39, 205.

110. Scanlon, *What We Owe to Each Other.*

111. Quong, *Liberalism without Perfection,* 208.

112. John Locke argued that the liberal state should protect civil interests such as "Life, Liberty, Health and Indolency of Body; and the Possession of outward things such as Money, Lands" and leave the salvation of souls to the care of individuals. John Locke, *A Letter concerning Toleration,* reprinted in *A Letter concerning Toleration in Focus,* ed. John Horton and Susan Mendus (London: Routledge, 1991), 17. John Stuart Mill generalized the point and argued that the liberal state should only prevent harm to others. John Stuart Mill, "On Liberty," in *Mill: Texts, Commentaries,* ed. Alan Ryan (New York: Norton, 1975), 48. Immanuel Kant had earlier sought to provide a justification of a categorical distinction between universally valid principles, which can be justified interpersonally, and ethical doctrines, which cannot. On Kant's doctrine of toleration, see Rainer Forst, *Toleration in Conflict: Past and Present* (Cambridge: Cambridge University Press, 2011), 314–329. John Rawls drew on Kant to design a contractual thought-experiment that showed that fairly situated persons would agree to live by principles of right (regulating their mutual interaction) but not by principles of good. Rawls, *A Theory of Justice.* Ronald Dworkin wrote that contractualist procedures do not establish, but instead assume, the basic liberal ideal that people should have politically guaranteed, equal rights to liberty as ethical independence. Ronald Dworkin, "The Original Position," in *Reading Rawls: Critical Studies on Rawls' "Theory of Justice,"* ed. Norman Daniels (Stanford, CA: Stanford University Press, 1989), 16–53.

113. Quong, *Liberalism without Perfection,* chap. 5.

114. See, for example, Gerald Gaus, "Sectarianism without Perfection? Quong's Political Liberalism," *Philosophy and Public Issues* 2, no. 2 (Fall 2012): 7–15.

115. Kent Greenawalt has designated them as the "borderlines of status." Kent Greenawalt, *Religious Convictions and Political Choice* (Oxford: Oxford University Press, 1988), chaps. 6–8.

116. For discussion, see, e.g., Micah Schwartzman, "The Completeness of Public Reason," *Politics, Philosophy and Economics* 3 (2004): 191–220; and Williams, "Public Reason."

117. For related criticisms of Quong that make the more general point that state enforcement of a particular conception of justice is as sectarian as state enforcement of a particular conception of the good, see Timothy Fowler and Zofia Stemplowska, "The Asymmetry Objection Rides Again: On the Nature and Significance of Justificatory Disagreement," *Journal of Applied Philosophy* 32, no. 2 (2015): 133–146; and Kevin Vallier "On Quong's Sectarian Political Liberalism," *Criminal Law and Philosophy* 11, no. 1 (2017): 175–194.

118. See Chapter 5.

4. Disaggregating Religion in Nonestablishment of Religion

1. In Chapter 5, I will turn to the issue of the respective jurisdictional claims of the state and religious associations. In Chapter 6, I will inquire into the Free Exercise Clause, and I will apply my disaggregating strategy to the ideal of freedom of religion.

2. I follow Rajeev Bhargava in defending what he calls *political* secularism (the proper state response to religious diversity) rather than *ethical* secularism (a substantively anti-religious, atheist, or scientist worldview). Bhargava's distinction closely maps onto Charles Taylor's distinction between overlapping consensus and independent ethical secularism (Taylor, "Modes of Secularism," in *Secularism and Its Critics,* ed. Rajeev Bhargava [New Delhi: Oxford University Press, 1998]), which itself is a gloss on Rawls's own distinction between political and comprehensive liberalism. For more on the distinction between the two secularisms, see Cécile Laborde, "Justificatory Secularism," in *Religion in a Liberal State: Cross-Disciplinary Reflections,* ed. Gavin D'Costa, Malcolm Evans, Tariq Modood, and Julian Rivers (Cambridge: Cambridge University Press, 2013); and Laborde, *Critical Republicanism: The Hijab Controversy and Political Philosophy* (Oxford: Oxford University Press, 2008).

3. Ran Hirschl, *Constitutional Theocracy* (Cambridge, MA: Harvard University Press, 2010).

4. Jonathan Fox, "World Separation of Religion and State into the 21st Century," *Comparative Political Studies* 39 (2006): 537–569; Fox, "Do Democracies Have Separation of Church and State?," *Canadian Journal of Political Science* (2007): 1–25.

5. Winnifred Sullivan and Lori Beaman, eds., *Varieties of Religious Establishment* (Farnham, UK: Ashgate, 2013); Winnifred Fallers Sullivan, Robert

Yelle, and Mateo Taussig-Rubbo, eds., *After Secular Law* (Palo Alto: Stanford University Press, 2011).

6. For different answers, see Simon Căbulea May, "Religious Democracy and the Liberal Principle of Legitimacy," *Philosophy & Public Affairs* 37, no. 2 (2009); Saladin Meckled-Garcia, "The Ethics of Establishment: Fairness and Human Rights as Different Standards of Neutrality," in *Negotiating Religion*, ed. Cécile Laborde, François Guesnet, and Lois Lee (London: Routledge, 2016); and Jean L. Cohen, "Rethinking Political Secularism and the American Model of Constitutional Dualism," Rajeev Bhargava, "Is European Secularism Secular Enough?," and Tariq Modood, "State-Religion Connections and Multicultural Citizenship," all in *Secularism and Constitutional Democracy*, ed. Jean L. Cohen and Cécile Laborde (New York: Columbia University Press, 2016).

7. My strategy here has been inspired by George Sher's penetrating engagement with liberal neutrality in *Beyond Neutrality*. Sher points out that liberal neutrality relates to different dimensions of an "incoherent" notion of conception of the good. Sher in effect disaggregates that notion into three distinct dimensions. See George Sher, *Beyond Neutrality: Perfectionism and Politics* (Cambridge: Cambridge University Press, 1997), 43–44.

8. A similar move inspires Veit Bader's important work on the priority of liberalism over secularism. See Bader, *Secularism or Democracy? Associational Governance of Religious Diversity* (Amsterdam: Amsterdam University Press, 2007).

9. An earlier sketch of this conceptual framework can be found in Laborde, "Justificatory Secularism."

10. In Chapter 5, I will explain the sense in which minimal secularism is, in addition, a doctrine that relies on democratic state sovereignty—and I shall address the jurisdictional boundary question in relation to the respective jurisdictional claims of state and religious associations.

11. Mark Lilla, *The Stillborn God: Religion, Politics, and the Modern West* (New York: Vintage Books, 2008). Critics such as William Cavanaugh, in *The Myth of Religious Violence* (New York: Oxford University Press, 2009), have argued that this enchanted story of the origins of the liberal state is a myth. This may well be the case. But as I pointed out in Chapter 1, the dubious genesis of an idea does not determine its truth or plausibility. I want to explain the sense in which liberalism must "take God out of politics," regardless of whether actual states in early modern Europe did so.

12. John Rawls, *Political Liberalism,* paperback ed. (New York: Columbia University Press, 1996).

13. On ecocentrism, see, e.g., Robyn Eckersley, *Environmentalism and Political Theory: Toward an Eco-centric Approach* (Albany, NY: SUNY Press, 1992); Ned Hettinger and Bill Throop, "Refocusing Ecocentrism: De-emphasizing Stability and Defending Wilderness," *Environmental Ethics* 21 (1999): 3–21; Adam Konopka, "Ecological Goods That Obligate," *Environmental Ethics* 31 (2009): 245–262.

14. For two thought-provoking criticisms of the idea that public reason is about justifying state coercion, see Colin Bird, "Coercion and Public Justification," *Politics, Philosophy, and Economics* 13, no. 3 (2014): 189–214; and Andrew Lister, *Public Reason and Political Community* (London: Bloomsbury Academic, 2013). Here I broadly follow Charles Larmore's suggestion that "the distinctive feature of political principles which sets them off from other moral rules" is that they are rules with which individuals can rightly be forced to comply. This is what justifies the requirement that political principles must be publicly justified. Charles Larmore, "Moral Basis of Liberalism" *Journal of Philosophy* 96, no. 12 (1999): 607.

15. The distinction between intelligibility, accessibility, and shareability is drawn from Kevin Vallier and Fred D'Agostino, "Public Justification," in *The Stanford Encyclopedia of Philosophy,* Spring 2014 ed., ed. Edward N. Zalta, http://plato.stanford.edu/archives/spr2014/entries/justification-public/. *Intelligibility: A*'s reason R_A is intelligible to members of the public if and only if members of the public regard R_A as justified for A according to A's evaluative standards. *Accessibility: A*'s reason R_A is accessible to the public if and only if all members of the public regard R_A as justified for A according to common evaluative standards. *Shareability: A*'s reason R_A is shareable with the public if and only if members of the public regard R_A as justified for each member of the public, including *A,* according to common standards. On this topic, I have benefited from conversations with Aurélia Bardon, Matteo Bonotti, Jeff Howard, Sune Laegaard, and Micah Schwartzman.

16. Or at least a weakly idealized constituency of Members of the Public, such as those formed by minimally rational moral agents. In Gerald Gaus's theory, for example, Members of the Public "are not so idealized that their reasoning is inaccessible to their real-world counterparts" (276), but instead are idealized in the following sense: they hold the beliefs that their real-world

counterparts would be justified in holding after engaging in a "respectable amount" of good reasoning (250). Gerald Gaus, *The Order of Public Reason: A Theory of Freedom and Morality in a Diverse and Bounded World* (Cambridge: Cambridge University Press, 2011).

17. For thoughtful reflections about what is lost when theological language (say, about gifts of God) is translated into secular language, see Albert Weale, "Public Reason of the Heart," in Laborde, Guesnet, and Lee, *Negotiating Religion*. See also Steven G. Smith, "The Roar of the Lion, the Taste of the Salt: On Really Religious Reasons," *Religious Studies* 48, no. 4 (December 2012): 479–496.

18. Robert Audi, *Democratic Authority and the Separation of Church and State* (New York: Oxford University Press, 2011), 67. Further, Audi clarifies: "I have not implied (and do not believe) that adequate reasons must be shared by everyone. . . . They need only be accessible to rational adults: roughly, appraisable by them using natural reason in the light of facts to which they have access on the basis of exercising their natural rational capacities" (70). Although I am indebted to Audi's general insight, I depart from him in important ways. I am skeptical that natural reason can alleviate the burdens of judgment identified by Rawls; I do not think that religious reasons uniquely exhibit inaccessibility, nor do I think that all religiously inspired reasons are religious reasons in Audi's sense. For a similar proposal, which focuses on the exclusion of what she calls "absolutist" reasons, see Aurélia Bardon, "Religious Argument and Public Justification," in Cohen and Laborde, *Secularism and Constitutional Democracy*.

19. The term "epistemic abstinence" is drawn from Joseph Raz, "Facing Diversity: The Case of Epistemic Abstinence," *Philosophy & Public Affairs* 19, no. 1 (Winter 1990): 3–46.

20. I lack the space to engage the burgeoning literature about the relationship between science and public reason. Let me simply note that the question of science further illustrates the epistemic content of public reason—too often ignored by liberal theorists. Most liberal theorists tend to collapse epistemic reasonableness into ethical reasonableness. A version of this, we saw in Chapter 3, was evident in Eisgruber and Sager's attempt to explain that teaching creationism in school is wrong because it "disparages" nonbelievers. On my view, the problem with the teaching of creationism in biology classes is not a problem of civic disparagement but instead a problem of official inculcation of epistemically inac-

cessible ideas. New work in this area includes Gabriele Badano and Matteo Bonotti, "Rescuing Public Reason's Accessibility Requirement," unpublished manuscript on file with author. For thoughtful reflections about the difficulties encountered by political liberal theories of public reason in justifying the special authority of science, see, e.g., Karin Jønch-Clausen and Klemens Kappel, "Scientific Facts and Methods in Public Reason," *Res Publica* 22 (2016): 117–133.

21. Gerald F. Gaus and Kevin Vallier, "The Roles of Religious Conviction in a Publicly Justified Polity: The Implications of Convergence, Asymmetry, and Political Institutions," *Philosophy & Social Criticism* 35, no. 1 (2009): 51–76.

22. For different versions of these criticisms, see Jeffrey Stout, *Democracy and Tradition* (Princeton: Princeton University Press, 2003), chap. 3; Christopher J. Eberle, *Religious Convictions in Liberal Politics* (Cambridge: Cambridge University Press, 2002); Kevin Vallier, "Liberalism, Religion and Integrity," *Australasian Journal of Philosophy* 90, no. 1 (2012): 149–165; Nicholas Wolterstorff, "The Role of Religion in Decision and Discussion of Political Issues," in *Religion in the Public Square: The Place of Religious Convictions in Political Debate,* ed. Robert Audi and Nicholas Wolterstorff (Lanham, MD: Rowman and Littlefield, 1997), 67–120; Michael J. Perry, *Love and Power: The Role of Religion and Morality in American Politics* (New York: Oxford University Press, 1993); Andrew R. Murphy, *Conscience and Community: Revisiting Toleration and Religious Dissent in Early Modern England and America* (University Park: Pennsylvania State University Press, 2001); Paul Weithman, *Religion and the Obligations of Citizenship* (Cambridge: Cambridge University Press, 2002).

23. Here I have been inspired by Charles Taylor, "Modes of Secularism"; and Taylor, "Secularism and Critique," http://blogs.ssrc.org/tif/2008/04/24/secularism-and-critique/.

24. Laborde, *Critical Republicanism.*

25. Jürgen Habermas, *Between Naturalism and Religion* (Cambridge: Polity Press, 2008), 130.

26. Laborde, "Justificatory Secularism," sec. 2. See also Habermas, "Religion in the Public Sphere," *European Journal of Philosophy* 14, no. 1 (2006): 1–25; Kent Greenawalt, *Private Consciences and Public Reasons* (New York: Oxford University Press, 1995); Richard North, "Public Reason, Religious Restraint and Respect," *Philosophia* 40 (2012): 179–193; Jonathan Chaplin, "Law, Religion and Public Reasoning," *Oxford Journal of Law and Religion* 1 (2012): 319–337.

27. For a defense of a bifurcated, indirect model of public justification that relieves ordinary citizens of the burdens of public reason and imposes them only on public officials, and especially on elected partisans, see Matteo Bonotti, *Partisanship and Political Liberalism in Diverse Societies* (Oxford: Oxford University Press, 2017), chap. 7.

28. Eberle, *Religious Convictions*. Kevin Vallier argues that both natural law and religious testimony are accessible (and therefore that the accessibility condition is incapable of ruling out religious reasons on epistemic grounds). I disagree: the crucial difference is that natural law argument can be discussed within a purely secular framework, whereas religious testimonies cannot. Kevin Vallier, "Against Public Reason Liberalism's Accessibility Requirement," *Journal of Moral Philosophy* 8 (2011): 366–389.

29. Personal experience is an important and too often underrated source of knowledge, and neglecting it can constitute an epistemic injustice. See Miranda Fricker, *Epistemic Injustice* (Oxford: Oxford University Press, 2007). But although single first-person experience can provide essential testimonies in court cases, for example, it cannot form the legitimate basis for laws, which by their very nature must be generalizable. An exception—put to me by Andy Koppelman—is that of diplomatic relations. Why should Angela Merkel not rely on the personal impression she has formed of Vladimir Putin when she makes foreign policy decisions? She can—but only because diplomatic relations rely on interpersonal rather than impersonal rules, and to that extent are about the rule of men—and women—rather than the rule of law.

30. Jeremy Waldron, *God, Locke, and Equality: Christian Foundations of Locke's Political Thought* (Cambridge: Cambridge University Press, 2002), 20.

31. For the view that utilitarianism contains "detachable" reasons that are both permissible and contestable in public reason, see Richard J. Arneson, "Neutrality and Utility," *Canadian Journal of Philosophy* 20, no. 2 (1990): 215. Note also that non-fideist (philosophical and rationalist) arguments for the existence of God (Aristotle, Aquinas, Averroes, Descartes, Kant) are publicly accessible in my sense. François Boucher and Cécile Laborde, "Why Tolerate Conscience?," *Criminal Law and Philosophy* 10, no. 3 (2016): 493–514. But this philosophical argument cannot provide an accessible political reason for any particular law or policy. Detailed accounts of the will of God (of the type "If God exists, this is what he demands") are intelligible only within self-contained traditions of thought, but not broadly accessible, in the way that

non-fideist arguments are. On this topic, I have benefited from illuminating conversations with Steven H. Shiffrin. Shiffrin's own engagement with public reason can be found in chapter 8 of his *The Religious Left and Church-State Relations* (Princeton: Princeton University Press, 2009).

32. Patrick Neal, "Religion within the Limits of Liberalism Alone?," *Journal of Church and State* 39, no. 4 (Autumn 1997): 697–722, at 712.

33. Robert P. George and Christopher Wolfe, eds., *Natural Law and Public Reason* (Washington, DC: Georgetown University Press, 2000); Robert Audi, "Liberal Democracy and the Place of Religion in Politics," in Audi and Wolterstorff, *Religion in the Public Square*, 1–66; Michael Perry, *Religion in Politics: Constitutional and Moral Perspectives* (Oxford: Oxford University Press, 1997), 72–82; John Finnis, "Is Natural Law Theory Compatible with Limited Government?," in *Natural Law, Liberalism, and Morality*, ed. Robert P. George (Oxford: Clarendon Press, 1996), 1–26, at 3. Critics of Natural Law theories, such as Stephen Macedo and Kent Greenawalt, "Natural Law and Public Reasons," *Villanova Law Review* 47, no. 3 (2002): 531–552, argue (rightly, in my view) that although Natural Law may not be persuasive, it is not inaccessible. For the contrary view, that Natural Law is incomprehensible without endorsement of a theistic framework, see Nicholas Bamforth and David A. J. Richards, *Patriarchal Religions, Sexuality and Gender: A Critique of New Natural Law* (Cambridge: Cambridge University Press, 2008).

34. Mohammed Fadel, "The True, the Good and the Reasonable: The Theological and Ethical Roots of Public Reason in Islamic Law," *Canadian Journal of Law and Jurisprudence* 21, no. 1 (2008): 5. See, more generally, Andrew March, *Islam and Liberal Citizenship: The Search for an Overlapping Consensus* (Oxford: Oxford University Press, 2009); and Abdullahi Ahmed An-Na'im, *Islam and the Secular State: Negotiating the Future of Shari'a* (Cambridge, MA: Harvard University Press, 2008).

35. Habermas, "Religion in the Public Sphere," 10.

36. Richard Rorty, "Religion as Conversation-Stopper," in *Philosophy and Social Hope* (New York: Penguin, 1999), 168–174.

37. Jeffrey Stout makes a similar point in his spirited engagement with Rorty from a pragmatist perspective. He notes that "[in] religiously divided societies such as ours, one is unlikely to win support for one's political proposals simply by appealing to religious considerations." He adds: "Is it true that religion is essentially a conversation stopper? I would have thought that the pragmatic

line should be that religion is not *essentially* anything, that the conversational utility of employing religious premises in political arguments depends on the situation. There is one sort of religious premise that does have the tendency to stop a conversation, at least momentarily—namely, faith-claims." Stout, *Democracy and Tradition*, 86.

38. Waldron, *God, Locke, and Equality.*

39. Stout, *Democracy and Tradition*, 70.

40. Larry Alexander, "Liberalism, Religion, and the Unity of Epistemology," *San Diego Law Review* 30 (1993); Chaplin, "Law, Religion and Public Reasoning"; Christopher J. Eberle, "Religion and Insularity: Brian Leiter on Accommodating Religion," *San Diego Law Review* 51 (2014); Boucher and Laborde, "Why Tolerate Conscience?"

41. For a useful typology of religious reasons in political debate, see Andrew March, "Rethinking Religious Reasons in Public Justification," *American Political Science Review* 107, no. 3 (2013). March also proposes that religion be "disaggregated": "the morality of the inclusion of a religious argument in public deliberation over a political decision differs, often radically, depending on the specific properties of each, namely the form and content of the religious argument and the subject matter of the political decision" (524). March's argument, like mine, is sensitive to the distinction between the *source, form*, and *content* of religious argument.

42. See, e.g., Bird, "Coercion and Public Justification."

43. Vallier, "Against Public Reason," 372.

44. I do not mean to imply that the liberal theorists I have referred to would all be equally happy with my conclusion about restricted neutrality. Dworkin's liberalism is not rooted in neutral foundations and does not imply neutrality about ethical independence, so my conclusion would not have worried him. Eisgruber and Sager (*Religious Freedom and the Constitution* [Cambridge, MA: Harvard University Press, 2007]) also freely accept that neutrality has a restricted subject matter and (in the case they discuss) is contingent on the particular sociological features of religious identity in the United States. Quong (*Liberalism without Perfection* [Oxford: Oxford University Press, 2011]), by contrast, follows through neutralist liberalism to its most logical conclusion: his "liberalism without perfection" explicitly rejects cultural subsidies and other perfectionist policies. My critique of Quong, then, is slightly different from my critique of Dworkin and Eisgruber and Sager. I claim, not that his theory is compatible with (even moderate) perfectionism, but instead that the

idea of foundational disagreement about the good does not succeed in grounding neutrality about the good. Admittedly, Quong's anti-perfectionism is also rooted in other ideals: his rejection of paternalism and his theory of legitimacy and equal respect. In the next two sections, I too ask what kind of neutrality about the good the liberal norms of freedom and equality imply. Thanks to Jeff Howard for discussions on this point.

45. Sher, *Beyond Neutrality;* Joseph Chan, "Legitimacy, Unanimity, and Perfectionism," *Philosophy & Public Affairs* 29 (2000): 5–42; Steven Wall, *Liberalism, Perfectionism and Restraint* (New York: Cambridge University Press, 1998).

46. I do not make this case here. For a range of recent, different lines of arguments, see, e.g., Martha Nussbaum, *Not for Profit: Why Democracy Needs the Humanities* (Princeton: Princeton University Press, 2010), chaps. 3 and 6; John Horton, "Why Liberals Should Not Worry about Subsidising Opera," *Critical Review of International Social and Political Philosophy* 15, no. 4 (2012): 429–448; Nick Martin, "Liberal Neutrality and Charitable Purposes," *Political Studies* 60 (2012): 936–952; Véronique Munoz-Dardé, "In the Face of Austerity: The Puzzle of Museums and Universities," *Journal of Political Philosophy* 21, no. 2 (2013): 221–242; Matthew Kramer, "Paternalism, Perfectionism, and Public Goods," *American Journal of Jurisprudence* (2015): 1–27.

47. Alan Patten has proposed a conception of liberal neutrality as equality of treatment. Neutrality of treatment improves on neutrality of both impact and justification. Patten explicitly derives the notion of equality of treatment from his reflections about religious establishment. Neutrality as equality of treatment, in his view, explains why some intuitively non-neutral policy, such as religious establishment, is wrong even though it can be justified neutrally. Alan Patten, *Equal Recognition* (Princeton: Princeton University Press, 2014), 113.

48. Jean Baubérot and Micheline Milot, *Laïcités sans frontières* (Paris: Editions du Seuil, 2011); Taylor and Maclure, *Secularism and Freedom of Conscience;* Eisgruber and Sager, *Religious Freedom;* Sune Laegaard, "Unequal Recognition, Misrecognition and Injustice: The Case of Religious Minorities in Denmark," *Ethnicities* 12, no. 2 (2012): 197–214; Laegaard, "Secular Religious Establishment: A Framework for Discussing the Compatibility of Institutional Religious Establishment with Political Secularism," *Philosophy and Public Issues* 3, no. 2 (2013): 119–157; Cécile Laborde, "Political Liberalism and Religion:

On Separation and Establishment," *Journal of Political Philosophy* 21, no. 2 (March 2013): 67–86; Laborde, "Laïcité, séparation, neutralité," in *Ethique et déontologie dans l'Education Nationale,* ed. Jean-François Dupeyron, and Christophe Miqueu (Paris: Armand Colin, 2013), 171–183.

49. Modood, "State-Religion Connections."

50. Laborde, *Critical Republicanism,* chap. 4; Jean Baubérot, *Laïcité, 1905–2005: Entre passion et raison* (Paris: Editions du Seuil, 2004).

51. For a more extended critique of the indeterminacy of liberal neutrality in conceptualizing equality between "religion" and "nonreligion," see Cécile Laborde, "The Evanescence of Neutrality," *Political Theory,* First Online, May 8, 2017 (symposium on Alan Patten's *Equal Recognition*).

52. See the different positions defended by Cohen, "Rethinking Political Secularism"; Bhargava, "Is European Secularism Secular Enough?"; and Modood, "State-Religion Connections."

53. Elizabeth S. Anderson and Richard H. Pildes, "Expressive Theories of Law: A General Restatement," *University of Pennsylvania Law Review* 148, no. 5 (2000): 1509, 1520.

54. Daniel Brudney, "On Noncoercive Establishment," *Political Theory* 33 (2005): 812–839; Laborde, "Political Liberalism and Religion."

55. Anderson and Pildes, "Expressive Theories of Law," 1523–1527.

56. See also Chapter 3 on Eisgruber and Sager.

57. David Miller, *Citizenship and National Identity* (Cambridge: Polity Press, 2000), 23.

58. Philip Pettit, *Republicanism: A Theory of Freedom and Government* (Oxford: Oxford University Press, 1997).

59. Martha Nussbaum, *Liberty of Conscience* (New York: Basic Books, 2008), 227.

60. For the view that the liberal concern for the expressive function of state institutions in promoting equal respect is best expressed in republican language, see Laborde, "Political Liberalism and Religion."

61. See, generally, Avigail Eisenberg, "Religion as Identity," *Law & Ethics of Human Rights* 10, no. 2 (2016): 295–317; Kevin Carnahan, "Religion, and Not Just Religious *Reasons,* in the Public Square," *Philosophia* 41 (2013): 397–409.

62. For a penetrating criticism of the non-endorsement test and the jurisprudence of symbolism and neutrality, see Steven D. Smith, "Symbols, Per-

ceptions, and Doctrinal Illusions: Establishment Neutrality and the 'No Endorsement' Test," *Michigan Law Review* 86, no. 2 (November 1987): 266–332. See also Ira L. Lupu and Robert W. Tuttle, "The Limits of Equal Liberty as a Theory of Religious Freedom," *Texas Law Review* 85, no. 1247 (2007); Lupu and Tuttle, *Secular Government, Religious People* (Grand Rapids, MI: Eerdmans, 2014), chap. 5; Simon May, "Democratic Legitimacy, Legal Expressivism, and Religious Establishment," *Critical Review of International Social and Political Philosophy* 15, no. 2 (2012): 219–238; Sune Laegaard, "What's the Problem with Symbolic Religious Establishment? The Alienation and Symbolic Equality Account," in *Religion in Liberal Political Philosophy*, ed. Cécile Laborde and Aurélia Bardon (Oxford: Oxford University Press, 2017).

63. I owe this point to Aurélia Bardon.

64. For different perspectives about this controversy, see David Miller, "Majorities and Minarets: Religious Freedom and Public Space," *British Journal of Political Science*, FirstView article, February 2015, 1–20; Alexa Zelletin, "Freedom, Equality, Minarets," *Res Publica* 20 (2014): 45–63; Cécile Laborde, "Miller's Minarets: Religion, Culture, Domination," in *Political Philosophy, Here and Now: Essays in Honour of David Miller,* ed. Zofia Stemplowska, Daniel Butt, and Sarah Fine (Oxford: Oxford University Press, forthcoming).

65. Rogers Brubaker, "A New 'Christianist' Secularism in Europe," http://blogs.ssrc.org/tif/2016/10/11/a-new-christianist-secularism-in-europe/.

66. Even though they do not infringe on human rights. See Meckled-Garcia, "The Ethics of Establishment." In "Political Liberalism and Religion," I also developed a two-tiered account of the legitimacy of symbolic religious establishment. There I argued that political liberalism is indeterminate between symbolic separation and symbolic establishment, and that the latter is ruled out by a specifically republican interpretation of political liberalism. As I suggested in a footnote, however, the argument implied (but did not develop) an account of why it is impermissible for the state to endorse a *religious* identity (as opposed to, say, a political or a national identity). I am now inclined to think that it is only when religious divisions map onto socially salient markers of vulnerability and domination that expressive symbolism is a problem; and that, in that case, it is a problem for basic liberal legitimacy as much as for the more demanding criterion of republican citizenship.

67. *Lautsi and Others v. Italy,* ECHR 2011.

68. Charles Taylor, *A Secular Age* (Cambridge, MA: Harvard University Press, 2007); Saba Mahmood, "Can Secularism Be Otherwise?," in *Varieties of Secularism in a Secular Age,* ed. Michael Warner, Jonathan Vanantwerpen, and Craig Calhoun (Cambridge, MA: Harvard University Press, 2010), 282–298.

69. Akeel Bilgrami, ed., *Beyond the Secular West* (New York: Columbia University Press, 2016).

70. Bhargava, *Secularism and Its Critics,* secs. 3 and 4; Bhargava, "Is European Secularism Secular Enough?"

71. For various perspectives on this challenge, see Christopher Eisgruber and Lawrence Sager, "Equal Membership, Religious Freedom, and the Idea of a Homeland," in *Religion and the Discourse of Human Rights,* ed. H. Dagan, S. Lifshitz, and Y. Stern (Jerusalem: Israel Democracy Institute, 2014); Hanna Lerner, *Making Constitutions in Deeply Divided Societies* (Cambridge: Cambridge University Press, 2011), chap. 3; Michael Karayanni, "Tainted Liberalism: Israel's Palestinian-Arab Millets," *Constellations* 23, no. 1 (March 2016): 71–83.

72. See, e.g., Michael Lambek, "Provincializing God? Provocations from an Anthropology of Religion," in *Religion: Beyond a Concept,* ed. Hent de Vries (New York: Fordham University Press, 2008), 120–138.

73. Alfred Stepan, "Stateness, Democracy, and Respect: Senegal in Comparative Perspective," in *Tolerance, Democracy and Sufis in Senegal,* ed. Mamadou Diouf (New York: Columbia University Press, 2013), 205–238. See also Souleymane Bachir Diagne, "The Sufi and the State," in Bilgrami, *Beyond the Secular West,* 28–44; Cécile Laborde, *La confrérie layenne et les lébous du Sénégal: Islam et culture traditionnelle en Afrique* (Bordeaux: CRNS-CEAN, 1995). For an account of more worrying recent trends, see, however, Natacha Tatu, "Sénégal: La contagion salafiste," *Nouvel Observateur,* June 23–29, 2016, 48–51.

74. On this theme, see also Bhargava, *Secularism and Its Critics;* Bader, *Secularism or Democracy?;* Ahmet T. Kuru, *Secularism and State Policies towards Religion: The United States, France, and Turkey* (Cambridge: Cambridge University Press, 2009); Elizabeth Shakman Hurd and Linell Cady, eds., *Comparative Secularism in a Global Age* (Basingstoke, UK: Palgrave, 2010), 94–115; Warner, Vanantwerpen, and Calhoun, *Varieties of Secularism.*

75. Will Kymlicka, *Multicultural Citizenship: A Liberal Theory of Minority Rights* (Oxford: Oxford University Press, 1995), 3, 111.

76. A note on Joshua Cohen's important essay "Establishment, Exclusion, and Democracy's Public Reason," which gets to the heart of many of the issues discussed in this chapter. Cohen describes the wrong of symbolic religious establishment as an "exclusion from the space of democratic reasons." Religion is special because it connects collective social practices with comprehensive and fundamental conceptions of the sacred. Because of the epistemic self-containedness of religion, religious reasons are radically different from political reasons, about which one can disagree without being excluded from the democratic community of citizens. Cohen's is a compelling account of the wrongness of religious establishment—and is notable for repudiating the theistic, obligation-centered view of religion and opting instead for a Durkheimian conception of religion as social practice. My approach departs from Cohen in fundamental ways, however. Whereas Cohen works with an "integrated" conception of religion, I disaggregate religion so as to bring out the different wrongs involved in establishment—epistemic exclusion from democratic deliberation (inaccessible reasons) should be distinguished from both equality infringement and liberty infringement. In his analysis of symbolic establishment, Cohen runs together the inaccessibility and the equality concerns (the first and the two concerns), yet they should, in my view, be kept separate. Because most policies of religious establishment are not justified by appeal to religious reasons *stricto sensu*, we need an account of their wrongness that attaches to how they treat citizens, regardless of the reasons brought forth to justify them. Furthermore, the wrongness of symbolic establishment in my view is not connected to the fact that excluded people share comprehensive meanings—as a Jew, I am not treated as an equal in a Christian state, regardless of whether my Jewish identity is a comprehensive or sacred identity for me. Finally, Cohen draws an unsustainable distinction between "religious" and "political-philosophical" disagreement (arguing that only the latter is tractable politically). On my view, foundational disagreement attaches to both, and reasonable citizens only share a general commitment to liberal norms such as equal liberty. See Joshua Cohen, "Establishment, Exclusion, and Democracy's Public Reason," in *Reasons and Recognition: Essays on the Philosophy of T. M. Scanlon,* ed. R. Jay Wallace, Rahul Kumar, and Samuel Freeman (Oxford: Oxford University Press, 2011). For another stimulating essay, which cashes out the "anti-theocratic principle" as containing both a reason-based ("secular independence") and an "equality-based" ("equal status") justification for

nonestablishment, see Corey Brettschneider, "Praying for America: The Constitutional Ban on Theocratic Reasoning in the Establishment, Free Exercise and Equal Protection Clause," unpublished manuscript, on file with the author.

77. John Stuart Mill, "On Liberty," in *Mill: Texts, Commentaries,* ed. Alan Ryan (New York: Norton, 1975).

78. To be sure, Michel Foucault's vision of liberty is markedly different from Mill's deceptively "simple principle" of personal liberty. Foucault's *The History of Sexuality* showed how the privatization of sexuality in the modern period was accompanied by the subjection of sexuality to historically unparalleled forms of scrutiny regulation and disciplinary regimes, crafted as a new object of knowledge, identity, and manipulation. In the last volume of *The History of Sexuality,* however, Foucault also explored the possibility of cultivating an "ethics of the self" that transgressed and at times transcended regulatory regimes of discipline. Michel Foucault, *The History of Sexuality,* vol. 3: *The Care of the Self,* trans. Robert Hurley (New York: Vintage Books, 1988).

79. Susan Moller Okin, with respondents, *Is Multiculturalism Bad for Women?* (Princeton: Princeton University Press, 1999); Clare Chambers, *Sex, Culture, and Justice: The Limits of Choice* (University Park: Penn State University Press, 2008); Monique Deveaux, *Gender and Justice in Multicultural Liberal States* (Oxford: Oxford University Press, 2007); Anne Phillips, *Multiculturalism without Culture* (Princeton: Princeton University Press, 2007); Ayelet Shachar, *Multicultural Jurisdictions: Cultural Differences and Women's Rights* (Cambridge: Cambridge University Press, 2001); Sarah Song, *Justice, Gender and the Politics of Multiculturalism* (Cambridge: Cambridge University Press, 2007); and Maleiha Malik, "Religion and Minority Legal Orders," Linda McClain, "The Intersection of Civil and Religious Family Law in the U.S. Constitutional Order: A Mild Legal Pluralism," and Alicia Cebada Romero, "Religion-Based Legal Pluralism and Human Rights in Europe," all in Cohen and Laborde, *Secularism and Constitutional Democracy.*

80. On ecocentrism, see, e.g., Robyn Eckersley, *Environmentalism and Political Theory: Toward an Eco-centric Approach* (Albany, NY: SUNY Press, 1992); Ned Hettinger and Bill Throop, "Refocusing Ecocentrism: De-emphasizing Stability and Defending Wilderness," *Environmental Ethics* 21 (1999): 3–21; Adam Konopka, "Ecological Goods That Obligate," *Environmental Ethics* 31 (2009): 245–262. For a political liberal defense of environmentalism, see, how-

ever, Derek Bell, "How Can Political Liberals Be Environmentalists?," *Political Studies* 50, no. 4 (2016): 703—724.

81. Chapter 3, section on "Ethical Independence."

82. The main difference between my account and Dworkin's is that the key normative distinction for Dworkin is between personal and impersonal values. I draw the line in a slightly different place: between comprehensive and noncomprehensive conceptions, where the former are explicated as connected to integrity-related liberties. This leaves open the possibility, on my account, that the pursuit of impersonal values (such as the protection of environmental diversity) can be central to a person's conception of her own integrity.

83. Gideon Sapir and Daniel Statman, "Why Freedom of Religion Does Not Include Freedom from Religion," *Law and Philosophy* 24, no. 5 (2005): 467–508. They write: "We propose that protection of freedom from religion should be limited to protection from coercion to participate in religious ceremonies. It is unreasonable to extend it to every instance of legislation motivated by religious reasons" (496). For the view that liberal neutrality properly conceived does not bar limitation of what he calls "non-basic liberties," see Peter de Marneffe, "Liberalism, Liberty, and Neutrality," *Philosophy & Public Affairs* 19, no. 3 (Summer 1990): 253–274.

84. On the generic value of freedom, see Ian Carter, *A Measure of Freedom* (Oxford: Oxford University Press, 1999); Matthew Kramer, *The Quality of Freedom* (Oxford: Oxford University Press, 2008).

85. In a recent UK case, an employment tribunal ruled that an employee's asserted belief that mankind is heading toward catastrophic climate change, and that he was under a moral duty not to contribute to it, is capable of being a protected belief for the purposes of the Employment Equality (Religion or Belief) Regulations 2003. *Grainger plc and Others v. Nicholson: Employment Appeal Tribunal*, November 3, 2009 [2010], I.C.R 360.

86. This is where I depart from Dworkin's emphasis on the distinction between personal and impersonal values.

87. This broadly maps onto the two theories of rights in Dworkin as explicated in Richard Pildes, "Dworkin's Two Conceptions of Rights," *Journal of Legal Studies* 24 (January 2000): 309–315.

88. For a good defense of shared days of rest along these lines, see Julie L. Rose, "Freedom of Association and the Temporal Coordination Problem," *Journal of Political Philosophy* 24, no. 3 (2016): 261–276.

89. The leveling down objection could be rebutted, however, if consideration of equal status and inclusiveness are relevant, as per the previous section.

90. http://theconversation.com/we-already-have-the-answers-to-humane-religious-slaughter-24428.

91. Sapir and Statman, "Why Freedom of Religion." Commenting on an Israeli case concerning the closing to traffic in an Orthodox Jewish neighborhood on the Sabbath, Sapir and Statman suggest that it makes no sense to speak of freedom *from* religion: "Secular people would not sense any offense to their *consciences* if they were forced to travel a long and circuitous route . . . they are not forced to participate in a ceremony of a clearly religious character. . . . There is nothing in the secular value system that is profoundly opposed to a circuitous drive, and therefore the journey is not an attack on their integrity" (494). As they note, "freedom of religion is usually perceived as narrower, and as having a different focus than freedom from religion. The former concerns *a right to engage in some practice,* while the latter concerns a right to be free of laws motivated by a certain set of reasons" (491).

92. A similarly motivated, but substantially different, proposal is Simon May's democratic principle of legitimacy—a principle that, on his view, "religious democracies" can meet. In a hypothetical state May calls Apostolica, religious establishment is deep and far-reaching. However, members of religious minorities enjoy basic (notably political) rights; and Apostolica is in other ways a well-functioning democracy (this is the main difference with Rawls's category of "decent hierarchical" societies in *Law of Peoples*). Apostolica is not a liberal secular polity committed to strict separation of religion and state; but (in May's reconstruction of the Rawlsian principle of legitimacy) it is an acceptably democratic polity. I differ from May in that I think of liberal and democratic standards as continuous, not conflicting. Democratic legitimacy is what allows the selection of one (among many) reasonable conceptions of liberal justice (not all of which require strict separation of religion and state). From this point of view, Apostolica does not meet all my criteria of minimal secularism. To be sure, some of its features are also found in Divinitia, such as the symbolic recognition of religion, the enforcement of a conservative social morality, and foundationally controversial positions about matters of bioethics. But other features of Apostolica are incompatible with liberal democracy: in particular, the fact that basic tenets of the religion are enforced to regulate people's intimate lives. This, in my view, violates both the accessibility and

NOTES TO PAGES 153–157

the personal liberty requirement of minimal secularism. See May, "Religious Democracy."

93. Robert Morris, "Alternative Futures for Formal Church Establishment: Two Case Studies from the UK," in Laborde, Guesnet, and Lee, *Negotiating Religion*; Tariq Modood, *Multiculturalism, Muslims and the British State* (London: British Association for the Study of Religion, 2003).

94. Micah Schwartzman, "The Completeness of Public Reason," *Politics, Philosophy & Economics* 3 (2004): 191–220, at 198, 201.

95. On the incompleteness of public reason generally, see David Reidy, "Rawls's Wide View of Public Reason: Not Wide Enough," *Res Publica* 6, no. 1 (2000): 49–72; Andrew Williams, "The Alleged Incompleteness of Public Reason," *Res Publica* 6, no. 2 (2000): 199–211; Schwartzman, "The Completeness of Public Reason"; John Horton, "Rawls, Public Reason, and the Limits of Liberal Justification," *Contemporary Political Theory* 2, no. 1 (2003): 5–23; Horton, "Reasonable Disagreement," in *Multiculturalism and Moral Conflict*, ed. Maria Dimova-Cookson and Peter Stirk (London: Routledge, 2010), 58–74.

96. See Fabienne Peter, *Democratic Legitimacy* (New York: Routledge, 2008). Some public reason theorists accept democratic procedures as a fair solution to the indeterminacy or inconclusiveness of public reason. See Schwartzmann, "The Completeness of Public Reason." See also Rawls: "While the idea of legitimacy is clearly related to justice, it is noteworthy that its special role in democratic institutions . . . is to authorize an appropriate procedure for making decisions when the conflicts and disagreements in political life make unanimity impossible or rarely to be expected." Rawls, *Political Liberalism,* expanded ed. (New York: Columbia University Press, 2005), 428.

97. Laborde, "Political Liberalism and Religion."

98. For various formulations of this account of the relationship between democracy and justice, see Jeremy Waldron, *Law and Disagreement* (Oxford: Oxford University Press, 1999); Richard Bellamy, *Political Constitutionalism: A Republican Defence of the Constitutionality of Democracy* (Cambridge: Cambridge University Press, 2007); David A. Reidy, "Reciprocity and Reasonable Disagreement: From Liberal to Democratic Legitimacy," *Philosophical Studies* (2006); Laura Valentini, "Justice, Disagreement and Democracy," *British Journal of Political Science* 43 (2012): 177–199; Paul Weithman, "Legitimacy and the Project of Political Liberalism," in *From a Theory of Justice to Political Liberalism* (Cambridge: Cambridge University Press, 2016), 62–71.

99. This is where I depart from advocates of purely procedural democracy, such as Jeremy Waldron and Richard Bellamy, who deny that democracy should be *externally* constrained by a conception of liberal justice: all liberal rights, in their view, are the outcomes of fair democratic procedures. See Waldron, *Law and Disagreement;* Richard Bellamy, *Liberalism and Pluralism: Towards a Politics of Compromise* (London: Routledge, 1999); and Bellamy, *Political Constitutionalism.* But as David Estlund has pointed out, "if political power is to meet the standards of liberal legitimacy, then disagreement can only be so deep; on at least some basic matters it must be the case that such disagreement as does exist is unreasonable, and in that sense less deep than [Waldron] suggests." David Estlund, "Jeremy Waldron on Law and Disagreement," *Philosophical Studies* 99 (2000): 111–128, at 116. See also Cécile Fabre, "The Dignity of Rights," *Oxford Journal of Legal Studies* 20, no. 2 (2000): 271–282; Thomas Christiano, "Waldron on Law and Disagreement," *Law and Philosophy* 19 (2000): 513–543.

100. In his later work, Rawls justifies political liberalism by appeal to the political culture of liberal democracies and limits the justificatory ambitions of the contractarian procedure introduced in *A Theory of Justice.* My own preferred view is a broadly constructivist method of justification, which suggests that the right moral principles should be reciprocally justifiable to free and equal persons. This constructivist agenda was inspired by Kant and pursued in the work of Rawls, Thomas Scanlon, Christine Korsgaard, Onora O'Neill, Jürgen Habermas, and Rainer Forst. Such approaches are often criticized for failing to justify a full set of liberal rights and a determinate conception of justice. For such a criticism of Forst's "right to justification," see, e.g., Adam Etinson, "On Shareable Reasons: A Comment on Forst," *Journal of Social Philosophy* 45, no. 1 (Spring 2014): 76–88. My approach is less vulnerable to this criticism because I concede that abstract constructivist justification can conclusively justify only minimal moral axioms ("Do not do unto others," etc.) and the validity of basic liberal rights. It is not an entirely vacuous principle, but it remains inconclusive about most reasonable disagreements about justice.

101. For a congenial republican theory that also construes democracy as legitimacy conferring, see Philip Pettit, *On the People's Terms: A Republican Theory and Model of Democracy* (Cambridge: Cambridge University Press, 2012), 142–145. Pettit sees distributive justice and democratic legitimacy as two distinct normative desiderata, whereas I prefer to see both justice and legiti-

macy as having democratic and distributive dimensions. Legitimacy is a less demanding standard, one that sets the bounds of reasonable disagreements about justice.

102. For a similar conception of the relationship between political theory and democratic politics, see Patten, *Equal Recognition*, 21–24.

103. Gerald Gaus, "Sectarianism without Perfection? On Quong's Political Liberalism," *Philosophy and Public Issues* 2, no. 2 (Fall 2012): 7–15. For Quong's response, see Jonathan Quong, "Liberalism without Perfection: Replies to Gaus, Colburn, Chan, and Bocchiola," *Philosophy and Public Issues* 2, no. 2 (2012): 51–79.

5. State Sovereignty and Freedom of Association

1. Thomas Berg, Kimberlee Wood Colby, and Richard W. Garnett, "Religious Freedom, Church-State Separation, and the Ministerial Exception," *Northwestern University Law Review Colloquy* 106 (2011): 175–190; Stephen D. Smith, "The Jurisdictional Conception of Church Autonomy," in *The Rise of Corporate Religious Liberty*, ed. Micah Schwartzman, Chad Flanders, and Zoe Robinson (Oxford: Oxford University Press 2016), 19–37; Richard Garnett, "The Freedom of the Church: (Towards) an Exposition, Translation and Defense," in Schwartzman, Flanders, and Robinson, *Corporate Religious Liberty*, 39–62; Victor Muniz-Fraticelli, *The Structure of Pluralism: On the Authority of Associations* (Oxford: Oxford University Press, 2014), 4.

2. Richard Schragger and Micah Schwartzman, "Against Religious Institutionalism," *Virginia Law Review* 99, no. 5 (2013): 917–985; Schragger and Schwartzman, "Some Realism about Corporate Rights," in Schwartzman, Flanders, and Robinson, *Corporate Religious Liberty*, 345–371; Jean Cohen, "Freedom of Religion Inc.: Whose Sovereignty?," *Netherlands Journal of Philosophy* 3 (2015); Jean Cohen, "Sovereignty, the Corporate Religious, and Jurisdictional/Political Pluralism," in *Religion in Liberal Political Philosophy*, ed. Cécile Laborde and Aurélia Bardon (Oxford: Oxford University Press, 2017); Lawrence Sager, "Why Churches (and, Possibly, the Tarpon Bay Women's Blue Water Fishing Club) Can Discriminate," in Schwartzman, Flanders, and Robinson, *Corporate Religious Liberty*, 77–101.

3. Anna Stilz, *Liberal Loyalty: Freedom, Obligation and the State* (Princeton: Princeton University Press, 2009).

4. Harold Laski, *A Grammar of Politics* (London: Allen and Unwin, 1982 [1925]). See also Cécile Laborde, *Pluralist Thought and the State in Britain and France, 1900–25* (Basingstoke, UK: Macmillan, 2000), chap. 4.

5. Here I should make it clear that I do not say more about which institutional form "the state" should take. It does not have to be centralized (see federal states); it can delegate areas of competence to supranational institutions (see the European Union); it must represent a wide plurality of interests and identities, not mere majoritarian will; and it should operate a division of powers (legislative, executive, and juridical). On my view, democratic sovereignty is not incompatible with popular "precommitment" to the constitutionalization of some basic rights—so democracy and rights are "co-original" in Jürgen Habermas's sense. For stimulating theories of sovereignty and democracy, see Jürgen Habermas, *Between Facts and Norms* (Cambridge, MA: MIT Press, 1996), 104, 118–130; Albert Weale, *Democracy* (New York: St. Martin's Press, 1999); Richard Bellamy, *Political Constitutionalism: A Republican Defence of the Constitutionality of Democracy* (Cambridge: Cambridge University Press, 2007); Jean L. Cohen, *Globalization and Sovereignty: Rethinking Legality, Legitimacy and Constitutionalism* (Cambridge: Cambridge University Press, 2012); Philip Pettit, *On the People's Terms: A Republican Theory and Model of Democracy* (Cambridge: Cambridge University Press, 2012); Pierre Rosanvallon, *La légitimité démocratique: Impartialité, réflexivité, proximité* (Paris: Editions du Seuil, 2008).

6. Interestingly, as early as the seventeenth century the Swiss used the very same term "competence-competence." A special, evenly divided Protestant-Catholic court was established to adjudicate whether a matter counted as religious and therefore had to be handled under the terms of the religious peace treaties. I am grateful to Benjamin Kaplan for pointing this out to me.

7. Hussein Ali Agrama, *Questioning Secularism: Islam, Sovereignty, and the Rule of Law in Modern Egypt* (Chicago: Chicago University Press, 2012); Markus Dressler and Arvind-Pal S. Mandair, *Secularism and Religion-Making* (New York: Oxford University Press, 2011); William T. Cavanaugh, *The Myth of Religious Violence: Secular Ideology and the Roots of Modern Conflict* (New York: Oxford University Press, 2009); Stanley Fish, "Mission Impossible: Setting the Just Bounds between Church and State," in *Law and Religion: A Critical Anthology*, ed. Stephen M. Feldman (New York: NYU Press, 2000), 383–410;

Saba Mahmood, *Religious Difference in a Secular Age* (Princeton: Princeton University Press, 2016).

8. For more on this theme, see Cécile Laborde, "Laïcité, séparation, neutralité," in *Ethique et déontologie dans l'Education Nationale,* ed. Jean-François Dupeyron and Christophe Miqueu (Paris: Armand Colin, 2013), 171–183. In Chapter 4, I explained another way in which the liberal state is "secular" in the sense of "nonreligious," by identifying the features of religion (and the good) that make religion impermissible as an object of state endorsement, for purposes of liberal legitimacy. In this chapter, I argue that once a state enjoys liberal legitimacy, it has, in addition, the prerogative to fix the more determinate boundary between what counts as religion and what counts as nonreligion, in more specific controversies about which there is reasonable disagreement about justice. This is what critical religion theorists refer to when they use the notion of "secularism" as a principle of meta-jurisdictional sovereignty.

9. For stimulating reflections, see Ronald Beiner, "John Rawls's Genealogy of Liberalism," in *Civil Religion: A Dialogue in the History of Political Philosophy* (Cambridge: Cambridge University Press, 2011), 283–300; Patrick Neal, "The Liberal State and the Religious Citizen: Justificatory Perspectives in Political Liberalism," in *Rawls and Religion,* ed. Tom Bailey and Valentina Gentile (New York: Columbia University Press, 2015), 133–151. For a pioneering discussion of the tension between liberal democratic citizenship and religious commitment, see Nancy L. Rosenblum, ed., *Obligations of Citizenship and Demands of Faith* (Princeton: Princeton University Press, 2000).

10. Wael B. Hallaq, *The Impossible State: Islam, Politics and Modernity's Moral Predicament* (New York: Columbia University Press, 2013).

11. J. N. Figgis, *Churches in the Modern State* (London: Longmans Green, 1914 [1913]), 72. Compare Laborde, *Pluralist Thought.*

12. Harold Berman, *Law and Revolution* (Cambridge, MA: Harvard University Press, 1983).

13. Brent Nongbri, *Before Religion: A History of a Modern Concept* (New Haven: Yale University Press, 2013); Kirstie M. McClure, "Difference, Diversity and the Limits of Toleration," *Political Theory* 18, no. 3 (1990): 361–391.

14. Cavanaugh, *Myth of Religious Violence.* The expression "Great Separation" is from Mark Lilla, *The Stillborn God* (New York: Vintage Books, 2008).

15. Michael W. McConnell, "Believers as Equal Citizens," in Rosenblum, *Obligations of Citizenship*, 91.

16. McClure, "Difference, Diversity," 384.

17. Cited in Andrew Koppelman, "'Freedom of the Church' and the Authority of the State," *Journal of Contemporary Legal Issues* 21, no. 145 (2013): 145–164, at 164. Available at SSRN: https://ssrn.com/abstract=2337116.

18. Saba Mahmood and Peter Danchin, "Immunity or Regulation? Antinomies of Religious Freedom," *South Atlantic Quarterly* 113, no. 1 (Winter 2014): 129–158.

19. For a penetrating criticism of the pervasive yet elusive meaning of "harm" in religious controversies, see Stephen D. Smith, *The Disenchantment of Secular Discourse* (Cambridge, MA: Harvard University Press, 2010), chap. 3. See also McClure, "Difference, Diversity."

20. For different perspectives, see Tariq Modood, T. R. Hansen, Eric Bleich, Brendan O'Leary, and Joe Carens, "The Danish Cartoon Affair: Free Speech, Racism, Islamism, and Integration," *International Migration* 44, no. 5 (2006); Talal Asad, Wendy Brown, Judith Butler, and Saba Mahmood, *Is Critique Secular? Blasphemy, Injury, and Free Speech* (Berkeley: University of California Press, 2009); Andrew March, "Speech and the Sacred: Does the Defense of Free Speech Rest on a Mistake about Religion?," *Political Theory* 40, no. 3 (2012): 319–346; Jeremy Waldron, *The Harm in Hate Speech* (Cambridge, MA: Harvard University Press, 2012); Christoph Baumgartner, "Blasphemy as Violence: Trying to Understand the Kind of Injury That Can Be Inflicted by Acts and Artefacts That Are Construed as Blasphemy," *Journal of Religion in Europe* 6 (2013): 35–63.

21. See, e.g., Peter Danchin, "Suspect Symbols: Value Pluralism as a Theory of Religious Freedom in International Law," *Yale Journal of International Law* 33 (2008); Susanna Mancini, "The Power of Symbols and Symbols as Power: Secularism and Religion as Guarantors of Cultural Convergence," *Cardozo Law Review* 30, no. 6 (2009): 2629–2668.

22. Smith, "Jurisdictional Conception"; Garnett, "Freedom of the Church"; Muniz-Fraticelli, *The Structure of Pluralism*.

23. David Nicholls, *The Pluralist State: The Political Ideas of J. N. Figgis and His Contemporaries* (Basingstoke, UK: Macmillan, 1994); Paul Hirst, *The Pluralist Theory of the State: Selected Writings of G. D. H. Cole, J. N. Figgis, and H. L. Laski* (London: Routledge, 1989); Laborde, *Pluralist Thought*; Marc Stears, *Progressives, Pluralists, and the Problems of the State: Ideologies of Reform in the*

United States and Britain, 1909–1926 (Oxford: Oxford University Press, 2006). Another European theory that has influenced U.S. religious institutionalists is that of neo-Calvinist Dutch writer Abraham Kuyper and his theory of sphere sovereignty. See Paul Horwitz, "Churches as First Amendment Institutions: Of Sovereignty and Spheres," *Harvard Civil Rights–Civil Liberties Law Review* 44, no. 107 (2009).

24. Berg, Colby, and Garnett, "Religious Freedom." See also Smith, "Jurisdictional Conception."

25. For other criticisms of religious institutionalists, see Winnifred Sullivan, "The Church" (2013), online at *The Imminent Frame*, http://blogs.ssrc.org/tif /2012/01/31/the-church/; Schragger and Schwartzman, "Against Religious Institutionalism"; Schragger and Schwartzman, "Some Realism"; Cohen, "Freedom of Religion Inc."; Sager, "Why Churches . . . Can Discriminate"; Sune Laegaard, "Disaggregating Corporate Freedom of Religion," *Netherlands Journal of Legal Philosophy* 44, no. 3 (2015): 221–230. For a thoughtful engagement with the jurisdictional boundary question from a multicultural perspective, see Ayelet Shachar, *Multicultural Jurisdictions: Cultural Differences and Women's Rights* (Cambridge: Cambridge University Press, 2001).

26. Muniz-Fraticelli, *Structure of Pluralism*, 117.

27. Cohen, "Sovereignty"; Dieter Grimm, "Sovereignty and Religious Norms in the Secular Constitutional State," in *Secularism and Constitutional Democracy*, ed. Jean L. Cohen and Cécile Laborde (New York: Columbia University Press, 2016), 341–357.

28. In the *Burwell v. Hobby Lobby* ruling (2014), the U.S. Supreme Court held that a family-held business corporation was exempt from the contraception mandate imposed under authority of the Affordable Care Act. Because the requirement to provide insurance coverage for contraception to their employees "substantially burdened" the owners of Hobby Lobby, they were exempted under the federal Religious Freedom Restoration Act.

29. Smith, "Jurisdictional Conception," 25–28.

30. Muniz-Fraticelli, *Structure of Pluralism*, 179. Italics added.

31. Ibid.

32. Laegaard, "Disaggregating."

33. For a defense of quasi-sovereignty for theocratic communities, see Lucas Swaine, *The Liberal Conscience: Politics and Principle in a World of Religious Pluralism* (New York: Columbia University Press, 2006).

34. *Hosanna-Tabor Evangelical Lutheran Church and Social v. Equal Employment Opportunity Commission,* 565 U.S. (2012); *Burwell v. Hobby Lobby,* 573 U.S. (2014).

35. For a historically detailed critique, see Cohen, "Freedom of Religion Inc."

36. F. W. Maitland, introduction to Otto van Gierke, *Political Theories of the Middle Ages* (Cambridge: Cambridge University Press, 1900); David Runciman, *Pluralism and the Personality of the State* (Cambridge: Cambridge University Press, 1997).

37. Christian List and Philip Pettit, *Group Agency: The Possibility, Design and Status of Corporate Agents* (Oxford: Oxford University Press, 2011).

38. Cohen, "Freedom of Religion Inc."; Schragger and Schwartzman, "Some Realism."

39. Laborde, *Pluralist Thought;* David Runciman, *Pluralism.*

40. John Dewey, "The Historic Background of Corporate Legal Personality," *Yale Law Journal* 35, no. 655 (1926).

41. Schragger and Schwartzman, "Some Realism," 360.

42. Mark Rosen, "Religious Institutions, Liberal States and the Political Architecture of Overlapping Spheres," *University of Illinois Law Review* 737 (2014): 737–783; Lesley A. Jacobs, "Bridging the Gap between Individual and Collective Rights with the Idea of Integrity," *Canadian Journal of Law and Jurisprudence* 4 (1991): 375–386.

43. Peter Jones, "Group Rights," *The Stanford Encyclopedia of Philosophy* (Summer 2016), ed. Edward N. Zalta, https://plato.stanford.edu/archives/sum 2016/entries/rights-group/.

44. Cited in Christopher C. Lund, "In Defense of the Ministerial Exception," *North Carolina Law Review* 90 (2011): 57–60.

45. For an early explication and defense of the ministerial exception, see Douglas Laycock, "Towards a General Theory of the Religion Clauses: The Case of Church Labor Relations and the Right to Church Autonomy," *Columbia Law Review* 81, no. 7 (November 1981): 1373–1417. The only exceptions from this broad sweep of exemptions are corporal punishment, criminal action, and sexual abuse and sexual harassment cases.

46. *Hosanna-Tabor Evangelical Lutheran Church and School v. EEOC* (2012).

47. Even authors otherwise critical of church autonomy defend the ministerial exception. See, e.g., Sager, "Why Churches . . . Can Discriminate";

Eisgruber and Sager, "Vulnerability of Conscience"; Schwartzman and Schragger, "Against Religious Institutionalism"; Ira C. Lupu and Robert Tuttle, "The Distinctive Place of Religious Entities in Our Constitutional Order," *Villanova Law Review* 46, no. 5 (2001); Cohen, "Freedom of Religion Inc."

48. As Leslie Griffin notes, "the favourite straw woman is that without the exception, courts will force denominations with all-male clergy to accept women priests. Using the ministerial exception to address that problem, however, is like swatting a fly with a sledgehammer." Leslie C. Griffin, "Ordained Discrimination: The Cases against the Ministerial Exception," *University of Houston, Public Law and Legal Theory Series* (2011): 19.

49. For instructive comparisons between American and European approaches, see Carolyn Evans and Anna Hood, "Religious Autonomy and Labour Law: A Comparison of the Jurisprudence of the United States and the European Court of Human Rights," *Oxford Journal of Law and Religion* 1, no. 1 (2012): 1–27; and the special issue *The Ministerial Exception,* ed. Pamela Slotte, *Oxford Journal of Law and Religion* 4, no. 2 (June 2015). For a critique of recent trends, see, e.g., Sjin Smet, "Fernandez Martinez v Spain: Towards a 'Ministerial Exception' for Europe?," https://strasbourgobservers.com/2012/05/24/fernandez-martinez-v-spain-towards-a-ministerial-exception-in-europe/. On UK law, see Julian Rivers, *The Law of Organized Religions: Between Establishment and Secularism* (Oxford: Oxford University Press, 2010); and Russell Sandberg, *Law and Religion* (Cambridge: Cambridge University Press, 2011).

50. Rosen, "Religious Institutions."

51. Andrew Shorten, "Are There Rights to Institutional Exemptions?," *Journal of Social Philosophy* 46, no. 2 (2015): 242–263.

52. Title VII of the U.S. Civil Rights Act of 1964, which forbids employment discrimination, exempts religious organizations from the prohibition of religious discrimination. The UK Employment Equality (Religion and Belief) Regulations 2003 accommodate employment where religion or belief are "genuine occupational requirements" and for other jobs "where an employer has an ethos based on religion and belief." See Russell Sandberg and Norman Doe, "Religious Exemptions in Discrimination Law," *Cambridge Law Journal* 66, no. 2 (July 2007): 302–312.

53. Lund, "In Defense." See also Jacob Levy, "Classifying Cultural Rights," in *Nomos XXXIX.*

54. For a case from the European Court of Human Rights, see *Obst v. Germany* (2010), where a Mormon director's employment was terminated because he was having an extramarital affair. For a U.S. case, see *Little v. Wuerl* (3r Cir 1991), where a teacher in a Catholic school was fired because she failed to have her first marriage annulled before she remarried. A good survey is Evans and Hood, "Religious Autonomy."

55. *EEOC v. Pacific Press Publishing*, 676 F2d 1272 (1982), cited in Nancy Rosenblum, *"Amos:* Religious Autonomy and Pluralism," in Rosenblum, *Obligations of Citizenship*, 169–170.

56. *Boyd v. Harding* 88 F 3d 410 (6th Cir 1996); *Ganzy v. Allen Christian School* 995 F. Supp. 340, 348 (1997); *Cline v. Catholic Diocese of Toledo* (2000).

57. Kent Greenawalt, "Freedom of Association and Religious Association," in *Freedom of Association*, ed. Amy Gutmann (Princeton: Princeton University Press, 1998), 109–144, at 116. But this does not mean that either should receive governmental benefits, or that they cannot be criticized or shunned. Compare Corey Brettschneider, *When the State Speaks, What Should It Say? How Democracies Can Protect Expression and Promote Equality* (Princeton: Princeton University Press, 2012).

58. Christopher McCrudden. "Multiculturalism, Freedom of Religion, Equality, and the British Constitution: The JFS Case Considered," *International Journal of Constitutional Law* 9, no. 1 (2001): 200–229; Haim Shapira, "Equality in Religious Schools: The J.F.S. Case Reconsidered," in *Institutionalizing Rights and Religion: Competing Supremacies*, ed. Leora Batnitzky and Hanoch Dagan (Cambridge: Cambridge University Press, 2017), 164–183.

59. Sacred Congregation for the Doctrine of the Faith, *Inter Insigniores*, Declaration on the Admission of Women to the Ministerial Priesthood (October 15, 1976).

60. For an excellent presentation of the theological debates, and a compelling case for women priests, see http://www.womenpriests.org/church /interlet.asp.

61. The UK Employment Equality (Sex Discrimination) Act 2005 provides that gender discrimination can be lawful "so as to comply with the doctrines of the religion" or "because of the nature of the employment and the context in which it is carried out."

62. For the view that ethnic groups lack clear identity and effective agency, and therefore are deficient right-holders (by comparison with formally consti-

tuted associations), see James Nickel, "Group Agency and Group Rights," in *Nomos XXXIX,* 235–256. See also Adina Preda, "Group Rights and Group Agency" *Journal of Moral Philosophy* 9 (2012): 229–254.

63. Avigail Eisenberg and Jeff Spinner-Halev, eds., *Minorities within Minorities: Equality, Rights and Diversity* (Cambridge: Cambridge University Press, 2005); Shachar, *Multicultural Jurisdictions.* On the republican theory of nondomination that I defended in *Critical Republicanism,* I also emphasized the importance of *voice* and contestability within associations. This, however, falls short of a demand of full democratization of associations.

64. For similar suggestions, see James D. Nelson, "Conscience, Incorporated," *Michigan State Law Review,* no. 5 (2013); Elizabeth Sepper, "Contraception and the Birth of Corporate Conscience," *Journal of Gender, Social Policy and the Law* 22, nos. 2/4 (2014): 303–342.

65. Most critics accept that Hobby Lobby can make a religious freedom claim, but argue that the claim should be rejected because it harms or burdens employees, or generates other unacceptable third-party costs. My criticism is more radical: I am interested in the first, qualification stage: Do organizations such as Hobby Lobby have a *pro tanto* claim of religious freedom? Can commercial associations put forward relevant coherence interests? For a pioneering discussion, see Cohen, "Freedom of Religion Inc."; and the essays in Schwartzman, Flanders, and Robinson, *Corporate Religious Liberty.*

66. See, generally, Alan J. Meese and Nathan B. Oman, "Hobby Lobby, Corporate Law, and the Theory of the Firm: Why For-Profit Corporations are RFRA Persons," *Harvard Law Review Forum* 127 (2014): 273–301.

67. Justice O'Connor's concurrence in the landmark case *Roberts v. U.S. Jaycees,* 468 U.S. 609, 623 (1984), distinguished between expressive and commercial association. In *Roberts,* the Court recognized that the power to determine its own membership is central to the free speech rights of expressive organizations. Nonetheless, the Court upheld a Minnesota public accommodation law requiring the Jaycees to admit women as members, in contravention of that organization's rules. Justice O'Connor, in a concurring opinion, found that the Jaycees were a commercial organization, and therefore subject to state regulation of its membership. On the other hand, she suggested, a predominantly expressive association has an absolute right to determine its own membership. For discussion, see Seana Valentine Shiffrin, "What Is Really Wrong with Compelled Association?," *Northwestern Law Review* 99, no. 2 (2005).

68. *Tyndale v. Sebelius,* 904 F. Supp. 2d 106, 117 (D.D.C. 2012). The case concerned a for-profit corporation that publishes religious books and Bibles. Cited in Sepper, "Contraception," 312.

69. Nelson, "Conscience, Incorporated."

70. Shorten, "Are There Rights?"

71. Meir Dan-Cohen, "Between Selves and Collectivities: Towards a Jurisprudence of Identity," *University of Chicago Law Review* 61 (1994): 1213; Shiffrin "What Is Really Wrong?," 852.

72. Nelson, "Conscience, Incorporated."

73. See Nelson Tebbe, *Religious Freedom in an Egalitarian Age* (Cambridge, MA: Harvard University Press, 2017), chap. 7, for a good, nuanced discussion.

74. Annabelle Lever, "Equality and Conscience: Ethics and the Provision of Public Services," in *Religion and Liberal Political Philosophy,* ed. Aurélia Bardon and Cécile Laborde (Oxford: Oxford University Press, 2017).

75. Kent Greenawalt, "Five Questions about Religion Judges Are Afraid to Ask," in Rosenblum, *Obligations of Citizenship,* 196–244.

76. Christopher Lund construes associational interests expansively. He has offered a tripartite distinction between what he calls the *relational, conscience,* and *autonomy* components of freedom of religious association. Relational components involve the rights of religious organizations to discriminate in hiring on the basis of religion, whether or not individuals are to perform religious or nonreligious activities. Conscience components involve the right to discriminate (on any ground) when such discrimination is one of the doctrinal tenets of the religious association. Autonomy components refer to the ministerial exception *simpliciter* and justify blanket immunity from interference with church appointments of ministers. As I explain below, I disagree with Lund's jurisdictional theory of religious immunity, defending instead a more minimal approach of judicial deference toward religious competence. But, for my purposes here, I do not think that Lund's further distinction between relational and conscience interests can be sustained. What I prefer to call coherence interests can be subsumed into conscience interests: associations do not have separate relational interests that would, in and of themselves, justify exemptions from employment laws. Lund, "In Defense." This permissive criterion is used in U.S. law: since 1972, Title VII exempts religious employers from all claims of religious discrimination, re-

gardless of whether the employees perform religious or secular activities. This has become even more controversial in the context of the debate over "charitable choice" and the mooted expansion of "faith-based welfare." See Emily R. Gill, "Religious Organizations, Charitable Choice, and the Limits of Freedom of Conscience," *Perspectives on Politics* 2, no. 4 (2004): 741–755. For a critical analysis of *Corporation of the Presiding Bishop v. Amos* (1987), see Nancy Rosenblum, "*Amos:* Religious Autonomy and Pluralism," in Rosenblum, *Obligations of Citizenship,* 165–195.

77. Bruce Bagni, "Discrimination in the Name of the Lord: A Critical Evaluation of Discrimination by Religious Organisations," *Columbia Law Review* 79, no. 1514 (1979): 1539–1529, at 1539–1540.

78. Greenawalt, "Freedom of Association," 116.

79. A good philosophical treatment of this question is Stuart White, "Religion and Employment Discrimination: The Latitude Issue," (unpublished manuscript, on file with author).

80. This semantic approach is pursued by Zoe Robinson, "What Is a Religious Institution?," *Boston College Law Review* 55, no. 181 (2014). For a compelling critique, which also disaggregates the various modes of religious association, see Ira C. Lupu and Robert W. Tuttle, "Religious Exemptions and the Limited Relevance of Corporate Identity," in Schwartzman, Flanders, and Robinson, *Corporate Religious Liberty,* 373–397. Another disaggregated theory of freedom of association, which distinguishes different types of group (intimate associations, community groups, and value organizations) and different types of relationship (leadership, membership) is Tebbe, *Religious Freedom.*

81. There is, however, an ambiguity in U.S. jurisprudence here. Strictly speaking, freedom of association implies the right to associate to engage in activities protected by the First Amendment, including speech, assembly, and the exercise of religion. The right of religious association, on this view, is derived, not directly from freedom of speech, but from the right to associate in activities connected to the exercise of religion. Many commentators, however, seek to derive the rights of religious associations directly from freedom of speech, via an expressive theory of freedom of association. For an extensive discussion and critique, see John D. Inazu, *Liberty's Refuge: The Forgotten Freedom of Assembly* (New Haven: Yale University Press, 2012).

82. Amy Gutmann, "Freedom of Association: An Introductory Essay," in Gutmann, *Freedom of Association,* 3–32, at 11–12.

83. *Roberts v. U.S. Jaycees,* 468 U.S. 609, 623 (1984).

84. *Boy Scouts of America v. Dale,* 530 U.S. 640 (2000).

85. Shiffrin, "What Is Really Wrong?"

86. Andrew Koppelman (with Tobias Barrington Wolff), *A Right to Discriminate? How the Case of Boy Scouts of America v. James Dale Warped the Law of Free Association* (New Haven: Yale University Press, 2009).

87. Andrew Koppelman, *Defending American Religious Neutrality* (Cambridge, MA: Harvard University Press, 2013); Koppelman, " 'Freedom of the Church.' "

88. For a general argument to this effect, see Caroline Mala Corbin, "Above the Law? The Constitutionality of the Ministerial Exemption from Antidiscrimination Law," *Fordham Law Review* 75, no. 4 (2011): 1965–2038.

89. Richard W. Garnett, "Are Churches Like the Boy Scouts?," *St. John's Legal Comment* 22 (2007): 515.

90. The connection between public reason and judicial restraint in epistemic assessments of religious beliefs is also noted in David Golemboski, "Judicial Evaluation of Religious Belief and the Accessibility Requirement in Public Reason," *Law and Philosophy* 35 (2016): 435–460. However, I reject the more comprehensive "symmetry argument" propounded by Abner Greene. Greene has developed an epistemic theory of state-church relations according to which it is the inaccessibility of religious belief that justifies the special treatment of religion, both for free exercise and for nonestablishment purposes. The basic thought is that because religious arguments are excluded from the lawmaking process, religious believers should be compensated through special exemptions, as a counterweight to the Establishment Clause gag rule. For my part, I reject the view that people should be compensated for the illegitimacy of some of the arguments they might present when acting in official capacity. More fundamentally, I do not think that there is a single conception of religion (whether epistemic inaccessibility or something else) that unites and justifies both clauses. My disaggregation strategy points to a plurality of normative dimensions of religion, and epistemic inaccessibility plays a very limited role. Accessibility is only one dimension (in addition to the more substantive values of freedom and equality) of what in Chapter 4 I called the secular state. And it plays no role at all in my justification of individual exemptions in Chapter 6, where I assume that it is irrelevant whether the arguments claimants present are accessible, intelligible, or even cogent or coherent, provided

they are connected to the ethical integrity of the claimant. What grounds the legitimacy of individual exemptions is not the epistemic status of individual beliefs, but the importance of certain practices to individual integrity. Matters are slightly different with groups because the issue of epistemic competence is bound up with the question of rightful authority (of leaders over members). There, it is not illegitimate for courts to inquire as to the properly "religious" nature of a claim—i.e., whether the claim correctly express a coherence or a competence interest. For Greene's theory, see Abner S. Greene, "The Political Balance of the Religion Clauses," *Yale Law Journal* 102, no. 1611 (1993): 1633–1639.

91. See *The Supreme Court's Hands-Off Approach to Religious Doctrine: An Introduction*, special issue, *Notre Dame Law Review* 84, no. 2 (2009).

92. In *Watson*, which concerned the split of a Presbyterian church over the issue of slavery, the Supreme Court rejected the English rule of awarding the property to the faction deemed to hold the "true standard of faith" and instead held that it would defer to the higher church authority's decision on this religious question.

93. Greenawalt, "Freedom of Association," 120–121; Kent Greenawalt, "Hands Off! Civil Court Involvement in Conflicts over Religious Property," *Columbia Law Review* 98, no. 1843 (1998). In the United Kingdom, the Free Church of Scotland of 1904 case was the *cause célèbre* that provoked the ire of pluralists. A dissenting minority of the church (the "Wee Frees") sought the assistance of the courts to forestall a merger with the United Presbyterian Church, a merger approved by a large majority of Free Church members. The House of Lords was called to interpret the terms of the original trust and, in so doing, sided with the minority, whose commitments it deemed continuous with the theological and ecclesiastical tenets of the founding ministers of the original church. In F. W. Maitland's words, it was there that "the dead hand [of the law] fell with a resounding slap upon the living body" of the Church. Pluralists such as Maitland argued that the state should let groups develop and grow organically. As Denise Réaume has shown, however, it is not clear that the hands-off approach to property disputes—what she calls the "Pontius Pilatius approach"—is always the best way to respect group autonomy, especially in case of internal constitutional dispute about which faction best pursues the original intentions of founders. See Denise G. Réaume, "Common-Law Constructions of Group Autonomy: A Case Study," in *Nomos XXIX*,

257–289, at 281. For further analysis, see Rivers, *The Law of Organized Religions,* 97–99.

94. See *NLRB v. Catholic Bishop,* 440 U.S. 490 (1979); *Serbian Eastern Orthodox Diocese v. Milivojevich,* 426 U.S. 696 (1976); *Gonzales v. Archbishop,* 280 U.S. 1 (1929). As Lupu and Tuttle have shown, the rationale is not one of sweeping "freedom of the church" but, rather, a limited claim of state incompetence about certain matters. Ira C. Lupu and Robert W. Tuttle, *Secular Government, Religious People* (Grand Rapids, MI: Eerdmans, 2014), chap. 2.

95. Cited in Corbin, "Above the Law?," 1980.

96. Lund, "In Defense." For other defenses of the ministerial exception by appeal to structural limitations on state competence, see Lupu and Tuttle, "Distinctive Place"; Lupu and Tuttle, *Secular Government, Religious People,* chap. 2.

97. Berg, Colby, and Garnett, "Religious Freedom," 188.

98. See Chapter 6.

99. Corbin, "Above the Law?," 2017. See also Griffin, "Ordained Discrimination." But see Lund, "In Defense," for a contrary view.

100. *Rweyemamu v. Cote,* 520 F. 3d 198, 208 (2nd Cir 2008), cited in Evans and Hood, "Religious Autonomy," 13.

101. Evans and Hood, "Religious Autonomy," 22.

102. The case was particularly egregious, with no reasons for termination given, no chance of refutation, and no appeal. Ibid., 20.

103. *Weinstock v. Columbia University,* 2000. For analysis, see Corbin, "Above the Law?," 2019.

104. Lupu and Tuttle, *Secular Government, Religious People,* 44. Claims to jurisdictional sovereignty in internal affairs are central to recent cases, such as *Hosanna-Tabor* (where the church claimed that its employee, by appealing to a secular court, had broken her terms of employment with the church) and *Sindicatul "Păstorual Cel Bun" v. Romania* (where the church denied the trade union rights of Orthodox priests on the ground that the priests had vowed to stay faithful to the church). On the latter, see Chiara Cordelli, "Democratizing Organised Religion," *Journal of Politics* (January 6, 2017), http://www.journals.uchicago.edu/doi/abs/10.1086/689284.

6. Disaggregating Religion in Freedom of Religion

1. For different versions, see Chapter 2 on Dworkin; Sonu Bedi, "Debate: What Is So Special About Religion? The Dilemma of the Religious Exemption," *Journal of Political Philosophy* 15, no. 2 (2007): 235–249; Gemma Cornelissen, "Belief-Based Exemptions: Are Religious Beliefs Special?," *Ratio Juris* 25, no. 1 (2012): 85–109; Brian Leiter, *Why Tolerate Religion?* (Princeton: Princeton University Press, 2012).

2. Conclusion 3 could be reached through a different argument—for example, an argument that purports to show that exemptions *per se* are incompatible with equality or the rule of law. Although I do not think those arguments generally succeed, I do not discuss them in detail here, as I focus on the specifically liberal egalitarian concern with religious exemptions *qua* religious.

3. Private correspondence with author.

4. See, on the three cases respectively, Corey Brettschneider, "A Transformative Theory of Religious Freedom: Promoting the Reasons for Rights," *Political Theory* 38 (2010): 187–213; Martha Nussbaum, *The New Religious Intolerance* (Cambridge, MA: Harvard University Press, 2012); Cécile Laborde, "Miller's Minarets: Religion, Culture, Domination," in *Political Philosophy, Here and Now: Essays in Honour of David Miller,* ed. Zofia Stemplowska, Daniel Butt, and Sarah Fine (Oxford: Oxford University Press, forthcoming).

5. T. Jeremy Gunn, "The Complexity of Religion and the Definition of 'Religion' in International Law," *Harvard Human Rights Journal* 16 (2003): 189–214, at 197–199. In practice, religious persecution is also often a placeholder for a web of discriminatory forces—religious minorities are often discriminated against on grounds that are ethnic, racial, economic, political, and national.

6. See, e.g., Dworkin, *Religion without God* (Cambridge, MA: Harvard University Press, 2013), chap. 3; George Letsas, "Accommodating What Needn't Be Special," *Law and Ethics of Human Rights* 10, no. 2 (2016): 319–340; Brettschneider, "A Transformative Theory."

7. Gerald Gaus, *Justificatory Liberalism: An Essay on Epistemology and Political Theory* (Oxford: Oxford University Press, 1996), 175.

8. John Rawls, *The Basic Liberties and Their Priority,* vol. 3 (Salt Lake City: University of Utah Press, 1982). See also Philip Pettit, "The Basic Liberties," in *The Legacy of H. L. A. Hart: Legal, Political and Moral Philosophy,* ed. Matthew Kramer et al. (Oxford: Oxford University Press, 2008), 201–224.

9. Charles Taylor, in *Sources of the Self,* called them "strong evaluations": evaluations about better or worse, important or trivial conceptions of the good life, views that are not reducible to mere preferences, desires, and inclinations, but are instead the standards by which desires, preferences, and inclinations can be judged. Charles Taylor, *Sources of Self* (Cambridge, MA: Harvard University Press, 1989).

10. Andrew Koppelman, *Defending American Religious Neutrality* (Cambridge, MA: Harvard University Press, 2013); Koppelman, "A Rawlsian Defense of Special Treatment of Religion," in *Religion in Liberal Political Philosophy,* ed. Cécile Laborde and Aurelia Bardon (Oxford: Oxford University Press, 2017).

11. Alan Patten, *Equal Recognition: The Moral Foundations of Minority Rights* (Princeton: Princeton University Press, 2014), 136. For commentary, see Cécile Laborde, "The Evanescence of Neutrality," *Political Theory,* First Online, May 8, 2017.

12. As I showed in my analysis of Dworkin in Chapter 2, this echoes the tension between the "reason-constraining" and the "immunities" views of rights. The former denies the state the power to appeal to certain impermissible reasons; the latter demarcates spheres of belief and conduct insulated from majoritarian preferences. See Richard Pildes, "Dworkin's Two Conceptions of Rights," *Journal of Legal Studies* 24 (January 2000): 309–315.

13. See Chapter 3.

14. Jonathan Quong, "Cultural Exemptions, Expensive Tastes, and Equal Opportunities," *Journal of Applied Philosophy* 23, no. 1 (2006): 60.

15. Cornelissen, "Belief-Based Exemptions"; Bedi, "Debate"; Anthony Ellis, "What Is Special about Religion?," *Law and Philosophy* 25 (2006): 219–241; Leiter, *Why Tolerate Religion?* Curiously, critics of exemptions often make this case without considering the obvious point, made in the previous paragraph, that freedom of religion is widely considered to be a basic liberal right or special freedom. The invisible premise in their argument is that the onus of proof is higher for a (positive) exemption than it is for a (negative) abstention from interference. But the plausibility of that premise relies on a broader account of the justice of exemptions, as I show below.

16. Robert Audi, "Religious Liberty Conceived as a Human Right," in *Philosophical Foundations of Human Rights,* ed. Rowan Cruft, S. Matthew Liao, and Massimo Renzo (Oxford: Oxford University Press, 2015), 407–422, at 414.

17. Ibid., 418.

18. For discussions of the interpretive method applied to freedom of religion, see Cécile Laborde, "Religion in the Law: The Disaggregation Approach," *Law and Philosophy* 34, no. 6 (November 2015): 581–600; George Letsas, "The Irrelevance of Religion to Law"; Enzo Rossi, "Understanding Religion, Governing Religion: A Realist Perspective"; Ronan Mccrea "The Consequences of Disaggregation and the Impossibility of a Third Way," all in Laborde and Bardon, *Religion in Liberal Political Philosophy*.

19. In this chapter I only focus on the political philosophy of *exemptions* and do not provide a general theory of freedom of religion. In line with the disaggregative strategy, other interpretive values come into play when religion is protected in different parts of the law. I agree with James Nickel that religious practices and activities need not be seen as normatively special to be protected under standard liberal rights of thought, speech, association, and commerce. I depart from Nickel, however, in not grounding *exemptions* from general laws merely in the value of conscience. See James Nickel, "Who Needs Freedom of Religion?" *University of Colorado Law Review* 76 (2005): 941–964; Laborde, "Religion in the Law." A tricky question concerns the doctrinal implications of my interpretive approach. Nickel seems to want to altogether dispense with the category of a right to freedom of religion, and he argues that freedom of religion can be adequately protected under other liberal rights such as speech, association, and conscience. This might well be the case, but I prefer to remain agnostic about the doctrinal implications of my IPC theory. The upshot of my theory is this. Whatever system of rights we opt for, we have to make sure that it adequately protects integrity-protecting commitments (IPCs)—no less, but no more. If we retain a conventional schedule of rights (*cum* freedom of religion), we must make sure that freedom of religion is not construed so expansively that religious individuals and associations can claim exemptions from any activity they undertake. If we imagine a new schedule of rights *minus* freedom of religion, we would have to make sure that the other rights—freedom of conscience, cultural rights, freedom of association—allow for IPC exemptions. In both cases, the moral value protected by religious exemptions is not directly religion but, rather, integrity. Now, in some local cases of religious accommodation, we can hold a *presumption* according to which when a practice is commonly and uncontroversially thought of as religious, this description can be used as a proxy for the protection of integrity. The presumption, roughly, is that the practices that ordinary language widely recognizes as religious are integrity-protecting. This presumption allows us to protect practices such as

the wearing of religious dress or the taking of sacramental wine or peyote, without the need for intrusive scrutiny into individual integrity. The presumption allows us to use religion as a proxy for a fairly well defined good, that of integrity (here I disagree with Andrew Koppelman, who argues that "religion" in "freedom of religion" is a proxy for a loose bundle of multiple goods). So we exempt some religious practices out of respect for integrity (instead of exempting "religion" as such, as Koppelman proposes). Let me illustrate. Because we assume that when a prison chaplain uses wine, he uses it purely for a sacramental purpose, we can have a blanket exemption from a ban on alcohol in prisons for all chaplains, without intrusive and individualized scrutiny of sincerity. Likewise, we might have a general policy exempting religious signs from workplace uniform regulations—this is easier to administer than an individualized approach, even if not every protected person will be actually motivated by an integrity-protecting commitment. But it is the integrity-protecting commitment we protect, not religion generally: it is only because of administrative convenience that we offer categorical protection to certain practices, not because something called religion is by itself respectable—what is respectable is integrity. The presumption makes it clear that the semantic category of religion is both too under-inclusive and overly inclusive in relation to the interpretive value it protects. What matters is not the protection of the category of religion as such but, rather, the protection of the value of integrity. This sometimes allows, but does not automatically entail, that religion be used as a rough-and-ready proxy for the value of integrity. For more on Koppelman's defense of freedom of religion as a proxy for multiple goods, see Andrew Koppelman, "Nonexistent and Irreplaceable: Keep the Religion in Religious Freedom," *Commonweal*, April 10, 2015; Koppelman, "Religion's Specialized Specialness," *University of Chicago Law Review Dialogue* 79, no. 71 (2013); Koppelman, "'Religion' as a Bundle of Legal Proxies: Reply to Micah Schwartzman," *San Diego Law Review* 51, no. 1079 (2014). On this subject, I have benefited from conversations with Andrew Koppelman, Larry Sager, Taruan Khaitan, James Nickel, Hans-Ingvar Roth, and Onora O'Neil.

20. Cheshire Calhoun, "Standing for Something," *Journal of Philosophy* 92 (1995): 235–260, at 235. See also Lynne McFall, "Integrity," *Ethics* 98, no. 1 (October 1987): 5–20.

21. Bernard Williams, "A Critique of Utilitarianism," in *Utilitarianism: For and Against*, ed. B. Williams and J. J. C. Smart (Cambridge: Cambridge

University Press, 1973), 108–118; Bernard Williams, "Persons, Character and Morality," in *Moral Luck: Philosophical Papers, 1973–1980* (Cambridge: Cambridge University Press, 1981), 1–20. Ronald Dworkin also places a notion of ethical integrity at the heart of his "challenge model of ethics." Ronald Dworkin, *Sovereign Virtue: The Theory and Practice of Equality* (Cambridge, MA: Harvard University Press, 2000), 270.

22. For a defense of the value of integrity along those lines, see Patrick Lenta, "Freedom of Conscience and the Value of Personal Integrity," *Res Publica* 22 (2016): 445.

23. McFall, "Integrity."

24. For recent skeptical accounts of the possibility of identifying such a category, see, e.g., Richard J. Arneson, "Against Freedom of Conscience," *University of San Diego Law Review* 47 (2010): 1015; Simon Căbulea May, "Exemptions for Conscience," in Laborde and Bardon, *Religion in Liberal Political Philosophy.*

25. Paul Bou-Habib, "A Theory of Religious Accommodation," *Journal of Applied Philosophy* 23, no. 1 (2006): 109–126; Jocelyn Maclure and Charles Taylor, *Secularism and Freedom of Conscience* (Cambridge, MA: Harvard University Press, 2011), 76–77; Martha Nussbaum, *Liberty of Conscience* (New York: Basic Books, 2008), 19–20, 53–55; Chandran Kukathas, *The Liberal Archipelago: A Theory of Freedom and Diversity* (Oxford: Oxford University Press, 2003), 55.

26. Bou-Habib, "Theory of Religious Accommodation," 119. Bou-Habib also provides an argument to the effect that integrity is a basic good.

27. See Chapter 2.

28. Nussbaum, *Liberty of Conscience,* 2008. See also Kwame Anthony Appiah: religious practices are "likely to represent deeply constitutive aspects of people's identity, rather than something like a taste for one candy over another. We can make distinctions between [those] who, with Luther, declare, *Ich kann nicht anders,* and the Mr. Bartlebys who simply "prefer not to." Kwame Anthony Appiah, *The Ethics of Identity* (Princeton: Princeton University Press, 2005), 99.

29. Winnifred Fallers Sullivan, *The Impossibility of Religious Freedom* (Princeton: Princeton University Press, 2005); Saba Mahmood, *Politics of Piety: The Islamic Revival and the Feminist Subject* (Princeton: Princeton University Press, 2005). For other attempts to provide a more inclusive conception of conscience, close to what I call here integrity, see Jocelyn Maclure, "Conscience,

Religion and Exemptions: An Egalitarian View" (unpublished manuscript, on file with author); Paul Bou-Habib, "Reconstructing Religion without God" (unpublished manuscript, on file with author).

30. For a defense of the objective view, see Avigail Eisenberg, *Reasons of Identity* (Oxford: Oxford University Press, 2009).

31. One could also argue that any assessment of religious belief by judges violates the accessibility requirement of public reason (defended in Chapter 4) and the competence interests of religious groups (defended in Chapter 5). For an argument along these lines, see David Golemboski, "Judicial Evaluation of Religious Belief and the Accessibility Requirement in Public Reason," *Law and Philosophy* 35 (2016): 435–460. Golemboski shows that attempts by judges to assess the moral salience of religious beliefs, by appeal to three commonly used standards (reasonableness, centrality, and substantiality), unavoidably entangle them in substantive theological questions. And this, in turn, violates the accessibility requirement of public reason.

32. In *Syndicat Northcrest v. Amselem* [2004] 2 S.C.R. 551, the Supreme Court of Canada asserted the deeply personal and subjective nature of religious belief, in relation to a demand by an Orthodox Jew to be allowed to build a personal *succah* on his balcony, in contravention of traditional Jewish practice (and of the rules of the Montreal condominium where he resided) that recommend communal *succahs*.

33. What I would concede to Eisenberg, however, is that appeal to objective religious or cultural tradition can serve as an epistemic proxy in cases of well-established, uncontested categorical protection—as per the presumption explicated above. However Eisenberg goes wrong in illustrating the limits of the sincerity approach by referring to the example of kosher exemptions. It would be absurd, she notes, to let individuals set their own kosher standards; therefore, any official kosher certification has to be validated by community objective standards. This is correct. But this is not an example of an individual exemption: it is, rather, a collective exemption. It therefore falls under the rights of groups discussed in Chapter 5. Kosher standards are examples of what I call "coherence interests" that allow organized Jewish associations to qualify for collective exemptions. Eisenberg, *Reasons of Identity*, 107.

34. Charles Taylor, *Sources of the Self: The Making of Modern Identity* (Cambridge, MA: Harvard University Press, 1989).

35. Consider, for example, the case of *SAS v. France* (ECHR, July 1, 2014), where a woman claimed she wore a niqab "occasionally," depending on her

mood. Admittedly, this is no justification for a ban (French law prohibiting the full face veil is difficult to justify, and therefore the infringement of this negative liberty was illegitimate), but such a halfhearted commitment to a religious practice might, in my view, not meet the more demanding IPC test, and therefore not qualify for a *pro tanto* exemption. For some discussion, see, e.g., Valérie Amiraux, "Visibility, Transparency and Gossip: How Did the Religion of Some (Muslims) Become the Public Concern of Others?," *Critical Research on Religion* 4, no. 1 (2016): 37–56.

36. Kent Greenawalt, *Religion and the Constitution,* vol. 1: *Free Exercise and Fairness* (Princeton University Press, 2006), chap. 7. For a discussion of how courts can assess the sincerity of religious claimants, notably by evaluating external objective evidence, see Ben Adams and Cynthia Barmore, "Questioning Sincerity: The Role of the Courts after *Hobby Lobby,*" *Stanford Law Review Online* 67 (2014).

37. Would a sincerity test exclude members of the Church of the Flying Monster Spaghetti, who have gone to great length to invent a plausible religion in Italy and in the Netherlands—with the intention of ridiculing the special protection of religion in the law? Possibly not.

38. The thick sincerity test I propose is thinner than the tests currently used by the European Court of Human Rights, which problematically adds more objective tests of "cogency" and "cohesion." In *Campbell and Cosans v. the United Kingdom* (1982), the European Court of Human Rights stated that in order for a person's conviction to qualify as a "belief" on the understanding of the right to freedom of religion or belief, the conviction must display "a certain level of cogency, seriousness, cohesion and importance." For insightful discussion, see Lucy Vickers, *Religious Freedom, Religious Discrimination and the Workplace* (Oxford: Hart, 2008), 14; and Rex Adhar and Ian Leigh, *Religious Freedom in the Liberal State* (Oxford: Oxford University Press, 2005), 123–125.

39. The latter are tellingly referred to as "intégristes" in French. For thoughtful commentary, see Jean-Yves Pranchère, "Intégrité, intégrisme, et (dés)intégration du religieux: Quelques remarques sur la 'stratégie dissociative' proposée par Cécile Laborde," *Raison Publique* 29 (February 2016), http://www.raison-publique.fr/article808.html.

40. See Andrew Koppelman, "Conscience, Volitional Necessity, and Religious Exemptions," *Legal Theory* 15 (2009): 215–244. For a full response, see Lenta, "Freedom of Conscience," 445.

41. In *Williamson* (2005), the British House of Lords turned down an appeal by some Christian schools that they be permitted to administer corporal punishment to pupils, banned in the UK since 1987 (*Williamson v. Secretary of State for Education and Employment* (2005) 2 A.C. 246 (H.L.) (Eng.).

42. On this topic, I have benefited from instructive discussions with Paul Bou-Habib, my colleagues at UCL Political Theory, as well as participants at the MANCEPT seminar in Manchester on November 9, 2016, and the Nuffield Political Theory Workshop at the University of Oxford on January 16, 2017.

43. https://www.theguardian.com/world/2016/may/25/switzerland-ruling-overturns-muslim-pupils-handshake-exemption-religion. For discussions of similar cases, see Nadia Fadil, "Managing Affects and Sensibilities: The Case of Not-Handshaking and Not-Fasting," *Social Anthropology* 17, no. 4 (2009): 439–454; Deniz Batum, "Handshaking in the Secular: Understanding Agency of Veiled Turkish-Dutch Muslim Students," *Generos* 5, no. 1 (June 2016): 962–985.

44. https://www.theguardian.com/uk-news/2016/oct/24/born-again-christian-ashers-bakery-lose-court-appeal-in-gay-cake-row. For a critique of the decision on free speech grounds, see Peter Tatchell's piece, http://www.independent.co.uk/voices/ashers-bakery-cakes-gay-marriage-discrimination-northern-ireland-a7377916.html.

45. For an argument, see Vaughn Bryan Baltzly, "Same-Sex Marriage, Polygamy, and Disestablishment," *Social Theory and Practice* 38, no. 2 (April 2012): 333–362. Generally, see Elizabeth Brake, *Minimizing Marriage: Marriage, Morality, and the Law* (Oxford: Oxford University Press, 2012).

46. Arneson, "Against Freedom of Conscience," 1015.

47. Jeremy Waldron, "A Right to Do Wrong," *Ethics* 92 (1981): 21–39.

48. In Chapter 4, however, I provided a more skeptical account of liberal legitimacy. Rawls's thought was that reasonable Catholics and reasonable Muslims (for example) should find, within their own doctrines, reasons to endorse the publicly affirmed liberal conception of justice. On my view, although reasonable citizens can and should converge on general liberal axioms (such as the moral equality of all individuals), there is no reason to think that they can and should converge on the specific liberal conception that is publicly affirmed. It is sufficient, on my account, that reasonable citizens endorse the broad liberal norm of moral equality, not the details of the publicly affirmed

conception of justice; and that they (in addition) accept the legitimacy of democratic procedures in fixing the public conception of justice.

49. Bou-Habib, in a more recent paper ("Reconstructing Religion without God"), has revised his conception of integrity, arguing that it does not rest only on the performance of "perceived duties" because "our critical interests, or strong evaluation, cover more than perceived duty." Therefore, freedom of religion should protect our "preponderant axiological commitments" (a phrase he borrows from Taylor and Maclure, *Secularism and Freedom of Conscience* (Cambridge, MA: Harvard University Press, 2011). Bou-Habib rightly concludes that "a qualification test that requires strong evaluation as a key normative feature of religious activity does not evince a bias toward a parochial or protestant conception of religious faith." This was in response to criticism put to him in Jonathan Seglow, "Theories of Religious Exemptions," in *Diversity in Europe: Dilemmas of Differential Treatment in Theory and Practice,* ed. Gildeon Calder and Emanuela Ceva (Abingdon, UK: Routledge, 2011); and Laborde, "Religion in the Law."

50. Patten, *Equal Recognition,* 168.

51. In Chapter 2, I analyzed two theories of ethical salience: the mainstreaming strategy of Eisgruber and Sager, and the narrowing strategy of Maclure and Taylor. Each captured a crucial dimension of religion: Eisgruber and Sager analogized religion with vulnerable identities; and MacLure and Taylor analogized religion with conscientious duties. Here I combine the two insights, suggesting that religion should be disaggregated into the two dimensions of what I call identity and obligation.

52. Andrew Koppelman, "Is It Fair to Give Religion Special Treatment?," *University of Illinois Law Review* 3 (2006): 572–603, at 586.

53. If religious practices are not salient for them, they are unlikely to request exemptions, so this is not a difficult case. But what if the state directly represses them, or discriminates against them? If it does so out of animus or hostility, this is clearly incompatible with neutrality, regardless of how people feel about the targeted identity—as I suggested earlier in the asylum case. But if it does so out of a good public reason, it is more difficult to explain where the harm lies.

54. Patten, *Equal Recognition,* chap. 2. For more critical assessment, see Anne Phillips, *Multiculturalism without Culture* (Princeton: Princeton University Press, 2007).

55. Jewel Amoah and Tom Bennett, "The Freedoms of Religion and Culture under the South African Constitution: Do Traditional African Religions Enjoy Equal Treatment?," *Journal of Law and Religion* 24, no. 1 (2008–2009): 1–20. See also Rosalind I. J. Hackett, "Traditional, African, Religious, Freedom?," in *The Politics of Religious Freedom,* ed. Winnifred Fallers Sullivan, Elizabeth Shakman Hurd, Saba Mahmood, and Peter G. Danchin (Chicago: University of Chicago Press, 2015), 89–98.

56. Gideon Sapir and Daniel Statman, "Why Freedom of Religion Does Not Include Freedom from Religion," *Law and Philosophy* 24, no. 5 (2005): 467–508, at 481.

57. Perhaps it will be useful to add here a reminder of how I conceive the relationship between democratic practice and political theory, on my dualist theory of liberalism. I think of substantive theories of *justice* as contributions to democratic debate—philosophers, like other citizens, articulate their preferred conceptions, but accept that there are alternative reasonable conceptions. By contrast, I think of theories of liberal *legitimacy* as constraints on democratic debate: here the role of political philosophy is to identify the rightful limits of democratic deliberation, and articulate the basic rights and entitlements for which—for example—there should be immunities from majoritarian impositions.

58. For liberty-based accounts, see Michael W. McConnell, "Accommodation of Religion," *Supreme Court Review* (1985): 1–59; Michael W. McConnell, "The Problem of Singling Out Religion," *DePaul University Law Review* 50 (2000); Douglas Laycock, "Religious Liberty as Liberty," *Journal of Contemporary Legal Issues* 7 (1996): 313; and for a critique, see Christopher Eisgruber and Lawrence Sager, *Religious Freedom and the Constitution* (Cambridge, MA: Harvard University Press, 2007), esp. 202–203.

59. Brian Barry, *Culture and Equality* (Cambridge: Polity Press, 2001).

60. Jeremy Waldron, "One Law for All? The Logic of Cultural Accommodations," *Washington and Lee Law Review* 59, no. 1 (2002): 3–34; Simon Caney, "Equal Treatment, Exceptions, and Cultural Diversity," in *Multiculturalism Reconsidered: Culture and Equality and Its Critics,* ed. P. Kelly (Oxford: Blackwell, 2002), 81–101.

61. Patten, *Equal Recognition,* 139–140.

62. Susan Mendus, "Choice, Chance and Multiculturalism," in Kelly, *Multiculturalism Reconsidered,* 31–44; Quong, "Cultural Exemptions, Expensive Tastes."

63. Peter Jones, "Bearing the Consequences of Belief," *Journal of Political Philosophy* 2, no. 1 (1994): 24–43.

64. This is an example provided by William Galston and discussed in Greenawalt, *Religion and the Constitution*, vol. 2, *Establishment and Fairness* (Princeton: Princeton University Press, 2008), 315.

65. Alternative typologies of theories of religious exemptions are Seglow, "Theories of Religious Exemptions"; Andrew Shorten, "Cultural Exemptions, Equality and Basic Interests," *Ethnicities* 10 (2010): 100; Stuart White, "Religious Exemptions: An Egalitarian Demand?," *Law and Ethics of Human Rights* 6, no. 1 (2012): 97–118; Alan Patten, "The Normative Logic of Religious Liberty," *Journal of Political Philosophy* (Early View, December 1, 2016); Peter Jones, "Religious Accommodation and Distributive Justice," in Laborde and Bardon, *Religion in Liberal Political Philosophy*. I should emphasize here that I am concerned only with exemptions granted on an individual, one-to-one, basis. In practice, of course, many exemptions are granted categorically—to groups of citizens (Muslims, Native Americans, Sikhs, etc.). But, as Peter Jones has emphasized, the rights underpinning individual exemptions can be group-differentiated without being group rights in the strict sense. As I conceded above, exemptions from workplace uniform regulations (for example) are granted to groups such as Jews or Sikhs for administrative convenience, but they are not rights enjoyed by groups as groups: they are enjoyed by individuals whose individual integrity is at stake. Peter Jones, "Cultures, Group Rights, and Group-Differentiated Rights," in *Multiculturalism and Moral Conflict*, ed. M. Dimova-Cookson and P. Stirk (London: Routledge, 2010), 40.

66. Quong, "Cultural Exemptions, Expensive Tastes," 60.

67. On a strict construal, a person waives her Article 9(1) right to manifest her religion or belief if she voluntarily enters an institution that restricts that manifestation in some way, typically through paid employment. One familiar objection is that, in case of gender or race discrimination, it is never acceptable simply to say that claimants must go and find another job. This is correct. But it merely confirms my suggestion that, in exemption cases, religion should not simply be analogized with race or gender. People must take some responsibility for their beliefs and commitments, and not all burdensome regulation is unfairly discriminatory.

68. Brian Barry, despite his mostly formal account of equal opportunity, also distinguishes between the two Sikh cases. See Barry, *Culture and Equality*, 49–50. For different theories of costs and opportunities, see Bikhu Parekh,

"Barry and the Dangers of Liberalism," and David Miller, "Liberalism, Equal Opportunities and Cultural Commitments," both in Kelly, *Multiculturalism Reconsidered;* Peter Jones, "Liberty, Equality and Accommodation," in *Multiculturalism Rethought: Interpretations, Dilemmas and New Directions,* ed. Tariq Modood and V. Uberoi (Edinburgh: Edinburgh University Press, 2015), 126–156.

69. On the broad notion of cultural obligation, see Bikhu Parekh, *Rethinking Multiculturalism* (Cambridge, MA: Harvard University Press, 2000), 272; James Tully, *Strange Multiplicity* (Cambridge: Cambridge University Press, 1995), 172.

70. *MEC for Education, Kwazuly-Natal and Others v. Pillay* 2008 SA 474 (CC).

71. *SAS v. France* (ECHR, July 1, 2014).

72. Ronan McCrea, "Religious Discrimination in the Workplace: Which Approach Should the CJEU Follow?," http://eulawanalysis.blogspot.co.uk/2016 /07/religious-discrimination-in-workplace.html.

73. See Tariq Modood, T. R. Hansen, Eric Bleich, Brendan O'Leary, and Joe Carens, "The Danish Cartoon Affair: Free Speech, Racism, Islamism, and Integration," *International Migration* 44, no. 5 (2006); Talal Asad, Wendy Brown, Judith Butler, and Saba Mahmood, *Is Critique Secular? Blasphemy, Injury, and Free Speech* (Berkeley: University of California Press, 2009); Andrew March, "Speech and the Sacred: Does the Defense of Free Speech Rest on a Mistake about Religion?," *Political Theory* 40, no. 3 (2012): 319–346; Jeremy Waldron, *The Harm in Hate Speech* (Cambridge, MA: Harvard University Press, 2011); Caleb Yong, "Does Freedom of Speech Include Hate Speech?," *Res Publica* 17 (November 2011): 385; Christoph Baumgartner, "Blasphemy as Violence: Trying to Understand the Kind of Injury That Can Be Inflicted by Acts and Artefacts That Are Construed as Blasphemy," *Journal of Religion in Europe* 6 (2013): 35–63.

74. Charles Taylor, "The Politics of Recognition," in *Multiculturalism: Examining the Politics of Recognition,* ed. A. Gutmann (Princeton: Princeton University Press, 1994); Will Kymlicka, *Multicultural Citizenship* (Oxford: Clarendon Press, 1995); Joseph Carens, *Culture, Citizenship, and Community: A Contextual Exploration of Justice as Evenhandedness* (Oxford: Oxford University Press, 2000); Patten, *Equal Recognition.*

75. For a thoughtful study of conscientious objection, see Kimberly Brownlee, *Conscience and Conviction: The Case for Civil Disobedience* (Oxford: Oxford University Press, 2012).

76. Ian McEwan's novel, *The Children Act* (London: Vintage, 2014), sensitively explores the relevant ethical dilemmas. The key question he asks is whether a seventeen-year-old Jehovah's Witness should be treated by the law as a child, and have a blood transfusion forced onto him.

77. An interesting question here is whether laws demanded by justice only protect rights, narrowly construed, or whether they also expressively affirm the equal civic status of persons. In that case, a publicly endorsed exemption can constitute something like an expressive or dignitarian harm. Consider, for example, a recent UK law that makes marriage available to same-sex couples (*Ladele v. London Borough of Islington* [2009] E. W. C.A, Civ 1357). If a civil registrar refuses, on conscientious grounds, to perform such marriages, she might be seen—as a civil servant—to be conveying the message that LGBTQ citizens are second-class citizens who cannot avail themselves of the rule of law. What in nonestablishment jurisprudence is called the non-endorsement test (that the state should not endorse messages that exclude some categories of citizens) applies to the behavior and speech of public officials. See Chapter 4. Also see Corey Brettschneider, *When the State Speaks, What Should It Say? How Democracies Can Protect Expression and Promote Equality* (Princeton: Princeton University Press, 2012).

78. *Eweida v. United Kingdom* (2013).

79. On the autopsy case, see Paul Gallager, "Coroners Must Send Bodies for Scans rather than Autopsies if Religion Demands They Stay Intact, High Court Rules," *The Independent,* July 28, 2015, http://www.independent.co.uk /news/uk/home-news/coroners-must-send-bodies-for-scans-rather-than -autopsies-if-religion-demands-they-stay-intact-high-court-rules-10422561 .html. For a defense of "pure balancing" when no issue of justice is at stake, see Alan Patten, "Religious Exemptions and Fairness," in Laborde and Bardon, *Religion in Liberal Political Philosophy.*

80. Leiter, *Why Tolerate Religion?* For further discussion, see Francois Boucher and Cécile Laborde "Why Tolerate Conscience?," *Criminal Law and Philosophy* (October 2014): 1–22.

81. José Woehrling, "L'obligation d'accommodement raisonnable et l'adaptation de la société à la diversité religieuse," *Revue de Droit de McGill* 43 (1998): 325–401.

82. Nussbaum, *Liberty of Conscience,* 19–20, 168–170.

83. *Fraternal Order of Police Newark Lodge v. City of Newark,* 170 F.3d 359 (3d Cir. 1999). Two Muslim officers challenged the Newark police department's

requirement that officers be clean-shaven, on the ground that their faith demanded that they wear a beard. As the Newark department already exempted officers with skin disorders, Eisgruber and Sager diagnose a failure of equal regard, as we saw in Chapter 2.

84. For compelling arguments to this effect, see Peter Jones, "Religious Exemptions and Distributive Justice," in Laborde and Bardon, *Religion in Liberal Political Philosophy;* White, "Religious Exemptions." See also Bou-Habib: "Religious freedom stands on its own distinctive ground. Its proper treatment does not therefore depend on how other (supposedly) similar needs are treated by the state or on its being subsumable under other traditional liberties" ("Reconstructing Religion without God," 27).

85. Martha Nussbaum, *Liberty of Conscience;* Cécile Laborde, *Critical Republicanism* (Oxford: Oxford University Press, 2008), 82–83.

86. White, "Religious Exemptions"; Quong, "Cultural Exemptions, Expensive Tastes."

87. Kymlicka, *Multicultural Citizenship,* 114, 115.

88. Patten, *Equal Recognition.*

89. Quong, "Cultural Exemptions, Expensive Tastes."

90. Jonathan Seglow has argued that citizens have a broad interest in "civic participation," in being "quotidian citizens" participating in social life on equal terms with others. Jonathan Seglow, "Religious Accommodation: Responsibility, Integrity, and Self-Respect," in *Religion in Liberal Political Philosophy,* ed. Cécile Laborde and Aurélia Bardon. The specific situation rule does not apply here because I assume there is a general (not job-specific) rule enforcing one shared day of rest.

91. On the Ahmad case, see Jones, "Bearing the Consequences."

92. Laborde, *Critical Republicanism,* chap. 4. For various perspectives, see Tariq Modood, "Establishment, Multiculturalism and British Citizenship," *Political Quarterly* 65, no. 1 (1994): 53–73; Sune Laegaard. "Unequal Recognition, Misrecognition and Injustice: The Case of Religious Minorities in Denmark," *Ethnicities* 12, no. 2 (2012): 197–214; Peter Balint, "Identity Claims: Why Liberal Neutrality Is the Solution, Not the Problem," *Political Studies* 63, no. 2 (2013).

93. See the argument in Chapter 4.

94. Patten, *Equal Recognition,* chap. 5. Patten, however, does not distinguish between obligation-IPCs and identity-IPCs in the way I do.

95. See Laborde, *Critical Republicanism,* esp. chap. 4. A complication arises from the fact that many Christian claims—e.g., Sabbatarian—are not mainstream and count as minority religions in some contexts (e.g., days of rest).

Conclusion

1. For a stimulating approach to the study of ideologies that also disaggregates their various building blocks, see Michael Freeden, *Ideologies and Political Theory: A Conceptual Approach* (Oxford: Oxford University Press, 1996).

Acknowledgments

I began considering the ideas behind this book during a stay at Princeton's Institute for Advanced Study in the academic year of 2010–2011. While there, I was fortunate to be part of a yearlong seminar on the theme of secularism. Over the course of that year, the group developed searching criticisms of Western theories of secularism and religion—the kind that liberal political theorists had not, in my view, sufficiently engaged. I extend my thanks to fellow participants in the secularism seminar for stimulating and thought-provoking conversations. Above all, I am grateful to Joan Scott for inviting me to the institute and for offering me the opportunity to set out a research agenda in such a unique environment.

Back in the UK, I developed the framework for *Liberalism's Religion* as part of a European Research Council (ERC) personal grant (Grant 283867, "Is Religion Special? Reformulating Secularism and Religion in Contemporary Political Theory"). As the recipient of both a graduate Erasmus grant in 1992 and an ERC grant in 2012, I belong to a generation of European students who have greatly benefited from the full participation of the UK in the wider EU academic community. At University College London (UCL), the Department of Political Science provided a welcoming home for my ERC-funded project. In addition to several research trips, the ERC supported the activities of the Religion and Political Theory (RAPT) Centre between 2012 and 2016. I am particularly grateful to my research associates at RAPT, Aurélia Bardon and Lois Lee, for their thoughtful and incisive academic contributions and their tireless and good-humored organizational work. Thanks also to RAPT workshop participants for their comments on various draft chapters: Cristobal Bellolio, Matteo Bonotti, François Boucher, Jennifer Brown, Nick Martin, Ronan Mccrea, and Dara Salam. Colleagues at UCL—in Political Science, Laws and Philosophy, as well as within the interdepartmental "Negotiating Religion" group—were wonderfully supportive. Albert Weale, in particular, was characteristically generous with his wisdom, time, and friendship.

It is somewhat embarrassing to me that, given the number of colleagues who commented on the manuscript, this book is not better. Micah Schwartzmann from the University of Virginia and Aurélia Bardon and Jeff Howard from UCL generously organized workshops on the manuscript in the spring of 2016. I am enormously indebted to colleagues who, in addition to them, took the time to read the full text during these or other occasions: Christoph Baumgartner, Paul Billingham, Colin Bird, Matteo Bonotti, Paul Bou-Habib, Corey Brettschneider, Jean Cohen, Chiara Cordelli, Peter Jones, Andrew Koppelman, Sune Laegaard, Stephen Macedo, Daniel Sabbagh, Larry Sager, Seena Shiffrin, Winnifred Sullivan, and Nelson Tebbe.

For comments on key chapters, I am grateful to Guy Aitchison-Cornish, Valérie Amiraux, Netta Barak-Corren, Rainer Baubock, Eric Beerbohm, Richard Bellamy, Maria Birnbaum, Eva Brems, Gwénaële Calvès, Emanuela Ceva, Matthew Clayton, Peter Danchin, Christopher Eisgruber, Luc Foisneau, Charles Girard, Rob Jubb, Benjamin Kaplan, Tarun Khaitan, Denis Lacorne, George Letsas, Annabelle Lever, Christopher Lund, Jocelyn Maclure, Saba Mahmood, Maleiha Malik, Tariq Modood, Tobias Müller, Pablo Muchnick, James Nickel, Avia Pasternak, Alan Patten, Philip Pettit, Roland Pierik, Andrei Poama, Jean-Yves Pranchère, Robert Prost, Michel Rosenfeld, Jonathan Quong, Alain Renaut, Russell Sandberg, Fabian Schuppert, Elizabeth Sepper, Julian Rivers, Jonathan Seglow, Elizabeth Shakman-Hurd, Andrew

Shorten, Jean-Fabien Spitz, Daniel Statman, Jeff Stout, John Tasioulas, Wibren van der Burgh, Greg Walker, and Lorenzo Zucca. Sections of the manuscript were presented to audiences in Amsterdam, Barcelona, Belfast, Bordeaux, Brussels, Cardiff, Cambridge, Charlottesville, Chicago, Copenhagen, Florence, Geneva, Ghent, Leuven, Lille, London, Manchester, Montreal, New York, Nottingham, Oslo, Oxford, Paris, Princeton, Rennes, Sheffield, Stockholm, Uppsala, Warwick, and York. Many thanks to the organizers and participants.

My editor at Harvard University Press, Ian Malcolm, was hugely supportive throughout the several years it took me to write this book and invariably offered timely and thoughtful suggestions. I am grateful to Kim Giambattisto and Wendy Nelson for careful editorial work, and to Gaby Nair for editorial assistance in the winter of 2016.

Writing a book takes one away from family and friends. It has been an immense source of comfort that they were, despite everything, always there. Mark held the fort, often adjusted his schedule to mine, and managed to write three books at the same time. I dedicate this book to him, to Anna, and to Camille, with all my love.

Index